Ken Wishaw is a doctor with specialist qu... Since his early childhood he has been passior... fortunate to be able to combine this with his medical career. His role in helping to pioneer aeromedical intensive care retrieval is his highest medical achievement. More recently he has been actively involved in teaching advanced resuscitation and crisis management skills to other anaesthetists, particularly those in country practice, through the emerging field of simulator technology.

He is also a dedicated husband and father and proud member of a successful blended family. When he needs a break he pursues his ongoing love of flying in the sport of gliding.

HELICOPTER

The true story of Australia's first full-time chopper doctor

RESCUE

DR KEN WISHAW

MACMILLAN
Pan Macmillan Australia

Donations to CareFlight can be made by calling 1800 858 505.

First published 2004 in Macmillan by Pan Macmillan Australia Pty Limited
St Martins Tower, 31 Market Street, Sydney

National Library of Australia
cataloguing-in-publication data:

Wishaw, Ken.
Helicopter rescue: the story of Australia's first full-time chopper doctor.

ISBN 1 4050 3568 4.

1. Wishaw, Ken. 2. Surf Life Saving Association of Australia. 3. CareFlight (Organisation).
4. Physicians – New South Wales – Biography. 5. Helicopter ambulances – New South Wales.
6. Helicopters in search and rescue operations – New South Wales. I. Title.

362.18092

Typeset in 11/15 pt Sabon by Midland Typesetters
Printed in Australia by McPherson's Printing Group
Cover design by Darian Causby/Highway 51
Front cover photograph: Pilot Ken Vote, crewman Bill Hollingsworth (at the door),
paramedic Steve Fraser and Dr Sean Beehan undertake the rescue
of two men near Stanwell Tops on 18 October 1991.
Photo: Hank van Stuivenberg, Fairfaxphotos.
Back cover author photograph: Dr Chris Shirley

Papers used by Pan Macmillan Australia Pty Ltd are natural, recyclable products made from
wood grown in sustainable forests. The manufacturing processes conform to the
environmental regulations of the country of origin.

To Jackie, my best friend, my inspiration and my wife, without whose constant encouragement and support this book would never have happened.

And

To all those crew who I had the privilege to work with over the years. Trusting your life to your friends builds a special bond. I hope this book can be accepted as a representation of all of you.

Foreword

So there we were: doctors who had finished our specialist training in anaesthetics and intensive care. We liked the emergencies; we liked being able to cope with them. We'd always felt we must do the hardest things. There was no way we were going to lose control! We could handle anything! We were young, fit, healthy, restless; we needed adventure in spite of the pressures of family, career and a mortgage . . . And with the helicopter rescue service, along came a chance. It gave us our 'adventure'; an opportunity to show that we could do it.

How different it was in reality. The fact was that, when confronted with a horrible medical emergency in hostile surroundings, we often wondered what we were doing there. Our minds screamed, 'Get me out of here!' and time stood still. Everything moved in slow motion, like struggling through molasses. It seemed like hours must have gone by, but only minutes had passed before we were back; very tired, but with everything under control. Our own good training and our discipline, and that of the team had succeeded, as it was meant to do. Next came the sense of relief. There was also wonderful camaraderie. We shared dreadful but very funny black humour, and some bravado: 'Well, that wasn't so bad! Where's the next job?'

What is it all about? A retrieval and primary response doctor works outside the hospital and away from all the support systems a hospital provides. It involves endless, uncomfortable nights travelling often long distances in emergency vehicles. Why on earth would anyone do this? Well, I have given you part of the answer, and Ken's book will tell you the rest.

There is also this reason. Sixteen years ago, there was a group of doctors who were concerned about the transport of critically ill patients. At that time it was difficult to get the right escorts and medical equipment for these people. The role of the doctor at an accident site was controversial and the notion of 'retrieval medicine' was not widespread. Implementing it would be hard, because we would need to involve many diverse organisations, some of which had good reasons to be suspicious of doctors moving outside their traditional niche.

This group of doctors, of which Ken Wishaw and I were members, was given a chance to put their ideas into action. Through the ensuing years, with the help of a lot of wonderful people and through all the ups and downs, I do believe we have made a difference in this difficult and challenging area of medicine. The transport of critically ill patients in New South Wales now proceeds, for the most part, smoothly and with appropriate attendants and equipment.

The medical profession is often cautious and conservative, which is both a strength and a weakness. As a doctor, the chance to work outside the system and at the same time become integrated with it does not happen often. The chance to meet and work with people you would not ordinarily have contact with, to go places you would not ordinarily go, and to widen your view of the world was something I appreciated very much, and I know I speak for Ken and all our colleagues, medical and non-medical, when I say that we wouldn't have missed it for the world!

Read on and see why.

Dr Fran Smith
Sydney, 2003

Author's note

All the stories in this book are true.

Wherever possible I have verified the accuracy of my accounts through medical and flight records. Where privacy laws and the limitations of written records have left gaps I have relied on my own recollections and records and, where possible, verified my accounts with others present at the time. It has been necessary to change some names. I apologise for any inaccuracies or omissions.

K.W.

Prologue

As the drugs I had injected coursed through the boy's bloodstream, the muscles beneath his bruised and bloodied skin began to twitch frantically. For five seconds the grotesque movements continued, until finally the anaesthetic took effect and the shudders subsided. The eight-year-old was unconscious and paralysed; he could not even breathe without assistance. He was utterly dependent upon those of us in the emergency room. If I didn't get my actions right in the next two minutes, he would probably die.

An hour earlier Paul Bowdler had been a normal, happy lad sitting in the back seat of his family's car. He was fastidious about doing up his seatbelt. Many of his injuries were probably due to that seatbelt, but without it he would have died instantly.

His mother and sister had suffered multiple fractures and severe bruising, but Paul had not been so lucky. In the fraction of a second after the car was rammed violently from behind, his body was thrown forward against the seatbelt, his spleen was torn and his pancreas squashed against his spine. The collision forces were so great that as his body weight shifted, his upper thigh snapped before the seatbelt gave way. He was catapulted around the cabin of the car, sustaining severe head injuries and multiple facial fractures.

For forty-five minutes the emergency service officers worked to free him from the mangled remains of the vehicle; then, sirens screaming, they raced him to the local hospital. There the attending doctors struggled to cope with his injuries. They were familiar with trauma and had begun to resuscitate him, but from the outset they knew Paul needed more expertise than they had. That was why I was there trying my best to stabilise his condition.

This kind of trauma was not new to me – accident resuscitation was my field. However, this was one of the worst childhood trauma cases I had seen. Paul was in an awful predicament. I knew his laboured breathing was due to his airway slowly closing over as the swelling and bruising around his head and neck progressed. I had only minutes to do something before the swelling blocked his airway altogether, and then it might be impossible to salvage the situation. Something else played on my mind, too. Paul was around the same age as my eldest son. I pushed this disturbing thought away and checked that everything was in place for the procedure.

I had taken the first step towards stabilising him by administering drugs to sedate him further and to paralyse his muscles. This was to ensure that he didn't unconsciously fight the second step – the insertion of a hollow plastic tube down his throat and into his windpipe. This would guarantee a clear airway regardless of how bad the swelling became. It would also allow us to give one hundred per cent oxygen and deliberately overventilate his lungs, which would in turn decrease the swelling of his brain.

I knew the procedure was not going to be easy. The combination of the swelling and the blood in his throat from his facial injuries would make inserting the tube extremely difficult. There was also the risk that the drugs, or the tube itself, would trigger one of Paul's severe asthma attacks. It was little wonder, then, that the hospital doctors were happy to leave the procedure to me and instead take an assisting role.

I had already selected three other people to help me and briefed them on their tasks. Now I stood at the head of the operating table, leaning over Paul's face. The nurse to my left was supporting the back of his neck while simultaneously pushing on his windpipe. This action, known as Sellick's manoeuvre, would minimise the chance of blood and stomach acid being regurgitated during the procedure.

The second nurse, on my right, would hand me instruments as I called for them. Kneeling on the same side was Brian Deen, our team paramedic. He had clamped his hands on either side of Paul's head to prevent any excessive movement of his neck while I inserted the airway tube. The emergency neck X-rays, taken as the boy struggled, were not clear enough to exclude a spinal fracture, so we had to assume there was one.

I opened Paul's mouth. There was a copious amount of blood in his throat. Without looking up I held out my right hand and asked for a sucker. It was promptly slapped into my palm and soon the airway was dry and relatively free of blood. My next request was for a laryngoscope. This instrument had a fifteen-centimetre curved metal blade attached to a battery handle. Halfway down the blade was a light. I needed the laryngoscope to push the tongue and soft tissues aside, and to illuminate the opening of Paul's windpipe. The experienced and very proficient nurse knew, of the three laryngoscopes I had prepared, which one I wanted to use first.

I carefully slid the laryngoscope blade backwards along the boy's tongue, looking for recognisable structures to guide me to the top of his windpipe. I couldn't recognise a thing. Between the blood still oozing down from the back of Paul's nose, and the swelling and distortion of all the soft tissues, none of the usual landmarks was visible. I wasn't sure where I was. I withdrew the scope and reinserted it. The view was no better. Without withdrawing the instrument I again asked for the sucker. I was hoping the removal of the blood from the area would help. It didn't.

Time was running out. Any moment Paul's oxygen levels would start to drop. The swelling of his face would make ventilating him with a resuscitation bag almost impossible. Struggling to keep calm, I pressed on, asking now for the straight-blade laryngoscope. I desperately hoped this rarely used instrument would give me a better view.

The beeping of the pulse oximeter changed tone, telling me that the oxygen levels in Paul's blood were starting to fall dangerously. I angled the unwieldy laryngoscope down his throat and was again greeted by a lake of blood. I slowly advanced the instrument with my left hand, continuously sucking away the blood with the sucker in my right. The oximeter beat was loud in my ears, an urgent reminder of Paul's precarious situation; but I could not afford to rush in case I overshot the entrance to his windpipe and lost my bearings.

A few seconds later I was rewarded with a good view of the top of his windpipe. The nurse was poised with the breathing tube and passed it to me immediately. The tube slipped in easily. Once I was satisfied it was in far enough, I held it tightly in position by bracing my hand against Paul's teeth. The falling oximeter tone urged me on. Fighting my instinct to hurry, I slowly and carefully extracted the laryngoscope, fearful that I might accidentally dislodge the tube if I didn't take the utmost care. The nurse was ready with the breathing bag, and after I connected it she gave the first few breaths. Paul's chest rose reassuringly.

Without letting go of the breathing tube, I inserted the earpieces of my stethoscope into my ears one-handed. Listening to each side of his chest I could clearly hear air entering each time the nurse pressed the bag.

'We're in!' I exclaimed.

Confirming this, the oximeter tone rapidly rose and the readout on the machine increased to a healthy ninety-nine per cent, better than before we had started.

The tension broke and everyone started breathing again. At that moment I was grateful for every one of the four thousand anaesthetics I had given – each one had helped me keep my cool today, in the worst of circumstances. I also reflected on the excellent training I had received, particularly from my former mentors, Dr Dick Young and Dr Susan Kelly, who had drilled me constantly to be prepared for all contingencies. Without that training and experience, securing Paul's airway and keeping him alive might not have been possible.

We still had a lot to do but the trickiest part was over. Soon we had the tube securely taped to his face. Then and only then did I let it go.

We continued to survey Paul, top to bottom, side to side, back to front, checking we hadn't missed any other injuries. Brian placed a rigid collar around Paul's neck. The hospital doctors had splinted his leg. They asked me to check his abdomen. It was as stiff as a board. He was bleeding internally. We had already inserted an intravenous line into the veins in the crook of his left elbow, and now we matched it with another on the right side and started to infuse more fluids.

While one of the hospital doctors inserted a tube into Paul's bladder, I reinserted the laryngoscope and passed a tube down into Paul's stomach to remove the blood he had swallowed.

'How's the cross-match going?' I asked.

'Another five minutes,' came the reply.

Paul was pale and his pulse abnormally high. He needed the blood soon but there was nothing I could do to make it appear any faster.

Now we faced the other huge problem for Paul. He was in the wrong hospital.

We were in a small outer-suburban hospital over fifty kilometres from the Royal Alexandria Hospital for Children in Camperdown, in inner Sydney, where the high-tech equipment and specialists he so desperately needed were located. If Paul was to have any chance of survival we would have to abandon the relative comfort of this hospital and journey across town. I estimated we could do the journey in fourteen minutes.

Outside on the hospital helipad was the only type of vehicle capable of transporting Paul so quickly and efficiently. A Dauphin 365C-2 helicopter, with twin 650 horsepower jet turbine engines. The CareFlight chopper, piloted by Alain Le Lec, could reach speeds of over two hundred and twenty kilometres an hour.

We had done as much as we could for Paul. It was now time to prepare and package him for transport. First we wrapped him in a large aluminium foil rescue blanket to minimise heat loss. Brian, two wardsmen and I stood on one side of the table and burrowed our hands under Paul's legs, neck and head. As one, we lifted him just far enough for Alain and Terry Mortimer, the chopper crewman, to slide the orange vinyl and aluminium aircraft stretcher underneath him. Gently we laid him down. To prevent any movement of his neck, large orange foam pads were placed on either side of Paul's head and secured by velcro straps.

We then lifted a large four-legged metal container, called a stretcher bridge, off the floor and attached it over the top of the stretcher. This recently designed bridge contained all the life-support equipment Paul needed for the trip. It would not be removed until he was in the intensive care unit at the Children's Hospital. We transferred him from the hospital monitors to those in the stretcher bridge. Finally, once we had connected his breathing tube to the ventilator on the bridge, we were ready to move. There was only time for a quick goodbye from Paul's mother Evelyn who, in spite of multiple fractured ribs, had struggled to be with her boy.

Alain and Terry hurried ahead to open the doors of the helicopter and prepare it for flight while Brian and I, with the help of a host of doctors, nurses and orderlies, moved out through the main entrance. Patients in the waiting room looked on in stunned silence.

We loaded Paul into the aircraft and attached the stretcher bridge to two umbilical cords. One supplied oxygen to the ventilator and the suction unit, the other supplied power to all the monitors. Throughout the trip I would be able to measure all Paul's vital signs. Any faults in the life-support systems would trigger alarms, which would be transmitted through the aircraft intercom into my flying helmet.

A nurse raced up and passed us the blood. While Brian and I commenced the transfusion, Terry ushered the helpers and onlookers well clear of the aircraft and Alain commenced the start sequence.

Two minutes later we were airborne. By our standards the trip passed uneventfully. Brian and I were busy continuously checking the life-support systems, administering drugs and pumping in blood through the drip. The uneventfulness of the flight was testimony to our team's meticulous preparation prior to transport, and after fourteen minutes we landed safely at the Children's Hospital.

We handed Paul over to the hospital's medical team. We had done everything we could, now it was their turn to continue the fight for his survival. I knew he was in good hands. As I turned back to the helicopter I felt the adrenaline drain from my system; my job was over.

When I made my final follow-up report ten days later, Paul was still alive. His brain injury had not required surgery. He had not completely regained consciousness, but each day he was improving. His torn spleen had not ruptured through its capsule, and although he had lost a considerable amount of blood around the organ, scans suggested that the bleeding had stopped. It was a risk not to remove it, lest it bleed again, but if it could be left in it would serve his immune system well for the rest of his life. His pancreas had been severely damaged but this, too, was resolving. Several operations had already been performed to correct the fractures to his leg and his facial bones, but many more lay ahead for him. I was cautiously optimistic for him, although I knew he was still a very sick young boy.

The frantic nature of emergency medicine makes routine long-term follow-up logistically impossible. If there is one thing that frustrates those working in the field, it is never knowing how patients recover in the long term. All I could do was trust that Paul had been given the optimum chance of surviving.

Twelve years passed.

I began the research for this book and asked the medical records department of the Children's Hospital to contact Paul's family for permission to review his case to see whether, first, he had survived, and if so, how he had fared. I knew that CareFlight had proven over and over that a senior paramedic and senior doctor working in conjunction provided the best possible outcome for trauma victims; but it was one thing to know this in theory and another altogether to put it to the test and find out whether one particular patient had ended up on the right side of the statistics.

Paul's mother Evelyn answered the phone when the medical records administrator rang. Her reply, when I heard it, brought tears to my eyes. 'Paul's at university today but I'm sure he wouldn't mind.'

That simple statement struck me to my soul. For years the team at CareFlight had battled to raise the money to keep flying. Government funds always fell well short of what we needed. The rest we received from corporate sponsorship and community fundraising. The Care-Flight team was driven by an intense desire to take the highest standard of emergency medicine to wherever it was needed, whether that was the bottom of a cliff, the remote outback or a small country hospital. We pulled brutal shifts to provide round-the-clock service and spent our rostered days off fighting for the service's survival as the knockers attempted to shut us down. Evelyn's statement made it all seem worthwhile.

She rang me two days later. After thanking me for what I had done, and clearly as emotional as I was, she told me Paul's story. It hadn't been easy. He had taken some months to recover fully from the head injury, and having a hip in plaster for seven weeks, followed by months of physiotherapy, had made school very difficult. He had required multiple operations to his thigh and facial bones, but Paul and Evelyn had battled on, accepting challenge after challenge, and rising above them all. Paul is now in his fourth year of university doing a double degree in science and electrical engineering. To my mind he and his mum are both heroes.

It was no accident that the CareFlight team was able to help save Paul that day. The standard of service was the culmination of many years of training, planning, negotiation and experience, often in the face of criticism and doubt. Just over three years previously various senior health professionals had told us that there was no need for a formal medical helicopter and retrieval service in New South Wales. We ignored them. Paul's case was mission number 1285. To date, CareFlight has amassed over eleven thousand such missions.

It is time CareFlight's story, and the development of retrieval medicine, came to light. I can only tell my side of that story. I do not hold myself out as the bravest or the best. Many other people have done braver deeds over a much longer time. Most have journeyed along a path as difficult as mine. But I was the first full-time rescue helicopter doctor in Australia and saw medical helicopter and retrieval medicine develop from the crude early days to the sophisticated service it is today.

I write what follows in the spirit of those people who have provided, and continue to provide each and every day, this essential, life-saving service the length and breadth of Australia.

PART I
Up and Away

Life's delays are not necessarily life's denials.

Tony Robbins

1

The first plane I ever flew was a Qantas Boeing 707. I was twelve years old.

I was obsessed by anything to do with aviation. I pored over books about flying, and dozens of World War II model planes dangled on fishing lines from my bedroom ceiling. My sister and I lived with my mother since our parents' divorce, and Mum had scrimped and saved to take us on our first big holiday, to New Zealand. It was on our return trip from Christchurch that I took control of the international airliner, albeit for the briefest of moments.

As we sat waiting for takeoff Mum encouraged me to ask the chief steward whether I could visit the flight deck.

'You'll need to write a letter to the captain,' he replied sternly.

I grabbed Mum's drink coaster and stood to read the captain's name on the board on the forward bulkhead.

Dear Captain Cook, I wrote. *May I please visit the poop deck of your* Endeavour?

The steward raised his eyebrow at my cheeky letter but agreed to pass it on. I knew that such requests were rarely granted but hoped my joke about the captain's name would help.

Midflight the steward said the captain had given his permission, and I was fit to burst as I walked up the aisle. My first impression of the flight deck was how small it was. How could the pilots achieve anything at all in such a restricted space, let alone fly more than a hundred passengers across the world? I was later to achieve far more complex tasks from a flight deck far smaller.

The captain and crew introduced themselves and seemed remarkably idle to me, considering they were supposed to be flying a jetliner. 'This is the altimeter, it tells us how high we are,' the captain told me. I already knew from all my reading what most of the instruments were, but I hung on his every word. When he had finished he asked me whether I had any questions.

'Why is the throttle on number two set lower than the other three engines? The exhaust gas temperature gauge on two is also a bit low, is there a problem with that engine?' I asked precociously.

The captain glanced at the flight engineer then silently adjusted the throttle so that it was in line with the others. 'It appears you know your stuff, young lad,' he replied. 'Perhaps you might like to tweak that knob to the left and see what happens.'

I was not familiar with the instrument he pointed to, but dutifully obeyed. No sooner had I turned the knob than the aircraft banked to the left and then levelled on a new course to the south-west. I had just turned a jetliner!

'Bring it back to 280 degrees,' Captain Cook requested. Again I twisted the knob till the dial read 280, and the plane banked to the right to resume its former course. My grin was almost wider than my face.

As soon as I returned to my seat I blurted excitedly, 'Mum, did you feel the plane bank left and right a few minutes ago? That was *me*. I was flying the plane!' This grabbed the attention of everyone around us, and under their curious stares I felt like a king. 'I'm going to fly one day, I'm going to be a pilot,' I declared to all around me.

But somewhere over the next five years the dream faded. My mum encouraged me to follow my heart but Dad wanted me to take a more secure path and follow him into medicine – he was a radiologist. With a year to go before finishing high school I was more interested in bushwalking, abseiling, or any other adrenaline sport I could pursue, than studying. One day my dad sat me down and repeated what had become a standard 'discussion'. I was too smart to be a pilot, I should become a doctor instead. I had heard this lecture many times before but for some reason my father's heroic tales of saving people from the brink of death caught my imagination that day. Suddenly I became determined to gain the grades required for medical school. I needed to be in the top five per cent in the final school exams. Achieving those marks became all consuming and when I look back now I see this as the start of an obsessive determination that would be both a blessing and a curse later in my life. The dream of flying disappeared into oblivion.

I achieved the grades but found medical school largely tiresome and boring, as did most of my fellow students. Learning about the branches of the external carotid artery, or the ten causes of an enlarged liver, was a far cry from the excitement and glory I had been expecting.

The exception was accident and emergency medicine. There I found the drama and thrill I craved; this was where people's lives were saved or lost on a single decision. It was challenging and exhausting, but I felt in my element. I spent many nights and weekends as an extra in the emergency room and as an honorary ambulance officer. While I was not allowed to do much in this role, it was common for ambulances to be dispatched with just one officer, and so in reality my services were very much appreciated.

The closest I came to flying again was in my fourth year at med school, at the annual airport disaster exercise. I had volunteered to be a victim and would be plastered with make-up to look injured and then be placed near the wreckage along with fifty other 'passengers'. The Bank of New South Wales rescue helicopter would fly the two highest priority patients across Botany Bay to Prince Henry Hospital. The chopper was a M*A*S*H style Bell 47 with two external stretchers. When volunteers were called for, my hand shot up so fast I nearly dislocated my shoulder. To my dismay forty-nine other hands joined it just as quickly.

I was placed next to the crashed aircraft and given a sheet describing my injuries and how I was to act. It was obvious my injuries were only minor and my chances of a helicopter flight nil. I ripped up the sheet and created a new script which gave me serious head and neck injuries. Surely that would guarantee my flight.

I was too convincing. As I was stretchered to the triage point the medical commander briefly examined me and assigned me a low priority tag. 'This one's too seriously injured to waste our scarce resources on,' he explained. I was put to one side with a few of my mates and we watched forlornly as the helicopter departed with the two lucky victims. For some reason I felt despondent. It seemed to me that the opportunity of a lifetime had passed me by.

I had yet to realise that life's delays are not necessarily life's denials.

2

To the person who stole my wallet in July 1979, I'd like to say a sincere thank you. At the time, though, the loss of my wallet felt like the last straw.

I was working as an intern in an inner-city hospital. Not a minute went by when I didn't ask myself what on earth I was doing. I had graduated from medical school but although I could call myself 'Doctor', my duties, apart from the prescribed stint in casualty, were largely pushing a pen – ordering tests, writing up notes, filling out forms – following orders, and getting out of bed when more senior doctors preferred to stay asleep. Eighty-hour working weeks were common yet the work was far removed from my high-school fantasies of saving lives.

On that fateful day I had briefly left a patient in one of the emergency ward cubicles in order to attend a resuscitation in the trauma room. I returned five minutes later to find the patient and my wallet had both disappeared. That one act of ingratitude triggered all the other stresses of my internship – the unrealistic workloads, the inhuman hours, the lack of respect despite the weight of responsibilities we were asked to shoulder. Suddenly it was all too much to bear. I raved and shouted while the nurses looked on in scared bewilderment. I thumped the desk and punched a large dent in the cubicle wall. Eventually my anger gave way to grief and I slumped into my seat and cried. What had I done to deserve this? No answers were forthcoming, and I remembered that real doctors don't cry.

Over the next few days I spent my scarce leisure hours replacing the wallet's contents: my driver's licence, my registration tickets and my licence to scuba dive.

'Yes, of course we can replace your licence,' the lady from the Federation of Australian Underwater Instructors told me. 'Do you have any other endorsements you would like to add to your licence – first aid, resuscitation, anything like that?'

No problem there, I thought, and confidently stated that I was, in fact, a doctor.

'I'm afraid we don't accept a medical degree as proof of first-aid competency,' she replied.

I was stunned. It was okay for me to run a casualty department single-handedly, but I wasn't considered competent in first aid?

'What you require is an advanced resuscitation certificate from the Life Saving Society.' No amount of explanation would convince her, and eventually I gave up. Just another hurdle, I thought as I slammed down the phone. In the face of such an absurd rule, I was determined to get that damned accreditation come hell or high water.

A couple of months later, having gone off and obtained the appropriate certificate from the Surf Life Saving Association, I called the FAUI once again.

'I'm sorry, sir, we only recognise certificates from the *Royal* Life Saving Society, not the *Surf* Life Saving Association.'

I didn't realise there was a difference, but it seemed the two organisations were unconnected. How could still-water rescue competency be better than surf rescue competency?

None of my pleading or explaining got me anywhere, and my scuba diving licence was reissued without any additional endorsements. It was so typical of my life, I thought, feeling very sorry for myself. It seemed as though everything was conspiring against me. When was something good going to happen?

Not long afterwards that question was answered. One evening, two weeks after completing the advanced resuscitation course, I received a phone call from Frank Best, one of the instructors.

'Look, I don't know if this will interest you but I work as a volunteer rescue crewman for the Bank of New South Wales rescue helicopter and right now we're short of volunteer doctors to work on the aircraft. I was just wondering whether you'd be interested in joining the crew.'

Would I be interested? Let me think about that for a moment. 'Yes!' I shouted. 'Absolutely! What do you want me to do?'

My association with rescue helicopters had begun, and all because a patient had stolen my wallet.

Before I could fly as a medical crewman I had to establish that I was qualified for the job and pass the flight training requirements. Establishing that I was qualified was easy. I just lied.

One evening I went to Balmoral to meet Dr Sue Rowley, the honorary medical director of the Bank of New South Wales Rescue Helicopter Service. Sue is extremely experienced in general practice and emergency medicine, and she deserves credit as one of the true pioneers of medically staffed civilian helicopters in Australia.

If she had been more impressed by my enthusiasm than my knowledge, she was kind enough not to mention it. However, she did say that all doctors on the helicopters required a minimum of two years' postgraduate experience. I wasn't prepared for this; Frank was obviously unaware that I had only completed one year.

'So you have completed two years of training?' Sue asked.

I just smiled woodenly and muttered, 'Second year is a lot easier than first year.' What I wasn't telling her was that I had only been a second-year resident for one month.

She went on to describe some of the cases she had been involved with, emphasising the need to be able to take dramatic action in some of the most difficult environments. I would have to be able to transfer my skills into very trying circumstances. Intubating a person's windpipe or inserting intravenous lines while halfway down a cliff was very different from performing these procedures in a well-equipped emergency room.

The truth was, I shuddered at the thought of having to perform these procedures even in the emergency room. As yet I had not done my term as an anaesthesia resident and with only five days of anaesthesia experience in med school I was hopelessly inexperienced at such advanced resuscitation procedures. It would be another three months before I completed my anaesthesia term, and every day of those three months I prayed that my skills – or lack of them – would not be put to the test. It was too late to turn back now, though, even if I wanted to. At the end of the interview Sue gave me the nod to continue with flight training and then, subject to satisfactory report by the crew chief, I would be approved to flight status.

The next step was to attend a crew training day at Long Reef Beach. The aircraft was stationed at the base there on the weekends, having transferred from its weekday base at Royal North Shore Hospital. I turned up five hours before the rest of the crew and met Bob Ford, the crew chief.

'First you have to do a run-swim-run to see that you're fit enough, so let's go down to the beach and get started,' he said.

Nobody had mentioned this. In the last few years I hadn't had time for even the most basic of fitness regimes – sport was one of the first things to be sacrificed. I kept my fingers crossed that my dashes between hospital wards would stand me in good stead.

The jog along the beach was straightforward but the pool swim was difficult. It was high tide and the sea pool was awash with choppy waves. I had to complete ten laps, and by the fifth lap I felt as though I had swallowed half the Pacific Ocean. Later that day I spent considerable time relieving myself of all that ingested sea water. I struggled on, completing the four-hundred-metre swim in slightly less than ten minutes. (The requirement was eight minutes for crewmen, but some leniency was granted to the doctors.) By the end of the second run I was just happy I had survived.

It was time to start on the helicopter training. This was the moment I had dreamed of for weeks.

'None of what you are about to do is difficult,' Bob told me. 'The difficult bit is doing it exactly as you're taught while the noise of the aircraft is frazzling your brain cells. No matter how easy this might seem now, when the aircraft is going you *will* make mistakes. You just have to repeat the training often enough so that those mistakes become less and less frequent.'

We walked up to the top of the headland where the aircraft was parked. This was my first close-up view of a helicopter. The Bell 206B

Jet Ranger had far sleeker lines than the flying goldfish bowl they had been using when I had been a 'victim' at the airport disaster four years earlier. The aircraft was painted in the blue and white colours of the Bank of New South Wales, the service's major corporate sponsor.

It was beautiful. Its lines were stylish and sleek, and it looked as though it was going fast even when it was just sitting on the ground. It seemed impossibly fragile, though. The blades rocked gently in the breeze. It was hard to believe they could lift the aircraft into the air, let alone carry five passengers on a magic carpet ride at over two hundred kilometres per hour.

Over the next hour Bob showed me around the aircraft. First he taught me how potentially dangerous helicopters are. At normal rotor speed the main blades and the tail rotors are all but invisible. 'The tail boom is totally out of bounds to all but the pilot,' Bob instructed. 'If the pilot is sitting in his seat you never, never, *never* come under the rotor disc without specific thumbs-up permission from him. Most dangerous of all, as the blades are slowing down to stop, they can rock down on their hinge just low enough to chop your head off.'

So the first thing I learned was that the crewman and doctor had to guard the aircraft whenever the pilot was on board. We had stations to maintain to ensure both the safety of the aircraft and of any bystanders who did not treat the rotors with the respect they deserved. Even standing near the aircraft could be extremely hazardous when it was landing on beaches – the resulting sandstorm could easily blind people and lead them to blunder into the deadly blades.

Next we passed on to basic respect for the helicopter's fragility. Because the aircraft weight needed to be kept to a minimum, the external cladding and doors were far less robust than those of a family car.

'Even leaving your seatbelt out the door when you climb on board can bang a hole in the fuselage in seconds. Make sure you never do it,' Bob warned.

Every item of equipment on board needed to be put away and secured, and it quickly became obvious that there was very little room left over once everything was in place. The aircraft was so small that the left side of the superstructure had to be taken apart to get the stretchers in, then reassembled once the stretchers were in place. Bob then showed me how the seatbelts worked and explained what I could touch and what was out of bounds.

'There are a number of flight skills to learn. The first one we call "in and out at the hover",' he said. 'Imagine finding a victim where there's no space to land. They might be on the edge of a cliff, a wharf, or even a boat. This simple technique is the easiest way to get to them. Knowing how to do this may save somebody's life.'

As it turned out, Bob and I would owe our own survival to this very technique several years later in the firestorms of 1983.

'Sit in the aircraft and let's pretend you're in a hover a metre above a cliff ledge,' Bob said. 'Tap the pilot on the shoulder to let him know you're going; remove your helmet, unclip your seatbelt and reclip it behind you. Now open the door, step out onto the aircraft step and then down to the skid.' He pointed to the ski-like base of the helicopter, then continued. 'Kneel down and close the door over your head, making sure you have a firm hold on the step. Now that you have closed the door, twist around and step off onto the ground, then walk in front of the aircraft so the pilot can see you're okay.'

I followed Bob's instructions to the letter.

'Now do it again,' he ordered.

I repeated the manoeuvre without a mistake.

'Now do it again,' Bob said.

I couldn't understand why; the technique was so simple. But I did as I was told.

'Fine, now let's do it the other way round.' I did. Three times. All faultless. When are we going to do something complicated? I thought.

'Now let's use this technique for a surf rescue. Imagine that somebody requires rescuing from the water. We use exactly the same technique to reach them. Get out onto the skid, this time stand upright and just step off the skid into the water. Don't jump, it will jostle the aircraft. The pilot should have you around two or three metres above the water; it's a simple procedure.'

I couldn't argue with Bob about that. We ran through the manoeuvre a few times without a hitch.

'Once you have the victim in the rescue strop' – he had already shown me the rescue harness, an inflatable webbing belt which passed under the victim's armpits – 'the pilot will fly over you and drop the rescue line.' Bob showed me the handle attached to one of the pilot's main control levers. It was just a simple pushbike handbrake, but when he squeezed it the canister underneath the aircraft opened like a small bomb-bay. Out fell a ten-metre rescue rope. Two metres from the end of the line was a soccer ball partially filled with lead to make it fall and partially filled with foam to make it float. From the far side of the ball two lines continued with stainless-steel snap links attached.

'The pilot will bring the line to you by looking into the mirror near his right foot. Once you have the line, attach yourself first and then the victim.' He showed me how to do this, acting the role of the victim. 'When you're both ready, put your hand to the side and give a thumbs-up to the pilot. He will then raise you both out of the water to approximately one metre. At this point, give him another thumbs-up. If you don't, he will assume something is wrong and return you to the water to start again.

'Once you're on your way, wrap your legs around the patient and engage them in polite conversation, as they're always terrified. Once you're over the beach, the pilot will lower you. It's very difficult for him to know when you're about to touch down, so when you have about one metre to go, give him another thumbs-up so he can set you down gently. If for some reason you see the landing point he has chosen is inappropriate, wave him off with both hands.'

We practised the technique together, pretending to jump into the water, placing the rescue strop, attaching the harnesses, giving the right hand signals. Again it was so straightforward that the repetitions seemed completely unnecessary.

I was then taught about the use of the helicopter rescue hoist. 'The hoist will only lift ninety kilos, that's why we have to use the static surf line for all water rescues, or when you need to retrieve two people, or a crewman and a stretcher at the same time. Winching operations are dangerous and there are no margins for error.' Bob's face was stern. 'Treat them with great respect – they're the most hazardous part of helicopter rescue work.'

Again we simulated the procedures and after three hours I thought I had it all perfectly memorised. I waited with mounting excitement for the rest of the crew to arrive and for flight training to commence.

Finally, once I'd been introduced to the team and had sat patiently as all the techniques I had learnt that morning were reviewed for the rest of the crew, it was time to put all my practice to the test.

As the Jet Ranger fired up for the first time, I felt adrenaline surge through my bloodstream. There was a high-pitched scream from the starter motor and the *tick, tick, tick* of the igniter circuit. As fuel flowed into the jet turbine there was a sudden *whoosh* at ignition and then the scream was replaced by the roar of acceleration and the thump and flap of the rotors. The delicate little machine had transformed into a raging monster.

After a minute of winding up, the tail rotor was invisible and the main rotors a greyish disk above the machine. 'See what I mean?' screamed Bob into my ear. 'Just because you can't see the rotors doesn't mean they won't kill you.' As the pilot increased power, the rotor disk slowly raised and dragged the aircraft up a metre from the ground. In spite of Bob's warning I was totally unprepared for the downdraft and the noise that assailed my senses. The blades thrashed the air and the sound was so violent it obliterated rational thought, instilling in me a vague disturbing fear at the power of this machine.

I barely registered as one by one the crewmen practised their 'in and out on the hover' technique, all without a single mistake. I waited, half excited, half terrified, for my turn. Bob gave me the all-clear and I crouched down as low as I could, much lower than I needed to, and ran to the aircraft. I climbed aboard the skid, which was hovering at waist level. I entered the aircraft, closed the door, and then after a few seconds reversed the procedure till I was standing back next to Bob. My knees were trembling a little but I thought I'd done a pretty good job.

Bob was shaking his head. I followed his pointed finger to where I had jammed the seatbelt in the door; it was banging against the aircraft's fragile skin. On his signal the aircraft returned to the ground and he put the belt back in place. I felt like a prize idiot. Now I realised why he had made me practise even the simplest of skills over and over. Confronted by the chopper's overwhelmingly powerful presence, the lessons I had learnt had evaporated, making me fall back on instinct. And that is one of the fundamental challenges of heli-copter flying – instinctive responses are often wrong. It's only through endless practice that you can be sure your first response will be the right one.

My last land-based procedure was to be winched back into the aircraft. Each of the crew had done this without incident. On Bob's radio instructions the aircraft flew away from the training area so he could talk to me about the sequence one last time. I listened atten-tively and with great humility.

Finally Bob signalled the aircraft to return and from fifteen metres above my head the rescue hoist cable snaked down. The crew were watching intently, and I quietly prayed that I would at least get this one right. I was anxious to get the manoeuvre over and done with, so as soon as the winch hook descended to waist height I grabbed the cable to attach it to my harness.

Twenty thousand volts jolted through my body and my arm jerked backwards. For a moment I couldn't work out what was going on, then I noticed that all the crew were smiling and laughing. I had no time to wonder at the joke as I attached the cable and was hoisted, spinning in a slow circle, up towards the aircraft. I kept my eyes on the skid and raised my arms to stop myself hitting it. Once I had pulled myself up and into the aircraft I began to grin idiotically, as though I had just pulled off some death-defying feat.

With a smirk on his face – the first time I had seen him smile – Bob later told me of my mistake. 'What you missed was that every other crewman let that winch hook touch the ground before he picked it up. A helicopter develops loads of static electricity. We all went through the same little ritual when we first joined. I doubt that you'll ever make that mistake again!' He was positively beaming.

After a short break and a few reassuring pats on the back, it was time for my first water rescue. The chopper pilot flew one of the crewmen and myself to about five hundred metres off the beach. By now I had begun to realise how difficult the most basic procedures were in this environment. My natural response was to rush, as if my thought processes had been speeded up; I never got used to it but I did eventually learn to consciously slow my actions down. That first day, however, in spite of mentally rehearsing over and over the procedures for exiting the aircraft, I would have leapt into the water still wearing my flying helmet had it not been for the quick action of the crewman!

I somehow managed to survive that first water jump and in fact it was exhilarating to launch myself out of the sky and into the ocean. The crewman followed me into the water and bobbed around next to me as we watched the Jet Ranger depart around the headland. I felt a sudden sense of isolation and trepidation as our only means of exit disappeared from sight.

'He's giving us some space so I can repeat the briefing,' the crewman explained. 'It's also worthwhile thinking what it would be like to be out here if you were a real victim.'

I tried to imagine how I would feel, scared and cold, lost somewhere amongst the waves. As the aircraft swooped around the headland and came into a hover just short of our position I was gripped by a sense of relief and, close on its heels, exhilaration. Helicopters have a gracefulness that makes all their manoeuvres seem effortless.

The canister below the aircraft opened and the soccer ball on the end of the static line dropped down to us. Soon we were attached, and with a thumbs-up I signalled for us to be lifted from the water. I could see the crew gathered on the beach nearby to watch our return. Everything seemed to be going well. With the aircraft and rescue line out of sight above us, I felt as though I was flying, zipping across the water like Peter Pan.

Suddenly the Jet Ranger mysteriously returned to the hover and we were unceremoniously dropped back into the sea, only to be dragged immediately out again. This was repeated several times until I was thoroughly waterlogged.

'This is called tea-bagging!' screamed the crewman in my ear. 'It's the pilot's way of welcoming you to the service!' He was grinning like a lunatic and I could tell even from this distance that the other crewmen were enjoying the entertainment just as much. I was beginning to wonder whether I wouldn't be happier playing golf or knitting during my precious time off instead of hanging around with this bunch of madmen.

Eventually we made it back to the beach and I received several hearty congratulatory slaps on the shoulder from crewmen clearly unable to contain their mirth. After the aircraft shut down we gathered for a final debriefing. I did not feel at all confident that I had performed satisfactorily, so I was very surprised when Bob announced that I had passed all the skill stations. 'Believe me, you've performed far better than most other doctors on their first day.' He smiled when he saw my dubious expression. 'You'll need to keep practising like we all do, but as far as I'm concerned, welcome to the crew.' He turned to a man I had not met before, a friendly and slightly balding bloke with a dark grey beard. He seemed to have enjoyed my dunking as much as everyone else. Bob introduced us. 'Ken, this is Ian Badham, the service director.'

'Welcome to the service,' said Ian. 'If you're good enough for Bob and Sue Rowley, you're good enough for me. Consider yourself part of the team.'

It wasn't until later that I learnt Ian was the pioneer of the surf rescue helicopter concept in Australia, having introduced it back in 1973. As a journalist and a member of the Australian Surf Life Saving Association, he'd been selected to participate in an instructional congress being held in New Zealand under the auspices of the newly formed World Life Saving Assoication. He'd seen a demonstration of the surf helicopter there and, convinced that Sydney needed this service, had persuaded the Bank of New South Wales to sponsor a rescue helicopter trial. At the time there were no civil rescue helicopter services in Australia, but nevertheless Ian made it become a reality in just eighteen months. The trial was a success and the service flourished under Ian's guidance; there were now six helicopters flying around Australia, one in each capital city. The Sydney service was the only year-round service with weekend medical, as well as rescue, crew. The other five performed summer weekend beach patrols.

Amidst applause I was handed my service uniform. In line with the casual style of the service in those days, it consisted of red shorts, white T-shirt with logo, and a pair of joggers. I was now a rescue helicopter medical crewman and I couldn't wait for my first day of duty.

3

'Train on platform four, if there is a doctor on board please contact the station master.'

The train had just pulled into Strathfield station. I was on my way home from work, exhausted, but this was a call I could not ignore. 'I'm a doctor, can I help you?' I asked the portly station master.

'Over this way.' He beckoned me to follow him across to the other side of the platform. Blood was dripping out of the doorway to the carriage of another suburban train.

Inside on the floor was a schoolboy, perhaps fourteen years old. He lay on his side in a pool of blood, which had obviously flowed from the fracture in the side of his head. He was pale and unresponsive; his breathing was shallow and irregular, his pulse rapid and thready. His skin was a pale cream without a hint of pink. He was severely shocked from the loss of blood and had clearly sustained a massive blow to his head.

'Passengers said he stuck his head out the open door as the train approached the station. He must have hit one of the stanchions next to the track,' the station master told me shakily. 'We've called the ambulance.'

As I pondered what to do next, another station attendant arrived with a large old brown suitcase. He stopped short of the carriage door and pushed the suitcase across the blood-stained floor to me. 'First-aid kit,' he stammered, then turned and ran.

I opened the battered suitcase, hoping for bandages, maybe even some intravenous fluids. I didn't know what to expect, but I wasn't prepared for what I found. Cotton wool. Just cotton wool. Not a small packet or even several packets. The entire contents of the suitcase consisted of one massive wad of cotton wool. I shook my head in dismay.

'Has anyone got something I can use as a bandage?' I asked the shocked onlookers. No reply. Remembering back to my first-aid course and the need to be resourceful, I looked at the women. 'How about some pantihose to make a head bandage?' The women backed away nervously.

Just then the ambulance paramedics arrived. I described the situation and they seemed to tolerate my presence. While one of them put an oxygen mask in place and bandaged the boy's head, another joined me in placing IV lines in both his arms. After strapping a collar around his neck in case he had any spinal injuries, we loaded the boy onto the stretcher. Soon he was on his way to the hospital where I worked.

First thing the following day when I went on duty I checked on the boy in intensive care. His parents were distraught. They had just agreed to the withdrawal of life support. He died soon after.

The horror of this accident brought home to me the irony of my situation at the hospital. I was the neurosurgery resident. The title sounded impressive, but in reality I was still a pen-pusher, although I occasionally got to hold a retractor for a neurosurgeon in theatre. My knowledge of the management of severe head injuries was next to nil.

What else could I have done? What immediate action could I have taken to improve the boy's chances of survival? Although I asked myself these questions endlessly, agonising over whether I could have done something more, I didn't know the answers. Perhaps it was true, as my superiors said, that he was too far gone before I arrived, but maybe, just maybe, a more aggressive approach to his treatment might have made a difference.

It would be some years before I really understood the nature of head injuries and the role of medical management at the accident scene. But the frustration and sadness of that day made me determined to search for answers, and although I didn't realise it at the time, it drove me over the next ten years to help create the world's most sophisticated head injury resuscitation and transport service.

■ ■ ■

Sydney turned on a spectacular day for my first outing as a medical crewman. It was February 1980. An unseasonable westerly wind had blown the city's usual smoggy blanket far out to sea, and as I crossed the Sydney Harbour Bridge in the train the city looked magnificent. Soon I would see it from an even better viewpoint, one that few people are lucky enough to experience.

At Royal North Shore Hospital I walked up the main road to the hilltop where the helicopter waited. Slowly, as I rounded the top of the hill, the aircraft revealed itself: first the rotors, impossibly long and delicate; then the round bubble body and extended tail fin; finally the skids, barely keeping the machine from taking flight. I was fit to burst with excitement and anticipation.

I headed for a building over to my left. To call this a rescue base was a gross exaggeration. In reality it was an old fibro shack that stood alone in the hospital car park. It was due to be demolished as soon as alternative accommodation could be found for the service. It looked as though the demolition job had already begun.

Inside I found Terry Lee, the pilot, and Dick Graham, the crew-man. Terry worked for one of the TV stations and did casual paid shifts for the service. Dick was a solicitor and a volunteer; only Bob Ford was a paid crewman. Dick and Terry had been warned that this was my first day, but if my ignorance frustrated them, it didn't show. They assumed I knew nothing, which was pretty close to the truth. (By contrast, CareFlight familiarisation training for doctors under-taking helicopter operations is now two weeks full-time!)

Over the next hour Dick talked me through the checks on the rescue equipment. We unloaded the static line and inspected it inch by inch, and then I discovered the frustratingly difficult challenge of repacking it into its little canister below the belly of the chopper. We checked harnesses, dive gear (the helicopter service carried out dive operations for the police, who in those days did not have a specialist unit) and the rescue hoist. When we moved to the medical gear, I started to feel a little more at home. Two brown fishing tackle boxes held drug ampoules, syringes, intravenous fluids, bandages, tubes and splints. An Oxy Viva portable oxygen and suction unit was kept in the aircraft boot behind the left rear door, while a larger cylinder was clamped behind the pilot's seat on the right side of the aircraft. Finally we took the Lifepak 5 heart monitor off the overnight recharger and strapped it behind the left rear seat. We didn't need to check the pulse oximeter syringe pumps or transport ventilator. Such things had yet to be invented.

As the three of us walked across the pad towards the helicopter, Terry turned to me. 'Doctors who are willing to fly with us are harder to find than rescue crewmen,' he said, 'so you get the honour of the front seat. Anyway, if we need to do a water rescue it makes more sense for the rescue crewman to be sitting in the back.'

Inside the chopper, perspex windows reached from above my head down to below my feet. I had a clear view all around me, as though I wasn't sitting inside a vehicle at all. This would provide a very different perspective from the tiny window in a commercial aircraft, or even the rear seat where Dick would sit. Terry took his seat on the right-hand side, saying, 'Later I'll give you a more complete brief on the aircraft but for our morning patrol just remember these three things. Firstly, don't touch anything except to push the intercom button to talk to us. Secondly, don't put anything, including that,' he nodded at my camera, 'under the collective control.'

'What's the collective control?' I asked.

Terry pointed to a large lever between our seats, where you would normally find the handbrake in a car. 'Pulling up the collective adds power to the rotors. This changes their angle, or pitch as we call it, to provide more lift. When I pull the collective up, the aircraft goes up; when I push it down, the aircraft goes down. If we have an engine failure, provided I can immediately push the collective right down, we'll glide quite well; you probably wouldn't even notice much difference from a normal descent. Then once we were just above the touchdown point, I would use the momentum of the spinning rotors to give enough lift to soften the landing. The technique is called autorotation. But if the engine fails and I can't push the collective down because you have put your camera underneath it, the rotors will slow down, stop and fold up. Then we will glide like a greased house brick. Is the message clear?'

It was. Crystal clear.

Terry pointed to the switch panel above our head. 'Thirdly and finally, if we crash and I can't do it, throw these switches off.' He pointed to two switches at the front of the panel. One was labelled 'battery', the other 'fuel'.

Crash? Crash! In all my excitement I had never even thought of the possibility. The realisation of the potential danger must have shown on my face because Terry smiled and said, 'This is not a commuter run, we fly fast and low and perform rescues where no one else can. There's little margin for error.'

Dick was standing at Terry's open door. He looked across at me and grinned. 'Don't worry about it.'

'Why not?' I asked.

'The insurance cover we have for the accidental death of the duty doctor is very good,' he chuckled.

'Great,' I replied. 'That's really reassuring.'

Terry went on to describe our patrol. 'We'll depart for Sydney Cove then proceed down the harbour, turn left at Sydney Heads and continue north to Palm Beach. There we'll turn around and head back to Long Reef Beach. You and Dick can then do a practice water rescue before we shut down. All of this should take about thirty minutes.' By car you would be lucky to do that same journey in four hours.

Dick and I helped each other into our wetsuits and rescue harnesses. He showed me how to adjust the sun visor and microphone on my flying helmet, then we took our guard positions. I stood five metres in front of the aircraft while Dick was standing five metres to the right, opposite Terry's door.

From his pilot's seat Terry asked whether it was clear to start by giving us a thumbs-up. Dick and I returned his signal, upon which Terry shattered the peace of the tranquil morning by starting the aircraft and winding it up to flight speed.

Several passers-by stopped to watch us, and I grinned behind my helmet visor, thinking, Am I lucky or what? How long had it been since I had thought that about my life? In a flash I remembered how hard it had been to become a doctor and how few rewards there had been so far. It looked as though the hard slog was about to pay off.

Terry gave another thumbs-up and we approached the aircraft. Following correct procedure, Dick had to walk around to my station so that Terry could see him before making his way to his side of the chopper. In spite of my reaching my seat next to Terry well before him, Dick called 'Seatbelt secure' while I was still fumbling with my harness straps.

'Don't rush,' said Terry kindly, 'that's how you get killed in this game. Just because it gets noisy doesn't mean you have to hurry.'

I nodded, took a deep breath and continued; eventually I called, 'Secure.'

People expect a feeling of acceleration and power as a helicopter takes off, but that's not what happens. Someone once described it as falling upwards, it is such a surprisingly gentle motion, especially in comparison to the power and noise that blasts observers from the outside. The aircraft simply hangs like a pendulum below the rotor disc and is lifted off the ground without any of the acceleration forces produced by a fixed-wing aircraft.

That first day we were hovering a metre above the helipad one moment, the next we were wafting over the car park and the earth was steadily receding below. I didn't feel a thing.

We climbed to the south-east. Suddenly the entire city was laid out before me. The air was so clear we could make out individual buildings over thirty kilometres away. The skyscrapers of North Sydney rose into the blue sky, revealing themselves from behind closer buildings in three-dimensional complexity. Through the perspex window at my feet I could see tiny people and cars moving through the shadowed canyons between the buildings. Looking up I saw the arch of the Harbour Bridge looming behind the skyscrapers; a small red train, just like the one I had caught earlier that morning, was crossing the Bridge. I felt as though I was floating above the cityscape unencumbered, distant enough to be an observer but with such an unobstructed, intimate view as to feel a part of the bustle below me.

Terry made a seemingly unintelligible call to air traffic control and as we passed the massive grey iron bridge spanning the harbour, we turned eastwards to track towards Sydney Heads. The air speedometer read ninety knots. Terry saw me looking at the instrument and seemed to read my mind. 'Double the figure to arrive at kilometres per hour.' We had been slowly accelerating while climbing but it was hard to believe we were travelling so fast.

As we descended to a mere two hundred metres above the harbour I was struck by the incredible beauty of the panorama before me. The sparkling water was dotted with hundreds of white sailing boats tracking between larger ships and ferries. We passed over the hydrofoil heading towards Manly. People waved up at us and I returned their greeting enthusiastically. There's something about helicopters – people always wave, perhaps because it feels as though the chopper's passengers are close enough to call out g'day to, or perhaps these man-made dragonflies catch people's imagination and they sense the swooping joy flying brings.

A few minutes later we reached the Sydney Heads, ten kilometres downstream from the Bridge. Terry made another radio call. All I could understand was, 'SAR watch terminated good-day.' He turned to me and said over the intercom, 'I've just terminated our search and rescue watch with air traffic control, and we are now on search and rescue watch with surf lifesaving. We are now required to remain east of the coast and below one hundred and fifty metres.'

We passed North Head and made a left-hand turn. As Terry descended even further, a flock of seagulls scattered as we invaded their airspace. We were now flying so low that our flight down the harbour felt like it had been in the upper stratosphere in comparison. Soon we were only thirty metres above the water, and a glance at the instrument panel revealed we were travelling at a hundred knots, over two hundred kilometres per hour. I felt an odd sense of disorientation to be waving at people standing on the cliff top above us as we streaked past them.

We swung gently around the headland and flew along Manly Beach. The surf line was a rainbow below my feet: sapphire blue water to the right, transforming to emerald green behind the waves, golden green under the breakers and the yellow of the beach. Board riders and swimmers were in the water; bronzed bodies lay on multicoloured beach towels.

Ahead the next headland reared up, and at what seemed the last possible moment Terry pulled us into a tight right-hand turn. My body was pushed down hard into the seat. 'This is the only feeling of acceleration you'll ever get – straight down,' he explained.

I looked across at Terry and couldn't believe my eyes. Where I expected to see sky outside his window I found myself looking down at a surfer catching a wave! A glance at the instrument panel confirmed we were leaning over at sixty degrees.

As we reached the end of the headland, Terry rolled the aircraft from a steep right bank to a steep left bank in one continuous movement. I caught brief glimpses of tidal pools and fishermen on the rocks below before we were skimming above the next beach. We repeated the sequence ten times, each headland and beach a little different. It would take many flights before I was as proficient as my crew mates at taking in the landscape at such high speed. By the time I recognised objects they were gone. Fishing boat. Rock pool. Car park. Beach patrol. Golf course. More sand.

The run north to Palm Beach, thirty kilometres from Sydney Harbour, passed in a blur of colour and movement. It ended at Barrenjoey Headland, which marks the entrance to Pittwater and Broken Bay, a beautiful waterway the equal of Sydney Harbour but surrounded by the untouched bushland of Ku-ring-gai Chase National Park. Here we banked right and headed out to sea. After ten seconds we turned right again, backtracking southwards but this time flying in a straight line from headland to headland. Below us were the orange marker buoys that supported the shark nets, and we waved down to several surfboats and inflatable rescue boats on their morning patrols.

Ten minutes later we arrived back at Long Reef peninsula, so called because of the lengthy tidal rock-shelf jutting past the headland. On its northern shoulder lies the little sheltered bay of Collaroy Basin. Soon we were in a hover above the basin and Dick was briefing me on our training jump. With nervous excitement I removed my helmet, undid my harness and prepared to exit the aircraft.

'Slowly, properly,' I muttered over and over. The desire to rush was barely controllable. A little voice inside me was urging me to go faster, fuelled by the unbelievable din created by the turbine engine and rotors a metre above my head. I remembered how I had left the seatbelt webbing outside the door on my training day, so once I was kneeling on the skid of the hovering chopper I double-checked that I had not made the same mistake.

The aircraft suddenly bucked on one side and I tensed, wondering what was happening. Then I saw the splash of Dick entering the water below. The chopper had merely reacted to the removal of Dick's weight from the skid on the other side. Terry instantly stabilised the aircraft. Now it was my turn. I took a deep breath, checked below to see that I was not going to land on Dick, pried my shaking hand from the footstep below the door, and leapt into space. There was a feeling of nothingness and a pause in time as I briefly went into free-fall, then the splash and cold of spearing into the sea.

As the cold brine slowly percolated into my wetsuit the canister below the helicopter opened and the weighted ball on the rescue line plopped into the water nearby. The helicopter edged forward, dragging the line within reach, and we hooked ourselves onto the snap links. Thirty seconds later we were standing on the beach, the line, which Terry had jettisoned after our safe landing, in the sand beside us. The chopper headed out to sea to make its approach to the nearby landing site on a grassy knoll further up the headland. Dick quickly washed the rescue line, then we took our guard positions as Terry made his final approach and landing. The trip was over.

We stood in our guard positions for nearly ten minutes while the rotors slowly wound down. While many helicopters were being fitted with rotor brakes that would allow the pilot to stop the rotors once the engine was shut down, we were not so lucky. The time, however, seemed to pass in a moment as I relived the last half-hour and the most amazing ride of my life. I was hooked.

While Dick and I waited for the rotors to stop, Terry walked down the short grassy path to the two-storey brick building that housed the northern beaches radio control room above and the jet-rescue boat base below.

Eventually the rotors ceased turning and gently rocked up and down. Dick retrieved a metal hook on the end of a five-metre length of red webbing tape. He inserted the hook into a hole in the end of one of the blades then pulled the blade round to the back of the aircraft so the rotors were now in line with the fuselage. He then wrapped the tapes around a rod protruding from below the tail fin. It must have been obvious to him that I had no idea why he was doing this.

'You always tie down the rotors so they don't sail around and hit someone or flap up and down and damage the rotor mast.' Dick grinned. 'It also helps to untie the rotors before you start the aircraft,' he said. 'Sooner or later you'll see that one happen! If you're on guard then, signal the pilot to immediately abort the start by slashing your hand across your throat, otherwise the aircraft will be stressed, or you'll cop a flying metal hook in the head!'

By the time Dick and I entered the control room, Terry had our coffee waiting. 'Enjoy that?' he asked, grinning. It was a rhetorical question: his beaming smile was a reflection of mine.

As we sipped our coffee Dick corrected me on my jump. 'Remember, it's a lot easier for the pilot to balance the aircraft during a water jump if we both leave the skids at the same. Also you leapt away from the aircraft, which really threw it around.' Terry nodded in agreement. Dick continued, 'Don't leap off, just step off; you'll still clear the skids and you'll make life a lot easier for the pilot.'

I nodded humbly.

Dick then took me into the radio room and introduced me to the two duty controllers sitting in front of a large panel of radios. It was their job to monitor the radios of each and every patrol team on the beaches between Sydney Heads and Palm Beach. Additionally they monitored the whereabouts of the various rescue assets; namely the inflatable and jet-rescue boats and the helicopter. They assisted in coordinating any inshore rescues on the northern beaches and acted as the contact point for emergency services to request the attendance of the rescue helicopter.

'So you're the guys we did the SAR watch for?' I asked, trying to sound intelligent. Their disapproving looks only confirmed my ignorance.

Dick turned to me. 'We weren't looking after them, they were looking after us. If we fail to make a regular radio report to these guys, they're the ones who initiate a search to find us. That's what a search and rescue watch means.'

Boy, did I have a lot to learn.

We had barely finished our coffee when we heard another helicopter approaching. I rushed outside to find the Channel Ten helicopter heading towards the base. Suspended underneath on a ten-metre cable was a boat engine. I was standing in the middle of the large concrete area adjacent to the building, looking up, dumbfounded. The crewman on board seemed to be a particularly friendly chap, vigorously waving at me. I enthusiastically waved back. He continued to wave, and I continued to wave back until Dick grabbed me and shouted in my ear, 'He's trying to tell you to get off the pad so they can put their load down!' I backed sheepishly out of the way, and they carefully set the engine down right where I had been standing.

After landing their aircraft up on the headland, Dan Tyler, the pilot; crewman Peter MacCormick and Dr Graham Harris sauntered down the hill. My embarrassed apology was accepted after Dick explained it was my first day, and I was introduced to them. I had no idea how closely my future would be entwined with Peter and Dan.

A crowd from the jet-rescue base had gathered around us, and the two explained the mystery mission. They had been the duty rescue crew on the helicopter the day before and had rescued people from a brand-new boat that had been washed up on the rocks near Palm Beach. Cunningly they had decided to hire the Channel Ten helicopter and salvage the engine out of the boat.

Just as they finished their story the rescue alarm sounded from the radio room. As I bolted up the stairs, I hoped that this was going to be the big moment – my first mission. The radio officer first very seriously but then with a widening smirk said that a woman had just rung in and told him, 'You'd better get ready for a rescue, because there's a helicopter flying down Narrabeen Beach and the engine is falling out!'

Although the rest of the day passed without a call for assistance, I was busy coming to terms with this new world. I had grown up in the inner west of Sydney and had never lived near the beach; it was all new territory to me. I had no idea what a massive operation the Surf Life Saving Association ran every weekend. Everyone patiently answered my questions into the late afternoon until it was time to return to the hospital.

We took off from the headland and climbed to three hundred metres before tracking westwards into the setting sun. The flight couldn't have been more different from the morning patrol. It was a gentle journey in the evening haze, a peaceful conclusion to my first day.

4

'Enjoy your practice jump,' Peter Howe, the service's chief pilot, called over the intercom. 'Bet you'll be doing it for real before the day is done.'

With these words ringing in our ears, Gary Connors, the rescue crewman, and I climbed out onto the opposite skids of the hovering helicopter then simultaneously stepped off and into the dirty churning waters adjacent to the Long Reef rescue base.

I had been flying with the rescue helicopter service for three months. I shared the weekend roster with seven other volunteer doctors, and this was my fourth day as a medical crewman. The previous two duty days had been much like the first. I met the crew at the hospital, checked the gear and, after our patrol and practice jump, lounged around while learning more about the workings of helicopters and the beach patrol scene in general. My limited medical experience had not yet been put to the test and for that I was extremely grateful.

I was, however, impatient to experience the excitement of a rescue mission. On my previous two duty days we had scrambled several times for beach rescues but invariably the inflatable rescue boats had completed the task well before our arrival. I was starting to wonder whether these inflatables had made the helicopter redundant.

Our surf patrol on this day, however, had been very different from the easygoing 'fun ride' of the last three duty days. We had undertaken a slow, deliberate review of the twenty-three beaches on the Sydney coastline. Large sea swells were pounding the shores, a result of a tropical cyclone off the south Queensland coast. As we examined each beach Gary radioed details of its appearance to the patrol down below. Simultaneously he pointed out to me the telltale signs of rips, gutters, sandbanks and sweeps, each a potential death trap for the unwary swimmer. Many beach patrols had decided to close their beach but remained on duty as they had no legal power to enforce the closure.

Most importantly to us, it was obvious that the surf would be too big to launch inflatable rescue boats, and so there was every likelihood of us being called upon for surf rescues.

After we had completed our practice jump and returned to shore, Gary reviewed the techniques for mass rescue with Peter and myself. 'If there are two victims to be rescued, we both go in,' he said to me. 'The stronger swimmer – that's me – will stay with the second victim while you take the first to shore. If there are more than two victims, Peter will ferry you backwards and forwards leaving only the last one to me.'

Seconds later the radio operators sounded the alarm. We raced into the radio room. While one operator continued to reply to numerous calls, the other briefed us. 'A sandbank has collapsed behind the surf line at Palm Beach. Several people have been washed out to sea. There is no rescue boat available.'

We turned as one and ran for the door. Within moments Gary and I were donning our wetsuits while Peter started the aircraft. This is it, I thought, my first real rescue! I was gripped with nervous excitement; my hands shook a little with the adrenaline rush, making me fumble as I adjusted my harness. Slow down and do it right the first time, I quietly admonished myself. Soon we were airborne and heading north at maximum speed.

We arrived overhead ten minutes after the first request to 'scramble'. At the southern end of the beach we found a cluster of seven people treading water and frantically waving. They were over five hundred metres offshore and caught in the current. Not even the strongest swimmer could have resisted such a strong sweep.

I was jolted by the gravity of the situation. This was no adventure ride. The survival of seven people depended entirely on Peter, Gary and myself. Perhaps they would not have been so relieved to see us had they realised that one of their rescuers had never done this before.

Peter brought the chopper into a hover three metres above their heads. My hands were moving constantly from buckle to buckle. Could I do this safely? What had I forgotten? I felt Gary tap me on the shoulder; his helmet was already off. He signalled me to take mine off and then flashed a big smile, gave a thumbs-up and mouthed the words, 'You'll be fine.' Those gestures gave me confidence and courage, as well as an enormous feeling of support.

Soon we were out on the skids and then Gary and I quickly dropped into the water amongst the victims. Immediately the five blokes and two girls, all in their teens or early twenties, struggled over to us and clung on for dear life. They were clearly distressed and I was afraid they would drag me underwater in their panic. I quickly followed Gary's lead and blew into the mouthpiece of my wetsuit, inflating its internal bladder till I bobbed around like a cork, giving the victims the support they needed.

Peter had backed the helicopter away several hundred metres to allow us to brief the group about their rescue. Gary's next move caught even me by surprise. Nonchalantly he put his hands behind his head and lay back in the water as though he was lounging on an airbed in a resort swimming pool. 'How's your day going?' he asked cheerfully.

If I was surprised, the victims were stunned. Yet this technique worked beautifully. The panic evaporated from their faces and soon they were all laughing with relief. Gary engaged them in conversation, pointing out that this far out to sea there was no surf or white water to endanger us. He explained that the helicopter could not winch each person into the cabin, rather that I would accompany them one by one to the beach, suspended on the static rope below the aircraft. He promised them that he would be staying out here until the last person had been rescued. As he talked he sorted out in his mind who were the weaker swimmers. One girl in particular seemed exhausted and he motioned for her to paddle away with me for the first pick-up.

When we were ten metres away from the rest of the group I repeated the details of the rescue procedure. Both Gary and I had brought a strop with us from the aircraft. I passed the blue and orange harness around the girl's back and under her arms then clicked together the metal links at each end. Holding the clips firmly in place with my left hand, I gave the thumbs-up to the approaching helicopter with my right. Following Gary's lead I continued to make gentle conversation about what would happen next, which seemed to reassure her considerably. All she needed to do was to hold her arms down by her side to keep the rescue strop in place, and I would do the rest.

Soon we were lifted from the water and thirty seconds later we were being lowered to the awaiting crowd on the beach. Once we had touched down I unclipped her harness and she walked into the arms of the nearest lifesaver. With a smile on my face I gave a thumbs-up and was promptly hoisted back into the air. My last image was of the girl looking up, exhausted, relieved and mouthing the words, 'Thank you.'

I had just done my first rescue! Had it not been for us that girl would almost certainly have drowned. The thrill of the moment was overwhelming. I had helped save someone's life! Not as a small cog in the immense medical wheel, where as a junior doctor my contribution often felt insignificant, but as a rescue crew member snatching a young, healthy woman from a watery death.

As I skimmed back above the waves I felt a sense of immense elation. All the work and effort over the last seven years had been worth it just to be here right now. I whooped with joy, knowing nobody could hear me above the din of the aircraft.

By the time I was dropped into the water next to Gary I had composed myself and was ready to repeat the procedure. Meanwhile Gary had the next person selected, briefed and placed in his rescue strop, ready for me. I was only in the water for ten seconds before my second charge and I rose into the air for the journey back to land and safety. It ran like clockwork and Gary and I repeated the procedure another four times.

With each return journey out to sea I experimented with my own 'flying' technique. I found that as I skimmed above the waves I could hold the empty rescue strop suspended from the other hook at arm's length and use it as a rudder to change the direction I faced. I turned backwards, looking at the crowd as I departed, then slowly rotated, taking in the view and scanning for other victims.

After my last trip I stayed on the beach, receiving numerous slaps on the back from onlookers, victims and members of the beach patrol. I was filled with pride at being the hero of the moment. We all turned to watch Gary and the last victim approach. So that was how I had looked to those waiting on the beach. It was indeed an incredible sight. Gary settled onto the sand next to me, while everyone else retreated from the sandblast from the rotor wash.

He shouted in my ear, 'We need to do several aerial sweeps of the beach in case there are others we've missed.'

I nodded in reply while he signalled to Peter to set the aircraft down nearby. With the aircraft still running he briefed Peter then sat in the left front seat. Incredibly he signalled to me to attach myself once again to the static line. Gary's hand traced a large horizontal circle – they wanted to experiment with me searching from below the aircraft!

It was the weirdest journey of my life. Even the beach patrols faded in comparison to this form of travel! The static line from my harness was clipped to a metal D-ring behind my head and I was suspended leaning slightly forward. With no visible means of support it felt like flying unaided. All I was missing was a cape and some underpants over my wetsuit!

Over the next ten minutes we slowly traversed the length of the beach twice, searching ever further from the surf line. Using the patient strop as a rudder again, I was able to rotate slowly left and right to scan the waters below. Eventually Peter and Gary must have been satisfied that there were no more victims and we returned to the beach. It was none too soon as my harness was restricting the blood supply to my legs, not to mention my testicles. My final landing was a great relief but my legs could not support my weight and I was unceremoniously dumped on my backside.

Several minutes later, having restowed the rescue line, we departed, this time with me in the relative comfort of the back seat. As we flew south back to Long Reef, words tumbled over the intercom as we relived the whole event, sharing each other's perspective of the rescue and enjoying the collective euphoria. We conceded that slinging me under the aircraft was not such a great idea but I had to admit it was a truly amazing way to travel.

Back on the ground we refuelled the aircraft, first testing the mixture for any contamination then cranking each litre in with a hand pump. Eventually we returned to the radio room to recount the mission to the radio operators. Scarcely had we begun when another rescue request was received. Two young lads had taken their surf skis into the awesome surf at Bateau Bay, sixty kilometres north of Sydney. Onlookers and surf lifesavers had watched helplessly as the surf skis were destroyed and both boys swept out to sea. Within minutes we were streaking northward, eighty metres above the white-capped waves and at two hundred kilometres per hour. The large ocean swells continued to roll in below. Peter set a course two kilometres out to sea to track a more direct route to Bateau Bay.

'Can I do one of the radio calls?' I asked him.

'Think you're up to it?'

Bubbling with confidence I said, 'Sure. I've been listening closely over the last three months.'

Peter hesitated for a few seconds, then said, 'Okay, call the ambulance; their call sign is 2KJ-Central. I've set the radios, you're ready to speak.'

'Rescue Helicopter One, this is 2KJ-Central.' As soon as I said these words I knew I had blown it.

'Other way around,' Peter hissed over the intercom.

'Station calling 2KJ-Central?' I heard through the ether. My confidence had taken a nosedive, but Peter motioned with his left hand to continue. 'Ah, this is Rescue Helicopter One. We're heading to the Central Coast for a surf rescue and will maintain contact through surf channels.'

The controller replied, 'Roger; we are aware of the situation at Bateau Bay and have dispatched an ambulance to the scene.'

'Thank you,' was all I could manage.

'Not bad for a first try,' Peter's voice piped up through my headphones. I knew he was being very diplomatic. 'Remember,' he continued, 'it is the controllers on the ends of these radios who decide whether we should be involved in a rescue situation. If we don't sound professional on the airwaves, we don't get respect – or jobs. We may be volunteers but we don't have to sound amateurish.

'Firstly say the station you are calling, to prick their ears up, then who is calling them. Tell them everything important but no more. Be precise about where we are, where we are going, why, when we will get there and what help we need. I'll give you a list of standard radio terms to learn back at base. Now listen to my call to the police and contrast it to your call.' Peter twisted the dials on one of the radios. 'VKG, this is Rescue Helicopter One.'

'Receiving, Rescue One.'

'Departed Long Reef for Bateau Bay. ETA 1510. Report of two surfers in difficulty. Will switch to Central Coast frequency at 1500.'

'Roger. We will notify Central Coast of your situation, out.'

Peter turned to me. 'Hear the difference? No more and no less than they need.'

I might have been eager to learn but that day I realised I had to be patient, to watch and observe rather than rush in headlong without the right preparation. I was extremely grateful that the other crew members were so generous in guiding me through my mistakes.

Twenty minutes later, as we approached Bateau Bay from the south-east, we were lucky to spot the two victims before even commencing our search. Once again Gary and I launched ourselves into the ocean. Gary had suggested that I take the lead, reassuring and instructing the two on the rescue technique. With all the practice from the earlier rescue, this one ran smoothly and efficiently, and within twenty minutes we had completed the rescue and Peter had joined us on the beach, having landed and shut down the aircraft. Several television crews had filmed the whole event and were interviewing the two lads about their experience.

Suddenly one of the beach patrol asked whether we had seen the surf lifesaver who had gone out to the boys' rescue. We looked at him in dumb astonishment. Nobody had told us there were *three* people who needed to be rescued.

Quickly we scrambled back into the helicopter and we were soon in the air. Fifteen minutes later our mood was growing sombre. I was beginning to realise how lucky we had been so far today and how difficult it could be to spot a head in the middle of a white-capped ocean. Without any sign of the missing lifesaver we were starting to wonder whether our search would be futile. The tragedy of one death could not be offset by the triumph of nine rescues.

We reached the southern limit of the initial search grid and were just turning north when Peter spotted a red and yellow surf cap five hundred metres further south. He quickly swung the aircraft around and within moments we were hovering over the missing lifesaver. He appeared to be calmly treading water, in contrast to our previous victims, who had been struggling and waving in panic. Gary graciously let me do this rescue on my own, and soon I was in the water beside the lifesaver.

'God, am I glad to see you,' he exclaimed. 'You flew straight past me when you first arrived thirty minutes ago. I thought you had me spotted and were getting the other two first. But when you shut down on the beach I started to get really worried.'

I had him in the rescue harness without any fuss, but as we were both lifted I shouted, 'I think we have a problem here!'

'Yeah, what's that?' he replied casually.

'Are you aware that you don't have any swimming trunks on?' The bloke was stark bollock naked!

'Yeah, lost the lot in the waves. Swimmers and brand new surf ski too.'

I smiled. 'Well I'd better warn you that there are TV crews on the beach.'

'Jesus, I'm not worried about that – I'm so bloody glad I'm alive, I don't care.' And that's the way he appeared on TV that night. A naked lifesaver with an arm around the two boys he had tried to rescue.

We had rescued ten people that day. There were no drownings reported, in spite of the treacherous conditions. The sense of achievement was overwhelming. The events naturally received considerable media coverage. I spent hours on the phone that night with friends and relatives who rang to congratulate me. For several days afterwards I remained euphoric, my only focus being to get back into the helicopter and do it all over again.

5

Whoever said that the practice of anaesthesia is ninety-five per cent boredom and five per cent sheer terror clearly had no experience of the speciality. For me it was the other way around.

Until I started my term as an anaesthesia resident, I believed, like most people, that anaesthetists did very little during an operation. I quickly learnt how wrong I was. The drugs used in anaesthesia are the most powerful known to medicine. Some induce immediate unconsciousness; a millilitre of another can instantly paralyse every single one of the body's muscles. All of them have little margin for error in their dosage. It is common to be juggling five or more drugs simultaneously to produce the optimal conditions for surgeon and patient. The consequences of getting it even slightly wrong are serious at best, fatal at worst.

I had to learn how to put needles and tubes into people's veins, arteries, windpipes, chest cavities and even around their spinal cords. There was no time for boredom, just terror, adrenaline and exhaustion. It suited me perfectly!

Despite this I still saw my long-term career plans elsewhere. I wanted to be an eye surgeon. I had done a term in ophthalmology the previous year and had the support of the hospital's eye specialists to follow this path. When not working or flying I was now studying for entry exams into ophthalmology.

Adding twenty hours of study and lectures to my sixty-hour working week left me barely any time to remember that I had a lovely fiancée waiting patiently for snatched moments with me. Amanda and

I had met in New Zealand while I was doing an elective term in my final year of med school.

Early in the term I had been treating a patient with a ruptured aortic aneurysm. The patient needed immediate surgery to stop the massive blood loss. I was told to organise the transfusion with the blood bank. Not having a clue what to order, I demanded twelve bags of whole blood and I demanded them immediately. The pathology technician, who sounded like a bad-tempered old harridan, told me to get nicked. After admitting my ignorance and asking for guidance she told me six units would be enough to start with and it would take fifteen minutes.

The operation was a success and I went over to the lab to thank the technician for her help. The old ogre was in fact an attractive young woman with a captivating smile. Within weeks Amanda and I were an item. By the end of my five-month stay we were madly in love and Amanda followed me back to Australia.

Her bright, lively personality was a welcome relief from my work and study, and she accepted she had to share my free time with the helicopter rescue service. I continued on the roster as much as possible. I was addicted. My childhood dream to be the pilot of a commercial jetliner seemed sedate in comparison. Some days we only landed to refuel and start the next mission.

Most of our work related to beaches and boating. As we did not charge for our work, relying entirely on corporate sponsorship instead, the police were happy to use our service for free. We spent many hours undertaking searches for missing boats at their request. Mostly the searches were fruitless but occasionally we had a success.

The cliffs and rocky headlands around Sydney were another source of work. Rock fishing is the most dangerous of pastimes and this was brought home to me again and again as we rescued survivors, or recovered the bodies of those not so lucky. One favourite rock-fishing spot was at the sewerage outfall at North Head. The fish apparently loved this nutrient-rich environment, and where there are fish there are usually fishermen close by. I became a member of the Exclusive Order of Turd Jumpers when I effected a rescue in the broiling smelly brown waters below North Head. Like all members I was inducted with a lengthy soaking by the fire hose as soon as possible after the rescue!

While most of the time I felt safe on our missions, there were times when I was truly terrified; none more so than when I was being winched on the static line over land. When I was over sea I knew that if the line separated from the aircraft I would merely splash into the waters below. Over land it was a different matter.

The loop of the static line was attached to the aircraft by a cargo hook. This hook could be sprung open by the pilot pulling a toggle next to his seat. It was essential that the rope not be permanently attached to the helicopter so that if it became snagged it could be released. The pilots always assured us that the hook could never accidentally release. But the pilots never had to trust their lives to it. Occasionally rumours of a cargo-hook failure circulated through the crew. Somebody had heard of someone who had read an article about an incident, but concrete evidence was never forthcoming. Perhaps it was an urban myth but it never stopped us worrying that one day one of us would be injured or killed after the hook unexpectedly released.

On a number of occasions I accompanied patients strapped in rescue stretchers on the static line as we lifted them from the base of sea cliffs to ambulances waiting up top. To an onlooker I may have appeared to be caring for the victim. In reality I was petrified and praying that I would survive the journey.

The hoist was worse. Being suspended on a wire that seemed thin enough to floss your teeth with was terrifying. Worst of all was the initial departure from the aircraft. There was no way to test your weight on the wire before starting the descent. If the harness or hook wasn't right before you started, you would fall.

One training day it was my turn to be winched off the ground, retrieved into the cabin and then winched back again. The aircraft hovered some fifteen metres above my head as the wire snaked down. After letting it touch the ground to earth itself – that was a lesson I had never forgotten! – I attached the hook to my harness and the ascent began. The wire transmitted every vibration of the hoist motor to my harness, so I could sense the steady pull of the winch. I looked up and fended off the aircraft skid to avoid being hit on the helmet, and soon I was sitting in the aircraft. I nodded to the crewman and we proceeded to reverse the exercise.

I descended between the skid and the aircraft, doing everything by the book, unsuccessfully trying not to think about the injuries I'd suffer if I fell from this height. I was perhaps two metres below the helicopter when I went into free-fall. In that fraction of a second I knew I was dead. My heart started to hammer in my chest and momentarily I was overwhelmed by the feeling that this was too soon, I wasn't ready to die yet. Then suddenly the cable jolted me to a stop.

As I peered up through eyes clouded by relief I could see the crewman examining the hoist, then he continued to lower me down. A few seconds later I arrived safely on solid ground and unhooked the winch with shaking fingers. The chopper landed next to me, and later we inspected the hoist to see what had happened. We ran the cable in and out several times and on one occasion the mechanism that laid the cable neatly on the drum jumped and let the cable overlap itself. When we unwound the cable the wire jumped as the overlap was unwound. The jolt had lasted only about a second, but try telling that to my panicked nervous system.

In spite of careful servicing this became a recurrent problem. When it happened again after that day at least we knew what it was, but being the first to experience it did nothing to instil confidence in me about 'riding the wire'.

While most of our medical calls came from beach patrols, and very few from the ambulance service, there was one area of medicine where we had an undisputed role. Research at the spinal unit at Royal North Shore Hospital had established that, in most circumstances, the helicopter was a safer way to move patients with injuries to their spine than by road ambulance, and we were routinely called for such cases.

It was heart-wrenching work. Usually the victims were active boys or young men whose luck had run out. Many had sustained their injuries through contact sports and the rest were daredevils who thought they were indestructible.

There was nothing worse than stabilising a patient with all the signs of a spinal injury while he pleaded to the universe for another chance to rewrite the events of the last hour. While I did my best to reassure them that it was too early to conclude whether or not they had done any permanent damage, I knew that often this would be the case. Their active days were over.

The camaraderie of the helicopter crew saw me through the heartbreak of traumas like these. Everyone was straightforward, dedicated and eager to make the team work. I felt comfortable trusting my life to them in times of danger, and we had a lot of fun together when the danger was over.

All of this was in stark contrast to the dog-eat-dog game of being a resident medical officer.

As an RMO the rules were simple and cruel, and this brought out the worst in people. The only way to become a specialist was to work at the teaching hospitals for three to four years until you were accepted onto a specialist training scheme and became a trainee registrar. This then required another four or five years of exams and apprenticeship. Provided that trainee registrars passed their exams, they stayed on the scheme until they qualified as a specialist. The trick was to stay around as an RMO long enough and to have enough good references to get a trainee post. This was difficult to achieve as each RMO appointment was only for one year. Every September we would apply to continue the following year. Only fifty per cent would be selected, as each rung on the ladder offered fifty per cent fewer positions. The rest went to small suburban or country hospitals or into general practice. It was a one-way street; without a teaching hospital appointment the chances of ever doing specialist training were nil.

Reappointment relied on a skillful interview technique and good references from medical administration and the specialists for whom you worked. It was little wonder, then, that we never complained about eighty-hour working weeks or even eighty-hour continuous shifts. Anyone who complained, no matter how justified, was labelled a whinger. Whingers never came back the following year.

A typical working week was eight in the morning till six at night, Monday to Friday. If my work wasn't finished at six, I stayed until it was, just like every other RMO. We were never paid for these extra hours. Medical administration would not pay 'unrostered overtime'; it was always our own fault if we couldn't finish the massive workloads in our normal working days.

At least once a week I would work straight through the night as one of the duty RMOs. On these nights I would admit patients and assist at operations. When not in theatre I would be busy reviewing patients whose condition had deteriorated, replacing countless clogged intravenous cannulas and filling out innumerable forms – blood tests and X-ray requests, consent forms for operations and death certificates. Every fourth week I would do a continuous shift from 8 am Friday till 6 pm Monday – eighty-two hours straight. Usually I could snatch a few hours sleep here and there, but there were never any guarantees.

I knew how draining this life was but I accepted it, we all did; there was so much to learn and we needed the experience as well as the good references. Some of our less scrupulous colleagues would use techniques other than hard work to increase the likelihood of a job the next year. One I remember had snooker lessons and mastered the art of just being beaten by the medical superintendent each evening in the RMOs' quarters, then teamed up with him to annihilate other residents who stayed back to play at the end of the day. He was a very average doctor but a bum-licker of the first degree. He gained a post as a surgical trainee two years before any of his colleagues.

Despite all this, at the end of my second year I was confident I would be able to continue to a third year as a senior resident in ophthalmology at my current hospital. 'The job's yours,' resounded in my mind. 'Don't even bother applying anywhere else,' the relevant specialists told me. Right up to the moment I looked at the list for the next year's appointments I was confident, almost cocky. The job and my future were in the bag.

My name was missing from the list. I read the names a dozen times but the list didn't change. They had appointed a resident from another hospital to the job.

I was devastated. On the basis of their promises I foolishly hadn't even thought of a back-up plan. I felt like throwing up. Anger surged through me. I hated this place, these people, this system that used you then discarded you.

With every teaching hospital having made their appointments on the same day, I was in big trouble. Even the suburban and country hospitals announced their staff for the next year that day. All the appointments across the state were full.

It took me several days to deal with my feelings of despair. It was nigh on impossible to continue to work the remaining three months of the year, but my sense of duty to my patients and Amanda's support kept me going. We were due to be married in six weeks' time – some wedding present this was.

I started the humiliating job of ringing every medical superintendent in New South Wales. I made dozens of phone calls; however, I knew that if my own hospital didn't want me any more, it would be hard to convince anyone else that I should even be considered if a vacancy came up. After a week I was still without any prospects.

A day at the helicopter base helped break my grim mood. I walked up the hill, waiting for my first glimpse of the rotors, which always set my heart racing. This time, however, the familiar dual blades were missing. In their place were three unfamiliar blue blades. As I continued up over the hill the rest of the gleaming white body of an AS350B Squirrel, built by the French company Aerospatiale, was revealed. I had only ever seen these helicopters in overseas flying magazines and was not aware that this one had been brought into the country to demonstrate its capabilities to various civilian and military services. Peter Howe explained to Rick Mailey, the crewman, and myself that we had the aircraft on trial for a few days and would be doing demonstration rescues for the heavies from the Surf Life Saving Association and the Bank of New South Wales that morning. Aerospatiale saw the helicopter rescue service as a likely customer and felt the purchase of one of their state-of-the-art aircraft by such a high-profile organisation would be a real coup.

The Squirrel was very different from the Jet Ranger. Nearly the whole aircraft was made from fibreglass, including the rotor blades. The inside was spacious and, most importantly, there would be room for me to sit behind the patient's head. This would allow full resuscitation access, a prerequisite for critical care transport and something impossible in the Jet Ranger.

The Squirrel had incredible stability and quietness in flight. Compared to the noisy and relatively shaky feel of our ageing Bell, flying in this was pure bliss. The engineers had tracked and balanced the rotor system the day before to minimise vibration, and the result was so smooth I could easily imagine I was sitting in a simulator watching the scene change on an enormous screen. The executive fit-out with deep cushions and extra sound insulation meant we flew in plush comfort and barely needed our helmet intercoms to talk to each other.

One significant feature of the aircraft was a sliding back door on the left-hand side. This could be kept open during flight which meant we didn't have to close the door while standing on the skid. The technique required by the Jet Ranger of closing the door from the outside while in the hover was at best tricky and at worst hazardous. Additionally, on the Jet Ranger we had to remove the left rear door altogether and leave it behind somewhere in order to undertake winching operations. Not so with the Squirrel. We could open and close the sliding door at any stage in the flight. We loved it.

We performed our demonstration surf jump at Wanda Beach, launching ourselves from fifteen metres above the water for added effect. Being heavier than the Jet Ranger, the Squirrel created significantly more downdraft to stay in the air, but the extra spray was a minor inconvenience compared to the aircraft's considerable advantages.

Rick and I hooked onto the static line and Peter lifted us out of the water and transferred us smoothly over to the beach. Just as we were about to be set down Peter hauled us back into the air where he hovered for a full minute, no doubt demonstrating the machine's stability. Looking out to sea I could see a new set of breakers on its way.

Suddenly we were moving across the water only to be smashed into the largest of the incoming waves. Some minutes later, back at the beach, Peter described to the waiting audience that, as planned, he had dunked us to show how precisely he could position the aircraft and its load below. It may have been his plan but it was never part of ours and we retaliated with the fire hose that afternoon. The SLSA representatives were impressed; the bank representatives were quiet, knowing this enthusiasm would equate to a request for increased sponsorship.

We returned to standby at Long Reef Beach. Only one thought intruded on the day – how was I going to survive my career crisis? If only the helicopter rescue service paid me.

The following Monday the medical superintendent from St George Hospital across the city called to say he had just had a senior RMO change his mind and knock back his appointment for the next year. Would I please come in for an interview?

Thankfully I got the job. It wasn't ophthalmology, just another general year, but it was money, and more importantly I would be back in a major teaching hospital. St George was a very progressive place and highly regarded – my career prospects were still alive.

In December Amanda and I were married. She had been a great strength during those dark days, and although the car had three punctures on the way to the church, I felt the wedding signalled a new starting point in our lives. Everything was turning out okay after all.

6

St George Hospital was very different from my previous hospital. It was smaller, busier and it received a lot more trauma cases. The standard of medicine was excellent and I soon realised my career had taken a turn for the better. Once again good had come from adversity.

One Saturday, when I was on shift as admitting officer in the emergency department, I unwittingly became the focus of the local police sergeant. We normally had a great relationship with the police but on that particular day I tested the sergeant's patience to its limits.

A young man had been brought in by ambulance after being bitten on the foot by a snake. A compression bandage had been applied and the man was clinically stable. On enquiry it was obvious that the snake was a red-bellied black. While usually not fatal to adults, these snakes can give a lethal bite to children.

'What happened to the snake?' I asked.

'I caught it and put it in an old fish tank in the back yard,' the young man replied. 'We're going to keep it as a pet.' His barefooted girlfriend nodded enthusiastically, obviously supportive of this plan.

'You can't keep poisonous snakes as pets in Sydney, it's against the law,' I warned. The resultant looks were as venomous as the couple's new family member.

As the young fellow's condition was stable, I decided that the safety of the rest of the city's population came first. I called the local police and they reluctantly agreed to go and destroy the snake.

Unfortunately the victim's girlfriend overheard my call, and when I got off the phone I looked up to see her and her hobbling boyfriend making a hurried exit.

'You can't kill our snake!' she yelled as the two of them disappeared through the front doors and sped off in their rusty old ute. I was powerless to stop them.

Twenty minutes later I was called back to the phone.

'Sergeant Delaney here. We're trying to carry out your instructions and shoot the snake, but this bloke has just appeared, with his leg all bandaged up, and he's draped himself over the top of the fish tank. Judging by his language we'll have to shoot him first to get to the snake.'

'What do you want me to do?' I didn't see how I could help.

'Nothing,' he replied. 'I just wanted to know who sent us out here.'

'I'm sure you'll handle the problem, Sergeant.' I tried to sound supportive.

He hung up without further comment. Ten minutes later the senior nurse said a Sergeant Delaney was on the phone for me.

'Dr Wishaw?' he asked.

'Yes,' I replied with some trepidation, wondering what would come next.

'His girlfriend called the National Parks and Wildlife Service. The ranger here tells me this is a protected species,' he stated flatly. 'We can't shoot it. What do you think we should do?'

Starting to get a bit annoyed, I said, 'I don't know, I'm not a snake expert!'

The line went dead.

After ten more minutes Sergeant Delaney was again on the line. 'Taronga Park Zoo is willing to take the snake.'

'That's great. Well done, Sergeant!' I exclaimed brightly.

He didn't share my enthusiasm. 'But not until Monday. Any ideas?'

'Nope, not my area of expertise.' Again the conversation went no further. Must go and thank him in person on Monday, I thought. As it was, I didn't have to wait that long.

Thirty minutes later I heard someone screaming and raving in the entrance to the emergency department. A burly police sergeant walked in dragging a dishevelled old man who was obviously hallucinating.

What little I could understand of his ranting, the old man was yelling that someone was out to get him.

'Who's Dr Wishaw?' the sergeant bellowed to everyone within earshot.

'I am,' I replied meekly.

'Good. Got a present for you.' He grinned. 'He was drying out in the cells after a heavy night on the booze. He woke to find himself sharing his cell with a black snake in a fish tank. This sort of problem *is* your area of expertise. Good day.' He turned and left.

I spent the rest of the afternoon trying to settle the poor old fellow. No doubt it would have been better for everyone if I had never mentioned the wretched snake!

Barrington Tops is Australia's Bermuda Triangle. Two hundred kilometres north of Sydney, this volcanic massif rises over fifteen hundred metres above the surrounding countryside.

The Tops is a barren windswept plateau from which basalt ridges radiate like the legs of a massive starfish. The fertile volcanic soil supports triple-canopy rainforest, thinning out in the most exposed areas and thickest in the intervening valleys. The dense vegetation means that visibility on the ground in these valleys is only ten metres. It is a place of contrast. Barren and fertile; hot and cold; stunningly beautiful; dangerous and unpredictable.

About halfway through my year at St George, it was to this wild and rugged landscape that we were dispatched in search of a missing light aircraft. For reasons I have never understood, the inland light aircraft lane passes directly over Barrington Tops. Apart from the ocean, I can think of no more inhospitable place to crash. Even in the unlikely event of surviving an impact there, the chances of walking to help or being found by a search party are impossibly remote. Many aircraft have crashed there and some remain lost in the impenetrable jungle.

It seems there are no Aboriginal legends concerning the Barrington Tops. Indigenous people, for reasons unknown, avoided the area. As we searched it was easy to believe that the place was possessed by an evil spirit. Barrington Tops is continuously bombarded from the skies. Storms, hail, snow and lightning strikes assail the plateau. In return, perhaps some unnamed spirit of Barrington seeks revenge on any friend of the skies. Light aircraft are its favourite prey. Every one of the aircraft involved in the search was hammered mercilessly by the turbulence around the Tops.

Two days before our arrival a light aircraft had disappeared over Barrington. The last radio call by the pilot described loss of control and severe icing of the wings. On board were four senior policemen and lawyers. All sorts of conspiracy theories sprang up, though in reality we knew that disorientation at night in the adverse weather was probably the real killer. Regardless, no limits were put on the effort to find the wreckage and its occupants. Over twenty aircraft – military and civilian, fixed-wing and helicopters – were involved in the search.

Our chopper had been out looking for the missing aircraft since the night after the search began and had returned to Sydney for a new crew and supplies. On day three of the search our team took off from Royal North Shore Hospital well before first light. I had been given a few days off by my clinical bosses at St George, who had an interest, even a respect, for my 'hobby'. Heavy on fuel reserves, rescue and medical supplies, and four crew, we limped through the skies and arrived in the little town of Gloucester two hours later.

Gloucester was the closest town to the presumed crash site large enough to accommodate and cater for the gaggle of aircraft and crew. The whole town seemed to be involved in supporting the search effort. Our briefing at the hastily convened command centre at the pub did little to give us hope for either the survival of the crash victims or the ease of our search. It had been snowing on Barrington on the night of the crash; the conditions remained cold with high winds, and severe turbulence was being experienced by aircraft already involved in the search. Fixed-wing aircraft were prohibited from flying at low altitude due to the severity of the turbulence. Helicopters, being less affected by such conditions, were designated to scour the valleys.

With this in mind pilot Dan Tyler decided to lighten our aircraft as much as possible and we agreed to leave all rescue and medical gear at the search centre and retrieve it once a positive sighting was made.

It was likely that whichever aircraft found the crash site, I would be the first winched in to ascertain the possibility of survivors. It was not a prospect I relished.

We were only a few minutes into the search when we spotted a burnt, broken tree trunk, possibly the result of aircraft damage. After hovering over the damaged tree without seeing any other evidence of a plane, we continued on. Almost immediately we caught a glint of something on the side of a nearby ridge. Hoping it was a metallic object we climbed to the location. It was a small drift of snow. Over the next hour we made a dozen similar sightings, and it became clear just how difficult this search was going to be. Every snow patch seemed to reflect the sunlight. Every second tree appeared damaged by lightning.

Phil Dunne, a volunteer crewman, sat in the back opposite me, while Bob Ford was up front with Dan. Our concentration was not helped by waves of nausea caused by the severe turbulence. The relatively cramped and claustrophobic confines of the back seat made it far worse for Phil and me, and after an hour the two of us could take it no more. We begged for some relief. Dan, being the considerate man he is, quickly came up with a solution.

Ten minutes later we landed in a vacant lot behind the chemist shop in the small town of Dungog, some twenty kilometres south of our search area. As I walked into the chemist all the customers were looking around anxiously for the source of the incredible roar coming from behind the shop. They all went quiet when they saw me stride towards the counter in my new dayglo orange flight suit and helmet. Their concerned expressions turned to smirks and chuckles when I asked the pharmacist what she had available for motion sickness.

As the light faded we returned to Gloucester. All search teams were debriefed and the evening was spent sharing flying adventures, both fact and fiction, to amaze and outdo each other. Every now and then my mind would wander from this warm bubbly gathering to those five poor souls possibly dying of hypothermia scant miles away. I saw others frequently staring off into the distance, no doubt having the same thoughts.

The next morning we resumed our search to the south and once again, in spite of having taken our motion-sickness tablets, Phil and

I were soon incapacitated. We were adding little if anything to the search and adding considerably to the fuel consumption. So Dan decided to drop us in a clearing near a deserted sawmill. I have never felt so grateful to touch down. The aircraft departed north-wards and Phil and I just lay flat on our backs in the long grass, helmets still on, basking in the warm sunshine and chuckling to ourselves at how good this felt compared to the previous hour of pukey purgatory.

After some minutes we decided to explore. On one side of the field stood a stately country residence that was obviously deserted. On the other side was a ramshackle shed with a wisp of smoke coming from its rusty old chimney. To the west of the field ran a small river, which we forded easily to enter the deserted sawmilling town. It appeared that the mill had not been in operation for many, many years and the cluster of adjoining cabins were also empty. The only evidence of recent habitation was a sparkling new public telephone box, one of the first of its type to be installed in New South Wales. I could not think of a more unlikely place to find such a thing. I rang Amanda, mainly to convince myself that the telephone box actually existed and I was not in some weird episode of *Dr Who*.

We crossed back over the river to wait for the chopper. It was then we realised we were not alone.

The door to the small shed was slightly open. As we walked towards it, it was shut quickly and then opened again for a few seconds, before being slammed shut once more. Although somewhat perplexed, we decided our best course of action was to sit down nearby and chat. Very soon an old weather-beaten face appeared in the doorway. Summoning our best manners, we introduced our-selves, and very, very slowly, a little old man emerged from the shed. He wore threadbare grey trousers held up by a length of hemp rope, an old checked shirt and horn-rimmed spectacles. It was evident that shaving was only a weekly affair. He was small and timid, but very curious; he reminded me of a small woodland creature from a child's storybook.

We apologised profusely for invading his privacy and eventually he came over to sit with us. I never found out his real name; to me he's always been Barrington Bill. We explained our reason for being there and he showed almost as much curiosity about the way we had arrived as we did about his life.

It turned out that Bill had lived there as far back as he could remember. We were right in suspecting the sawmill had long been abandoned – it was over twenty years since it had last cut timber. The stately home belonged to a doctor from Newcastle who came up most weekends. Apart from this, Bill's only contact was with a woman from Dungog who drove up each fortnight with his groceries. It was obvious that he shunned even her company, as he had erected a flying fox across the creek to carry the food. On the allotted day he would send over a list of his needs and this helpful lady would retrieve the list without disturbing him, return to Dungog, cash his pension cheque and bring the groceries later that afternoon. These would be duly placed in the flying fox and sent over to Bill.

Incredibly our helicopter was the first aircraft Bill had ever seen close up. He said he was petrified when such a strange contraption landed in his paddock. He was even more scared when two creatures with white heads stepped out. He knew aircraft existed but that was about it. He had seen them fly over thousands of metres above, usually little more than vapour trails; seeing a helicopter land outside his shed was almost more than he could cope with. The more he spoke, the more apparent it became how isolated his life had been.

'Haven't you ever been to the city?' I asked.

'Just the once,' he replied. 'At the end of the Second World War. I thought I'd go to the city to celebrate, but those city fellas, they were too much for me. After an hour in Dungog I had to get back home to me shed.'

When the chopper returned half an hour later, we convinced Dan to give the 'owner' of the clearing a brief joy-ride.

Bill was bubbling with excitement as we helped him don one of our flying suits. We placed a helmet on his head, then led him by the hand to the noisy aircraft. Once he was strapped into the front left seat he sat perfectly still and was incredulous as he was taken for a gentle circuit two hundred metres above his little piece of the planet.

On his return to earth Bill was lost for words but beaming, obviously awestruck by the whole experience. We took lots of photos, some of which we sent to him, some of which remained on our walls for years to come.

We then turned back to the task at hand. News came through of a possible sighting of wreckage and we left to make a closer inspection. It was just another snowdrift.

It was two days and nights before the search was scaled down. The crews gathered for a final sombre lunch, leaving behind only a few aircraft and ground parties to continue the search.

We ate that day with an air force crew who had searched from their Iroquois helicopter based out of Williamtown, north of Newcastle. We all reflected on the great camaraderie shown by everyone in the face of what was becoming an increasingly grim task. After lunch, we said our goodbyes and headed back to Sydney, dismayed at our lack of success but at least consoled that we had done our best. To this date, and in spite of dozens of searches, no trace of the missing aircraft has ever been found.

The idea that there might be an evil spirit possessing Barrington Tops continued to trouble me. My disquiet was not helped by what I learnt over the next few days. It seems the air force Iroquois crew made a precautionary landing while returning home. The pilot believed the aircraft had developed a vibration and he was not willing to fly it further. Inspection by engineers could find no fault. Two days later the pilot and one of the crew with whom we had had lunch took off with a test pilot and technician to investigate further. During the flight a bizarre sequence of mechanical failures occurred and both the tail and main rotor separated from the aircraft. The aircraft plummeted over three hundred metres. Although all the crew had parachutes on, none of them made it out of the doors. There were no survivors.

PART II
Call Sign, 'Chickenman'

You cannot move things forward without exposure to risk and criticism. As a pioneer people will laugh at you before they applaud you.

Rachel Remen

7

As I approached the end of my third year as RMO at St George, my career direction was once again in total chaos. I still had visions of becoming an eye specialist but had recently failed the primary entrance exam for specialist training. Like eighteen of the other twenty candidates, I was devastated. Without that exam, another year as a senior resident was just marking time.

For my final term I was attached to the anaesthesia department. Unlike my previous term in anaesthesia, here at St George I was also involved in the resuscitation teams and the intensive care unit. I revelled in the management of critically ill patients, particularly the major trauma victims. More than anywhere else other than the helicopter rescue service, my contribution appeared to make a dramatic and significant difference to people's lives.

Within a few weeks I started seriously to doubt whether a lifetime of prescribing glasses and eye drops would satisfy my lust for adventure. Again fate struck. While I pondered whether I should abandon my plan to be an ophthamologist and somehow pursue a career in emergency medicine, or anaesthesia and intensive care, an offer came from a totally unexpected direction. Ian Badham and Sue Rowley asked me whether I would like to work full-time for the helicopter service.

To be paid to fly was beyond my wildest dreams! This had never happened before in Australia, but it seemed there was now money to pay for this position from an anticipated cost-recovery program for interhospital transfer of patients. To date Royal North Shore Hospital had allowed their emergency room registrar to go on weekday missions from time to time, but this way I would be employed by, and give first priority to, the helicopter service.

The reaction of my medical peers to my new job ranged from amusement to ridicule. Most thought it was suicidal, literally and career-wise. On several occasions during the past year I had arrived on Monday morning at the residents' quarters to find pinned to the noticeboard an article about my exploits from the morning papers, usually accompanied by comments that were less than complimentary. What drove them to do this was a mystery.

Dr Dick Young, the director of anaesthesia at St George, was the only doctor who saw any merit in the new position. He was years ahead of his time in recognising the need for a coordinated disaster plan for the state and was prominent in the creation of the paramedics service in New South Wales. If he thought the role was worthwhile, that was good enough for me. Amanda, too, saw how much this opportunity meant to me and so with her encouragement I agreed to become Australia's first full-time helicopter doctor.

I could barely contain my excitement. If it was adventure I was after, this was a job tailor-made for me.

I arrived at Rotary Lodge at precisely 8 am on my first day of work. Sue Rowley and Ian Badham arrived midmorning and we spent most of the day working out my job description and responsibilities. That was typical of our approach to any project: make it happen, then figure out the details and the paperwork later. It always seemed to work and was a refreshing change from the bureaucratic approach I had experienced as an RMO over the previous three years.

The Helicopter Rescue Service had abandoned the fibro shack in the middle of the car park. The local Rotary Club had built a motel adjacent to the hospital helipad for accommodation of patients' relatives, and they kindly donated to us the centre unit on the second floor to use as our office. On the north side our balcony overlooked the helipad ten metres away. The south-facing windows overlooked the hospital tennis courts and the pool. It wasn't unusual for the service binoculars to be trained on the swimming pool, just in case one of the young nurses needed rescuing.

Bob Ford was now the full-time crewman as well as the crew chief. We would work together Mondays to Fridays and cover midweek after-hours calls, while the volunteers would cover Saturdays and Sundays. We referred to them as the 'weekend warriors'. I no longer did weekend work, except for the occasional shift to fill the roster.

Bob had been a volunteer surf lifesaver for many years. His competence as a rescue crewman was unequalled. He was calm and easygoing and it would have been easy to mistake his approach to any task as relaxed; to those of us who knew him, however, it was meticulous and always correct. Nothing annoyed Bob more than someone rushing a job and getting it wrong. Sometimes I suspected his measured pace was a slight exaggeration to remind us all to slow down and get it right the first time.

Peter Howe had resigned as chief pilot and had been replaced by Dan Tyler. Until recently Dan had flown part-time with the rescue service and part-time for Channel Ten. In spite of a slap on the wrist for using the company helicopter for the engine salvage mission on my first duty day, he had remained at the TV station till now.

Dan was originally from Nebraska but had immigrated to Australia after marrying a local girl he met on R and R leave from the Vietnam War. In Vietnam he had flown Bell UH-1s, or 'Hueys', in the US Cavalry, carrying infantry troops. He amassed over forty medals during his time in service, including the Distinguished Flying Cross and the Purple Heart. When he moved to Australia he studied law at Sydney University and became a barrister, but he soon returned to flying. Still, he was never short of the most complex opinion on even the simplest legal question!

Dan had spent some of his time in Vietnam working as a combat assault leader. This required coordinating assaults from the air and being the first chopper into a landing zone. The others followed once they saw that he had survived. Dan's planning abilities were awesome – they had to be to keep him alive.

'Rescue base from Helicopter One,' he called one day as we headed off to a motor-vehicle accident.

'Base, go ahead,' came the reply.

After nibbling on one of his fingernails, he said, 'Could you order five drums of fuel?'

'Will do. Base out.'

I was silly enough to ask, 'Why five?'

He inspected a nail. 'Simple. It will take another twelve minutes to reach the accident. The report said one of the patients had been ejected from the car, so a spinal injury is likely. It will take you around twenty minutes to stabilise the patient. There are two spinal units in Sydney. The one back at North Shore will be closer, but that would bring us in just as the thunderstorm you can see down to the south will be over the hospital. So you will decide to go to Prince Henry Hospital. Allowing for the extra flight time, and the inevitable delays transiting back to base through Sydney International Airport airspace, along with heavy seas predicted for the weekend, we will need five drums to see us through to the next routine fuel drop next Tuesday.'

'Right,' I replied slowly with what must have been a bemused look on my face.

Each day I caught the train to work barely able to conceal my pride at wearing a shirt emblazoned with 'Helicopter Rescue Service'. Often I would meet Bob on the way and we would discuss our cures for the ills of the world. On arrival we would check the aircraft, lay out our wetsuits, neoprene boots and harnesses on the helipad at our guard stations, and brief the media on any interesting events. For several years Bob had had a regular five-minute interview spot on radio station 2UE with their top-rating breakfast announcer Gary O'Callaghan. This was part of the sponsorship deal. We would notify the newsroom of any missions we were en route to, thereby giving 2UE the scoop over other radio stations.

My days were split between office work, flying missions and working as a supernumerary anaesthesia resident in the operating theatres at North Shore. The hospital anaesthetists were happy to receive my free services (it shared the theatre workload and provided someone to look after the patient while they had tea breaks during long cases) and it kept my procedural skills current. Their reaction to what I was doing ranged from indifference to curiosity, but none of them ever thought it was a worthy medical role. Like the St George doctors, they thought I was committing career suicide. It wasn't that I had given up the idea of becoming a specialist, I just couldn't resist the offer of flying full-time. As soon as I started, any fears I might have had of leaving the traditional career pathway melted away. I was doing something I felt passionately about, something worthwhile. I couldn't wait to get to work each day.

After completing the aircraft and equipment checks, I would go over to the hospital to spend the morning in the operating theatres. If I was needed I could be contacted via a pager on my belt. In those days radio pagers merely beeped. They could not give a message. Mine was fancy by 1982 standards, being able to give several different tones, which by agreement meant different degrees of urgency. For routine and noncritical missions a particular tone would be activated, meaning 'Ring the helicopter office'. A different tone meant, 'We need you immediately!'

In the urgent cases, having sprinted from the hospital corridors up the hill to the helipad, I would breathlessly take my cue from Bob as to what to wear. If he was in his wetsuit and harness I would don the same. For non-water missions he would be in his yellow flame-retardant suit and, without fail, he would have laid mine out and stowed my wetsuit in the aircraft boot. Bob always seemed to have it all figured out.

My first mission as a full-timer involved a resuscitation of a heart attack victim on Manly Beach. The beach lifeguard called us. It was a complete surprise to the ambulance officers when we arrived. Paramedics were few and far between in those days, and the ambulance officers were only able to give basic life support. I was able to insert a breathing tube down the victim's windpipe to allow far more effective delivery of oxygen and prevent the possibility of highly acidic and corrosive stomach secretions from backtracking into his lungs. I was also able to shock his heart and administer drugs such as adrenaline. We worked furiously together for twenty minutes, but the man did not respond. Eventually we had to concede that it was too late. Giving up on a resuscitation is one of the hardest decisions to make: I always feel that if only I could keep going long enough, the victim would eventually revive.

The ambulance officers weren't sure how to respond to our presence. Our agreement with the ambulance service was only to respond to medical emergencies if requested by them; however, we maintained the right to respond to beach emergencies at the discretion of the lifeguards and SLSA. While the ambulance service hierarchy and controllers were aware that the helicopter now had a full-time doctor on the crew, it was obvious that this information had not yet disseminated out to the road crews. I sensed an undercurrent of suspicion and confusion when I asked the officers to spread the word that the helicopter service was only too happy to support them when needed.

A few days later we were called to a motor-vehicle accident: a head-on collision between a Volvo and a small Japanese car had occurred on the Western Freeway. After the accident the Volvo driver had merely opened the door and stepped out to assess the damage, but the nurse in the other car had had her leg impaled on the broken steering column. A doctor had been requested to assess the need for amputation. While speeding to the scene I naively believed that the ambulance service was immediately going to embrace our enhanced medical capability and that ambulance call-outs would become a regular occurrence. How wrong I was.

As usual finding the accident was easy. As we approached the general area the traffic below was at a standstill for several kilometres. All we had to do was follow the traffic jam to its end. By contrast the road beyond the scene was deserted and the police had kept a clear space without emergency vehicles about fifty metres from the accident. We approached from the far side of our designated landing site so that our rotor wash wouldn't blow the smashed glass from the wrecked cars into the air.

We could see a member of the Nepean rescue squad standing in the clearing with his two arms raised and pointing slightly to the south, indicating wind direction. We descended into the clearing and soon I was running over to the scene, medical equipment in hand.

Once I had introduced myself to the ambulance officer with the most pips on his epaulettes, I injected local anaesthetic around the victim's leg and made some incisions into the tissues with a scalpel to free her leg from the steering column. She had several leg fractures and was in a great deal of pain, but fortunately amputation was not required. In consultation with the ambulance officers we decided to fly her to Westmead Hospital.

Several television helicopters had attended the scene and one of the media pilots asked whether he could help us repack the aircraft. I was a little surprised but I smiled and said, 'Sure. My name's Ken, by the way.'

'David Jones,' he replied with a roguish grin. 'We've got some good footage and still shots. I'll make sure you get copies.'

'Thanks, appreciate that.' Nice guy, I thought, then forgot all about him.

On the return flight to the base I commented to Dan and Bob how frustrating the Jet Ranger was. We had only been able to transport the woman because her injuries were confined to her legs. Had there been injuries that affected her chest or airway the aircraft would have been too small to do anything during flight and I would have been forced to accompany her by road ambulance. The Bell allowed us to get our medical expertise to the patient but severely restricted which patients we could carry.

Some photos of the accident arrived at the base and over the next few weeks any footage or photos of our missions that had been taken by Channel Seven would somehow turn up on our doorstep. These were invaluable to us for promotional work, but the precise source remained a mystery.

It was not until a few weeks later, when we started to look around for a second full-time pilot, that the mystery was solved. We had decided to extend duty hours into the weekend, and thanks to an increase in sponsorship were able to advertise for another pilot. David Jones was one of the applicants. 'Have you received all the stuff I've been sending you?' he asked. As well as his considerable flying skills, we had to be impressed by his creativity. He got the job.

David was the opposite of Dan. Dan was serious and method-ical, David was easygoing and carefree. Dan was a steady progress man, David a sprinter. Dan was a man for the organisation while David just wanted adventure. Dan had learnt to fly in the military,

David had learnt to fly chasing deer around New Zealand. To Dan the fuel tank was half empty, to David it was half full. Both were extremely capable pilots.

I was forced to forgo my anaesthesia assisting for a few days, and instead the four of us flew to Long Reef each day to train David. Somebody was paying me to go swimming and flying and have a great time in the outdoors. It was bliss.

8

I had barely settled into assisting the anaesthetist with the first patient on the day's operating list when my pager started beeping. It was the urgent tone, which meant, 'Don't ring, just run'.

'Got to go,' I stated. Waiting just long enough to get a nod from the anaesthetist, I bolted for the door. Racing down the corridor and two flights of stairs, then through another fire escape door I ended up in the main foyer of the hospital. People stopped abruptly as I ran past them, still dressed in my pale blue cotton theatre shirt, baggy drawstring trousers and paper cap. As the automatic doors at the main entrance opened I received my first clue as to the nature of the forthcoming mission. I could already hear the rotors spinning. That meant there was no time for a pre-flight briefing. Probably a water rescue. By the time I was running past the hospital chapel I had removed my shirt. (There were no nearby phone boxes!) As I topped the rise I could see Bob in the front guard position, wetsuit and harness on. I tugged the drawstring to remove my trousers, leaving just the swimming trunks I always wore, then stuffed them under an empty fuel drum to prevent them blowing into the rotors. After I had scrambled into my wetsuit and wetsuit boots, Bob helped me into my harness. Adrenaline was surging through my veins and I needed consciously to slow everything down so as not to make silly mistakes.

We turned to the aircraft and David gave us the thumbs-up, meaning the aircraft was ready to go. Then things got curious. Instead of letting me go to my usual position in the front left, Bob pointed to the rear right, his usual position. Evidently I was going to be doing the rescue.

I forced myself to walk calmly under the rotor disc – it still made my heart pound to be so close to such lethal spinning blades, the engine raging in my ears. Inside I buckled my harness and put on my helmet. 'Ready in the back,' I indicated over the intercom, reaching forward and tapping David on the shoulder to confirm this. David nodded to let me know the message was received, and the aircraft lifted to a low hover and turned left towards the sea.

'VKG, this is Rescue Helicopter One,' Bob called.

'Rescue One, go ahead,' came the reply from the police radio room.

'Departed Royal North Shore Hospital, en route to your request for assistance off Palm Beach. Estimated time of arrival 0930.'

'Copy, Rescue One,' was the only reply.

Bob repeated the information to the ambulance service then switched to radio station 2UE.

'2UE News from Rescue Helicopter One.'

'Go ahead, Bob.'

'Roll a tape.'

'Rolling.'

'Five, four, three, two, one,' Bob counted down, allowing the radio technician to prep the tape and calibrate reception levels. 'We have departed Royal North Shore Hospital at the request of the police to assist a fishing vessel thirty kilometres east of Palm Beach. On board one of the deckhands has received injuries after becoming entangled in the nets. Our crew doctor will be treating him prior to transfer to hospital.' That was enough for the newsroom to create a scoop. Bob was smooth – there wasn't a glitch in his report.

'Channel Ten news, this is Rescue Helicopter One,' said Bob, calling our sponsors.

'We're already on our way,' came the reply. Obviously their eaves-dropping radio scanners were working that day.

'Ken, that's all we know,' Bob told me. 'When we get a bit higher we should be able to talk direct to the trawler on Marine UHF radio.'

The logistics of a mission this far out to sea were daunting. As the coastline disappeared behind us I ran the scenario through my head, trying to anticipate what treatment might be required.

'Nuovo Guiseppe, Nuovo Guiseppe, this is Rescue Helicopter One, do you copy?' Bob called.

'This is the Nuovo Guiseppe reading you loud and clear,' came the reply.

'Hey, a boat with a radio that works!' quipped David.

'Your radio, Ken,' said Bob.

'This is Dr Wishaw on board the helicopter, could you describe the accident and the condition of the patient?'

'He was caught in the nets and before we could stop the winch he was lifted up into the hauling gear. It cut off three fingers and then he dropped to the deck,' came the reply. 'We've wrapped his hand and we are looking for the fingers amongst the fish.'

Gawd, I thought, hope they're not too hungry. I could just imagine a snapper in its death throes swallowing the fingers and reaping revenge on its killer. 'Does he appear to have any other injuries, and has he lost much blood?' I asked.

'I don't think there are any other injuries. He's lying down, pretty pale and in pain.'

'Good, you're doing a great job. Now, here's what I want you to do. Raise his hand, which will slow the bleeding. Keep searching for those fingers. When you find them put them in the cleanest plastic bag you have and put the bag in a bucket of half ice, half water. We will be there in ten minutes.'

'We'll have the decks cleared for you by then. Nuovo Guiseppe out.'

The Channel Ten helicopter appeared out the left window, in close formation with us as we sped to the accident site.

Soon we arrived overhead. Below us the twenty-metre fishing trawler flopped around helplessly. The waters around the boat were stained red – the crew had gutted their catch while awaiting our arrival. That was how they kindly had cleared the deck for me! This made my job considerably harder as it was now very likely there would be hungry sharks circling the vessel.

David decided a winching operation was too dangerous because of the limited deck space and the boat's pitch and roll in the north-easterly swell. I readily agreed.

'This is what you're going to do,' said Bob. 'Get out onto the skid and step over onto their lookout tower. We'll lower your medical gear once you know what you need.'

Considering the amount of blood and guts in the water, this seemed a pretty good idea. I removed my heavy communications helmet and the scream of the turbine assaulted my unprotected ears, making clear thought well nigh impossible. Stay calm, don't hurry, I told myself. This is just a normal hover transfer – you've done dozens of them before, the only difference is that this one is fifteen metres further up in the air.

After securing my seatbelt behind me, I reached forward and tapped David on the shoulder to warn him to adjust the balance of the aircraft as I moved out the door. Carefully I opened the door and lowered my feet to the skid. I rotated to face inside the cabin and while my left hand hung grimly onto my seatbelt, I bent my knees till my groping right hand found the footstep projecting out below the door. Slowly I lowered myself further, releasing the seatbelt and finally closing the door above my head. I was outside. As I swivelled on the skid to assess the situation, David began to hover closer to the lookout tower. It was now simply a matter of stepping across the void ten metres above the deck of the boat.

As a result of the sea swell, the lookout tower was swinging backwards and forwards in a ten-metre arc. Too close and it would swat our chopper from the skies. This transfer would require leaping through space onto a rapidly moving target with the distinct possibility that if I missed I would join the dead fish on the deck below.

I watched the tower closely for a good minute, timing the swings and the speed at which it passed, calculating how much ahead I would have to jump to get the timing right. I finally realised there was nothing to be gained by watching any longer and I sprang into action. I opened the door to the chopper and got back in.

Disregarding howls of protest from Bob and David, I insisted that we hover away from the boat and, bloodstained water or not, I would swim to it. David's white helmet in front was shaking from side to side in dismay, but he obediently moved the aircraft to the side of the trawler. Again I went out onto the skid. I looked anxiously into the water below me. There didn't seem to be any fins cruising through the burly. I dropped into the sea and sprinted through the swells to the boat, where three pairs of massive hands flung me aboard like a tuna on the end of a line. I had swum twenty metres in what must have been a world-record time, but I had made it.

Inside the cabin the young bearded seaman was pale and scared, but otherwise okay. Surprisingly he had survived the fall with only a few bruises. The missing fingers were all accounted for and packed as instructed.

While Bob and David were not prepared to lower me by winch, they were able to lower the medical box onto the bow of the trawler, and soon I was giving my patient some much-needed pain relief. Once he was more comfortable, I unwrapped his hand. The finger stumps were remarkably clean. Good news. The sharper the cut and the less local damage, the more likely that microsurgery would succeed in reattaching the severed fingers.

There was no way the two of us could be winched back on board the helicopter, so we spent the next hour steaming into Pittwater Bay, and there we transferred the deckhand into the chopper. We flew our patient and his fingers to the Prince of Wales Hospital and delivered them to its microsurgery unit. Several weeks later we heard that the surgery was a complete success and the young fisherman had regained full use of all his fingers.

While the mission was not particularly heroic it was nevertheless a job well done. I was proud of my efforts. Apparently the skipper was very grateful too, because after landing back at the base we opened the boot compartment to have twenty-odd large fresh snapper fall to the ground. We all ate well for the next week.

It came as a complete surprise, after refuelling the aircraft and enjoying a welcome cup of coffee, to have Bob and David chastise me for my efforts. With huge grins across their faces they related the story again and again to all the office staff and anyone else who would listen. I'd chickened out on their grand plan (even though they had quietly admitted I'd shown good judgement). 'How dare you put your personal safety ahead of some great TV news footage?' they joked. With every telling David became more animated, and each time he looked at me he began strutting around like a chicken, squawking insanely.

Then, in a stroke of unsurpassed brilliance, he turned to me, flapped his wings and howled, 'C-h-i-c-k-e-n-m-a-n!'

Everyone knew Chickenman, a fictional radio character who could never do anything right. The joke continued all through the day, and every now and then David would emit a '*buck buck bacaaw*' followed by a chuckle. When he finally left for home, he called out, 'See you, Chickenman!'

That night our story was the lead article on the TV news, confirming that good pictures always come ahead of any other news.

The next morning I wondered what the papers would do with the story. I did not realise that Steve Grove, the cameraman aboard the Channel Ten chopper, had also taken still pictures. We scored the entire front page of the morning paper. DOC DIVES TO RESCUE, the headline read. At the bottom of the page it was stated that the potential dissolution of state parliament was reported on page two.

'Good morning, Chickenman,' Dan greeted me cheerfully as I entered the office. News travels fast, I thought. The nickname, or call sign as it is called in flying circles, stuck for years. Thanks, boys! We had no missions that day but I was asked to retell the story many times, complete with hilarious sound effects from David and Dan.

On the train home I looked at the dull-eyed commuters shuffling from their routine jobs. I felt privileged and blessed that my job was so different from theirs. As the train crossed the Harbour Bridge my pager started beeping. Again it was the urgent alert signal. I left the train at the next stop and a quick phone call to the base confirmed that I was needed. I was only a few minutes' walk from the Darling Harbour heliport and we agreed to rendezvous there.

On arrival at the heliport I told the operations desk what was going on, then, knowing I had several minutes to wait, turned back to the chairs behind me. Seated there were four executives who had the privilege of living on the Central Coast fifty kilometres north of Sydney and the financial means to commute by helicopter. It was over two hours' drive; by helicopter it was only fifteen minutes. To commute each day by chopper meant they must all have been loaded.

Yet they seemed as numbed to life as the train crowd. A more hangdog bunch of people I had never seen; their grey pinstriped suits reflected their glum grey expressions. I could not let their suffering continue any longer, it was time to have some fun.

I covered my badge with my arm and sat down amongst the suits. Their sideways glances told me they were miffed at being joined by someone wearing jeans. After sitting perfectly still and staring blankly straight ahead like the rest of them for thirty seconds, I reached down and removed my left sock and shoe and stuffed them in my bag. I resumed my solemn upright position, noting a few sideways glances in my direction. Thirty seconds later I repeated the act on the right side. Again I sat still for a while, then I removed my shirt. Finally I took off my jeans and sat there quietly in my swimmers. In the distance I heard the chopper approaching. The commuters thought it was their ride home and walked out to the pad. By now they were exchanging puzzled grins and trying to figure out this stranger's game.

The helicopter landed, silhouetted by the sun. It was not the commuter chopper they were expecting. Right type, wrong colour scheme. As soon as it had touched down Bob leapt out and helped me into my wetsuit and harness. As we took off to another successful water rescue, I grinned and waved as the suits stared, dumbstruck.

9

'Mayday! Mayday! Mayday!' came the call. 'Eleven kilometres east of Kiama, two on board. Going down, we're going down!' There followed an ominous silence.

A few seconds later, we learnt afterwards, the fishing boat had disappeared beneath the waves. Dave Milne and his mate Bill Sparks had only one life jacket and a few seat cushions to keep them afloat. Everything else was gone. Dave got the life jacket because he was a poor swimmer.

The authorities never heard the call. Jack Attwood, a keen ham radio operator who had turned retirement into an around-the-clock listening vigil as a volunteer for the Royal Volunteer Coastal Patrol, was just sitting down to his radio at home when he picked up the weak signal. He immediately rang the Shellharbour Water Police and soon the search was underway. Police launch *Scott* set out to sea a few minutes later. The south-westerly winds had picked up and were gusting to thirty-five knots. With a heavy chop and whitecaps forming on the top of each wave, the chances of finding the two were slim.

Once again my day assisting in the operating theatres was cut short by my pager beeping urgently. After another mad dash through the hospital, David, Bob and I left for the south coast to join the search. We tipped off our new television sponsor, Channel Nine, which jumped at the opportunity to join the search. Forty minutes later we were over the reported site, accompanied by a navy Huey helicopter and the Channel Nine chopper.

We knew that with each passing minute the cold seas would be sapping the fishermen's ability and will to stay alive. Hypothermia could have set in by now. The first warning sign is uncontrollable shivering; however, it's when the shivering stops that the real trouble begins. In severe hypothermia the shivering is replaced by a strong yearning for sleep, followed by coma and eventually death. It was vital that we get to the men as quickly as possible.

David conferred over the radio with the other pilots and devised a search pattern. This was years before the advent of Satellite Positioning Systems and the pattern would be flown by best guess. David allowed for wind drift and currents and drew up a prospective search area. High winds and strong currents meant we would have to search almost one hundred and sixty square kilometres.

The larger navy Huey, with five pairs of eyes on board, went south, while we shared the northern sector with the Channel Nine chopper.

The odds were against us finding the two fishermen. While locating lost people on a search mission was incredibly rewarding, ninety per cent of the time we didn't succeed. Sometimes we found the bodies but usually they disappeared forever.

An hour passed and hopes for the two men were fading. We were all becoming tired and hypnotised by the task. Whitecaps on the waves started to look like heads and wreckage in the water. Without reference points it was hard to know whether we had scanned the same area of sea twice or whether we had missed a sector. Several times we asked David to divert his course to check out a possible siting, but each time it turned out to be sea foam.

The search area extended well out to sea to allow for wind and current drift. Five kilometres north of our location, the Channel Nine chopper had just reached the north-east and remotest corner of the search area, some twenty-five kilometres out to sea, and started to turn west. We were eight kilometres further south.

The media chopper banked over steeply to start its turn for the next leg of the search. The Channel Nine cameraman's window was angled to look down below the aircraft, not only at the sea but, by an incredible stroke of good fortune, at two orange seat cushions. A second careful look and he made out two men waving frantically. Had it not been for the cushions he would not have seen them.

'Two men in the water!' came the call from the media chopper. We were there within a minute.

Bob and I quickly discussed the options with David, then we removed our helmets, went out onto the skids and leapt into the water. We swam over to the fishermen warily, knowing that their first reaction might be to panic and try to climb on top of us, but they were so incapacitated by the cold that there was little struggle left in them. We each carried a rescue strop which we immediately passed around their waists to help them stay afloat. It was obvious that if they had been left much longer, this would have been a body recovery mission.

Both of the men were shivering violently from the cold and were exhausted but they were otherwise able to talk to us. Bill told us, 'Y-Y-You f-f-flew over us half an hour ago, that's when we really started to w-w-worry.'

A voice boomed from above. It was David on the aircraft loud-speaker. 'The navy chopper will pick up two of you and I will sling the other two to the police launch.'

Bob shouted over the noise of the aircraft hovering above. 'You take Dave; we'll wait for the navy.' We could see the Huey fast approaching from the south.

I attached myself and Dave to the static line underneath our aircraft and we were hoisted into the air. To give him a further sense of security, and to warm him up, I wrapped my legs tightly around him as we started our journey underneath the helicopter to the police launch *Scott*. Shortly afterwards the Huey dropped a net into the water and scooped Bob and Bill up and on board.

Dave and I had an eight-kilometre journey to the police launch. Dave was still shivering violently but there was little I could do to treat his hypothermia while we were in the air. By experimenting with holding my arms out I found a way to rotate so that I was in front of him and shielding him from the chilling slipstream. In spite of his weakened condition he was still overwhelmed with relief at being rescued.

'We had hooked a yellow fin t-t-tuna and were so intent on getting it on b-b-board, we didn't see the southerly b-b-buster till the waves started coming over the stern. The b-b-boat sank thirty seconds after t-t-taking on the first wave.' He told me how cold and desperate they had been and how all he wanted to do now was hug his two children.

'It was Channel Nine who spotted you,' I told him.

'How will I ever r-r-repay you all?' he stammered.

'Easy,' I replied. 'From the police launch I'm going to arrange for you to be taken by ambulance to the hospital for a check-up. Every television station will be filming you. Just as you're about to get into the ambulance, one of you should turn and say, "Thanks Channel Nine!" That will prevent the other stations from showing this slice of footage and give Channel Nine an exclusive story. As they've just started to sponsor our service, they in turn will be grateful to us and will hopefully continue their sponsorship.'

Soon we neared the police launch. I told Dave we would have to be dropped into the water ten metres away from the launch and swim over to it. Naturally he wasn't too keen on re-entering the water but I assured him I would be with him the whole way. All he had to do was relax and I would tow him to the boat and lift him out. There was no other way to do it and he resigned himself to another dunking.

The drop-off went uneventfully, and with the help of the police we soon had him on board the launch. Immediately we carried him below deck and removed his clothes. A quick examination revealed he had no injuries and so we dressed him in a dry pair of overalls and wrapped him in a blanket.

An hour later, on dry land, Bob and I talked to the reunited mates. Bill was in much better condition than Dave, who could now walk unaided but was still weak. Dave got into the ambulance first, too exhausted to speak to the media, but Bill, having been briefed by Dave, followed our plan to perfection. Just as he was about to step into the ambulance he turned and from underneath his blanket gave a big double thumbs-up and said his line: 'Thanks Channel Nine!'

The groans of disappointment from the other TV crews were audible, but the Nine crew was delighted. The exclusive story and graphic rescue footage led the Channel Nine news around the country that night and was sold overseas to be shown around the world.

We were on a high. We had received national and international recognition for our rescue service. In spite of our frustrations, we were proud of the difference we made to so many people. Yet, despite this, we were more conscious than ever of the shortcomings of our operation.

'There's got to be a better container than fishing tackle boxes for our medical gear,' I complained.

Bob sighed. 'We were just lucky it wasn't a winch job,' he said, referring to our latest surf rescue. 'At least we didn't have to return to shore to take off the door.' Usually we had to find a place to store the left rear door while we used the winch, and this sometimes meant flying back to shore before we could begin the rescue.

'The aircraft doesn't hold that much fuel,' added David. 'If we had taken a full tank, with all the equipment you guys want to carry, we would have been too heavy to hover. To drop the door we would also have had to return to refuel.'

The shortcomings were endless. I started to think of better ways to hold our medical gear. We all started to yearn for a better aircraft. The Jet Ranger performed valiantly, but it was getting old and tired and was woefully inadequate for the multiple roles we assumed.

The weight problem meant that if we didn't burn off enough fuel en route to a rescue, the engine's power output was not great enough to carry the extra weight and allow for prolonged hovering. Hovering takes more power than cruise flying because the aircraft rotors battle their own turbulence. To avoid overstressing the engine we would sometimes abandon the hover and fly a circuit. Once we had forward speed and the rotors were in smooth air, the power required to stay aloft would drop by forty per cent, the engine would cool down and we could then return to our task.

Once, however, this worked to our advantage. We had responded to a report of a body in the water near the Sydney Opera House. Being only four minutes' flying time from our base, we were still heavy as we searched the waters off Sydney Cove. Dan looked at the instruments every few seconds. They were well into the red zones. 'We're overtorqueing! We need to do a circuit.'

I nodded.

He cracked a smile. 'Of course, the tide's coming in, so looking for the victim up the harbour would make sense.'

'Makes a lot of sense to me,' I said. 'You okay with that, Bob?'

'Sounds great!' He grinned.

Dan swung us around to the west and we joined the select few aviators who have flown under the Sydney Harbour Bridge. As we flew out of bright sunshine into the Bridge's shadow, I was awed by the fact that this immense structure arcing above us was man-made, put together, bolt by bolt, by human hands. It seemed somehow a monument to human tenacity. After twenty seconds or so we turned around and probably became the first aviators to fly under the bridge in both directions.

Soon we were called by Sydney Water Police, who by now suspected the report to be a hoax and offered to continue the search themselves. We returned to base, all smiles for the rest of the day.

A few days later we were unable to start the aircraft due to a flat battery. Our external battery cart was so old it was useless. Eventually, with the help of two cars and two sets of jumper leads, we got going. The situation was pathetic; something had to change.

One problem – finding a better way to carry our medical equipment – was relatively easy to solve. After much thought I bought a Lowes brand backpack with two detachable minipacks. Airway equipment was kept in one minipack, intravenous access equipment in the other, and the rest was stored in the main pack. To make access to items in the main pack easy, I purchased a number of Tupperware boxes to divide items into drugs, bandages, IV fluids and so on.

The pack was an outstanding success. It was much more robust than the old fishing boxes and it left us with our hands free while doing our jobs. We could also now winch or abseil with our medical gear. I had grand visions of the concept being developed much further, little knowing that one Dr Frank Thomas from Salt Lake City, Utah, was going to beat us to the final solution in future years.

Apart from frustrations with equipment, I was also disappointed by the lack of calls from the ambulance service. While we continued to transport patients with spinal injuries, other calls for assistance were few and far between. In spite of the aircraft's limitations, I was at a loss to understand why.

These frustrations were forgotten the day Dan and I nearly crashed. We were to affect a mock rescue near the Sydney Opera House for the benefit of Water Safety Week. Our lucky crewman was to jump into the water adjacent to an inflatable life raft and rescue a scantily clad fashion model. The two would then be transferred on the static line to the waiting police launch.

Apart from the fact that the rescue strop removed the model's bikini during the rescue, requiring our crewman to use his hands to maintain her modesty, the simulation went without drama. However, we were then asked to create more footage by winching our crewman off the rear deck of the launch and back up into the helicopter. Dan and I were somewhat hesitant, not least because I was in the front co-pilot seat, which was not our normal winching position. There was no way I could climb through to the back seat. We reluctantly accepted the request and the winch cable was lowered as I watched from the half-open door.

Our crewman waited on the rear deck with the rescue strop looped and clipped to his own harness. He attached the winch hook and gave the thumbs-up signal, at which point Dan put the aircraft into a slow climb. Just as the tension was taken up, our crewman stepped towards the back of the boat and in the process the strop hooked under the stern rail of the twenty-ton launch. With the winch wire caught up, the chopper jerked to a stop then rapidly rolled to the left and back-wards. There was a slight swell in the harbour and at that moment the boat dropped another metre into a trough between the waves, dragging the helicopter even further down and stressing everything way beyond its design load.

The aircraft was rapidly tilting beyond its flying limits. Sliding backwards into the harbour seemed inevitable. I looked across at Dan in horror. He was furiously trying to control the chopper. Then, incredibly, just before the roll became uncorrectable, the winch cable snapped some three metres above the crewman's head. The force of the separation flung him several metres off the rear of the launch. Twenty metres of cable came looping and coiling rapidly skywards towards our main rotors. I watched in speechless terror. If the cable tangled in the rotor blades they would be ripped off the aircraft and we would plummet into the harbour.

The bundle of wires seemed to hover in front of us for an eternity, mere centimetres below the rotor disc, before dropping back down. Dan and I stared at each other; if I looked as ashen as he did I must have been an awful sight. Dan just wanted to get away from the place and, after making sure that our crewman had been rescued and was okay, we proceeded up the harbour back to base.

We were only a few seconds into the flight when, looking back over my shoulder, I was horrified to see that the winch cable was now flapping wildly just beside our tail rotor.

'Hover!' I screamed at Dan. 'Bring us into a hover!' The panic must have sounded in my voice because he slowed immediately and we hovered in stunned silence until the cable had been fully retrieved.

It was a very sombre flight home that afternoon and as we shut down the aircraft our usual camaraderie and black humour was absent. I don't know about Dan but my mind played over and over the image of the helicopter being pulled inexorably into the blue waters of the harbour.

10

'Let's get our own aircraft, something bigger, something we own,' declared Ian Badham, out of the blue.

I wasn't sure I was hearing right, knowing the state of our finances. The Sydney Helicopter Rescue Service could barely pay our wages and ran on a total annual budget of $350,000; how on earth were we going to be able to afford a new aircraft?

Ian *did* have a point, though. There was a growing realisation that transportation of patients both from accident scenes and between hospitals was going to become an increasing part of our duties. With its cramped confines, the Jet Ranger did not allow for sufficient access to the patient during transfer to make this viable for all but the most trivial of medical conditions. The helicopter itself was leased and there had never been any prospect of us owning it outright.

Ian, along with Peter MacCormick, the treasurer of the service (whom I had met salvaging the boat engine on my first day), were never ones to stand idle for very long, and despite our precarious financial position, they decided to go for broke. There was no hope of increased government assistance so it was down to their ability to negotiate greater financial support from our corporate sponsors to make this upgrade possible. It was, however, the right time to make the play. The Bank of New South Wales had just changed its name to Westpac (short for Western Pacific Banking Corporation) and it would be using the helicopter services it sponsored in all capital cities as a major part of its public relations and advertising campaign. As the flagship of the services we felt that the time was right to put pressure on the bank.

The negotiations were long and tough. The bank had always been very supportive of us, but naturally this was a business decision for them – they were not a charity and they would have to be able to justify the increased expenditure to their shareholders. Eventually Westpac agreed to fund a single-engined Squirrel. It wasn't the twin engine we'd hoped for, but it still represented a quantum leap in our capabilities and also signalled a fundamental change in our philosophy. To date, the Sydney Helicopter Rescue Service had been a low-cost enterprise with a low-cost aircraft flying daily beach patrols, partly so that all members had flying experience but mainly as a form of banner advertising for our sponsors.

Daily beach patrols would now be a thing of the past. More complex operating systems and a push into critical care transport capability required a far more professional and dedicated crew, and the beginning of the end of the weekend warrior mentality.

Our new aircraft arrived at Bankstown Airport in mid-1982. Its call sign was Hotel, Romeo, Sierra, the same initials as helicopter rescue service. We spent many days designing and overseeing its modifications. Being the first aircraft of its type in the country, and without the finances to visit overseas services that already flew Squirrels in a similar role, we based the interior fit largely on pictures from international magazines. All the necessary modifications were made to allow us to carry patients, and only the pilot retained the standard executive seat! The rest of the seating was spartan. I insisted the seat cushions be bright orange and the internal foam made from life-jacket padding, a result of our experiences with Bill and Dave, the fishermen. Maybe one day that would be us in the water.

By far the biggest challenge was the radio fit. Dan had opted for the most advanced gear on the market. It was cutting-edge technology for its time, allowing us to talk on every emergency service frequency used in New South Wales. We would be able to claim confidently that it was the most advanced communication vehicle in the country.

With our new aircraft's arrival we were becoming more and more frustrated by the old one's limited capability, but we still had to fly. Part of our job included public relations work. We had to grasp every opportunity to get the sponsors' names in the media. Sometimes we would do film shoots for various organisations, to be shown within the industry or on television or at cinemas.

The National Safety Council of Australia wanted to produce a short film on industrial safety, which would open with us flying to a building site and stabilising an injured construction worker. The theme of the film was to avoid hazardous situations before they became an accident.

The film director briefed us at our base; the pilot noted the written approval given by the Department of Civil Aviation. We assumed this meant they had surveyed the site and it had adequate clearances.

The film crew was coordinated and we flew to the scene. Upon landing, Bob and I rushed to the victim's aid and commenced treatment. The cameras then panned to the commentator who gave his opening lines.

'Cut,' called the director. 'Perfect! Well done first time.'

The film crew moved on and we were left to pack up our kit. As our pilot ambled over we looked back to where the aircraft was parked. We all burst out laughing. This was meant to be a film about avoiding hazardous situations, yet the supposedly surveyed landing site was an alleyway between two high-rise buildings. The distance between them was only a few rotor diameters wide. It was one of the tightest and most dangerous spots we ever flew into.

We had received a rare call from the ambulance service – could we assist with an injured man on a submarine? That made sense, I thought. It seemed the service only called us in if there was no other way to get the job done. Bob had already started to discuss the logistical difficulties, but eventually the controller cut him short, explaining that the submarine was in dry dock! It was being refitted at Cockatoo Island just three kilometres west of the Harbour Bridge, and six kilometres from our base. The logistics of accessing the island by boat were proving difficult and time was of the essence.

We accepted the mission and ten minutes later were in the forward torpedo room of the sub. Somehow a maintenance technician had not quite left one of the torpedo tubes before a torpedo slid down its loading rack into the same tube, crushing his hand. He was still trapped and in severe pain.

With numerous helpers we were able to support him as the torpedo was removed from the tube to release his jammed hand. Then we laid him down on the deck. His fingers were badly crushed and again it looked like a case for the microsurgery unit at Prince of Wales Hospital. Navy medics and an ambulance team who had just arrived by boat set to bandaging his hand while I established an intravenous line and gave the submariner some morphine. Within a few minutes he was feeling much more comfortable.

The next problem was getting him out of the submarine. We discussed our options, then bound him tightly into our confined-space rescue litter and hauled it backwards up the torpedo loading tunnel. By comparison the rest of the mission was easy, and twenty minutes later he was in the emergency room at Prince of Wales Hospital.

The mission involved ten minutes of flying time. What was a logistical nightmare for the ambulance service was a smooth and fast operation for us. Not all missions, however, had such successful outcomes. Sometimes it was bodies we were recovering, and often these were suicides.

One of the most popular suicide spots was at the Gap, a beautiful yet notorious cliff at the southern headland of Sydney Harbour. The cliff there is over seventy metres above the sea or the rocks below, depending on whether the tide is in or out. Bodies sighted on the rocks needed to be retrieved within hours before the incoming tide washed them out into the ocean. Unluckily for us, helicopter was by far the fastest way to retrieve these bodies. Most that were washed away soon sank and became all but impossible to find unless they resurfaced days later, considerably bloated by the effects of gas-forming bacteria on the internal organs. It was far preferable for everyone concerned to retrieve the body as soon as possible. Sharing the rescue line with a dead body was a very unpleasant but necessary part of the job.

On one occasion we were called to the Gap after reports of a person jumping from the cliff top. As we flew over the scene it was obvious from the angle of the limbs that this was not going to be a survivor. Dan radioed the police to say that the person was deceased and there was no need for their rescue squad to continue to the location at high speed under lights and sirens. The police, however, were obliged to continue until a medical practitioner declared the patient dead.

The closest we could get to the body was about fifty metres north along the cliffs. Even here there was not enough space to land and Dan was only able to hover near one of the rock ledges and drop us off. Bob and I jumped off the skids and onto the rocks, then walked southwards, ever wary of freak waves that could wash us out to sea. At least if that happened Dan could immediately drop the rescue line to us.

We were below the level of the ledge on which the victim lay so we had to climb up a three-metre wall then scramble up onto the ledge. I went first, finding it difficult to gain a hold on the slippery rock face. I struggled to lift my head above the lip of the ledge and as I did so I came face to face with half a human brain. I jerked back in shock, only managing to hold on by my fingertips. The body was sprawled two metres away. After clambering onto the ledge I examined the gruesome remains. Every bone in the body seemed to have suffered multiple fractures and when we touched it, it moved like a rag doll.

I turned around and warned Bob of the scene, then turned away and vomited into the sea. Dan, hovering overhead, recognised what this meant and promptly radioed the police and advised them that he had received confirmation from the crew doctor that the victim had died.

Bob and I stared up at the cliff. Ten metres above our heads a small blood-soaked ledge marked the site of initial impact. We took photos for the police records; then, with great difficulty, stuffed the remains into a body bag. It took some time searching the rocks for the missing pieces of the skull bones and brain, but eventually I was satisfied that all the pieces were accounted for.

We wanted to get out of that place as quickly as possible but neither of us was keen to be lifted to the top of the cliff with the body. So instead we sent it on the static line by itself and Dan returned to pick us up, hovering next to the rocks.

Bob and I strapped ourselves in, white-faced and silent. We were confronted with ghastly injuries on a regular basis, but somehow, because these injuries were self-inflicted, I could not stop thinking what desolation and despair must have led to such an annihilating act. I felt a deep sadness settle on my shoulders, and not even Dan's gentle consideration back at base could shake it.

11

'There's no time to roll a tape and edit your report,' the radio station producer stated. 'The news is just starting; you will be going live to air in five, four, three, two . . .' In the background I heard, 'Crossing to Dr Ken Wishaw aboard the 2UE Westpac Rescue Helicopter.'

In a flash of doubt I panicked; there was no time to rehearse. Even experienced news reporters sometimes needed several takes to get a report right. Could I do this?

'We're ten kilometres off Dee Why Beach and almost alongside the container ship *Manchester Star*,' I started, swallowing my nerves. 'Crew aboard the ship reported sighting distress flares some three kilometres south of their position. Along with the water police we are searching for the possible craft in distress. Winds are gusting to forty knots and the seas are over four metres with extensive white caps and spray, which is hampering the search effort. We are now turning south to search the next sector of the search area. This is Ken Wishaw aboard the 2UE Westpac Rescue Helicopter.'

After a few seconds the producer came back on. 'Excellent! That went nationwide. Keep us posted.'

'Will do,' I replied, breathing again. Next, with a little more confidence, I turned to the water police frequency. 'Sydney Water Police, Sydney Water Police, Sydney Water Police, this is Rescue Helicopter One.'

'Receiving, Rescue Helicopter One.'

'Our present position is three kilometres east of your launch, turning south to continue the search.'

'Copy Rescue One,' the radio crackled. A few minutes later the launch came onto the radio. 'Rescue One, we have sited a vessel with smoke flare two kilometres north of our position. Suggest you proceed to meet us.'

Dan nodded and we immediately swung north. Several minutes later we were overhead the ten-metre half-cabin cruiser. The craft did not respond to our radio calls. A man on board wearing a bright orange life jacket appeared. Dan brought us in close and low.

I switched my radio to the public address system speaker mounted below the aircraft. 'Do you have a radio?' I asked.

The man cupped his ear.

I repeated more slowly: 'Do you have a radio?'

He shook his head.

'Are you okay?' was my next question.

He nodded enthusiastically.

'Are you the only person on board?'

Again he nodded.

I continued, 'The water police will be here in ten minutes.'

He gave me a thumbs-up and a broad grin.

I relayed the information to the water police then Dan pulled us back to await their arrival. Ten minutes later the boat was under tow. As we headed back to base I did an update report to 2UE. I forgot to mention on the radio that I thought this guy was an idiot to be out here in these conditions.

How far I had come over the last nine months! With the help of the rest of the team I was taking an increasingly active role in every part of the operation. When I flew in the co-pilot's front left seat I assumed co-pilot duties, assisting with navigation and making all the radio calls, save for the air traffic control requests, so the pilot could concentrate on flying. My confidence and ability had developed enormously. The perfect live cross to national news was testament to my abilities to handle the radios under pressure. To me it was symbolic of the improvement in all my helicopter capabilities.

When we returned to base I received a visit from Dr Dick Young, the director of anaesthesia at my old hospital, St George. He had been at Royal North Shore on other business and had decided to come over to our office for a quick tour. He asked how the job was going for me personally.

I thought carefully about my reply. Dr Young was one of three specialists responsible for overseeing the ambulance paramedic program and I was not sure where his loyalties lay. 'I love the job but I think we're underutilised. I know there are a lot more cases the ambulance service could be calling us to, but it only seems to happen if certain controllers are on duty, or if there is no other way for the job to be done.'

He looked at me for a few seconds. '*I* know why you aren't being called as often as you'd like. I'll organise for you to attend one of the monthly paramedic review meetings, and then let's talk about this again.'

No sooner had we turned to walk over to the aircraft than Bob and Dan came running down the stairs. 'Rock fisherman in the water at Blue Fish Point!' Bob yelled as he scrambled into his wetsuit. Two minutes later we lifted off from the pad. From the front left seat I waved to Dr Young as we turned and climbed skywards.

A few days later I attended the paramedics' meeting. I was amazed by what unfolded. Afterwards I asked a number of questions and complimented the paramedics on their excellent case reviews. They accepted the compliments graciously but cautiously. The next week Dr Young and I talked again.

'Well?' he asked as we walked out of the office.

I shook my head. 'I had no idea. It was almost like an evangelical meeting, or a mutual admiration society. They seemed so full of themselves. Then I started to really listen to the cases, and it began to make sense. I'd have trouble dealing with any of those cases in the controlled environment of a hospital with unlimited resources on hand, yet they're doing it on the streets. My respect for what they do has gone through the roof. They told me that they first go on the road after just twelve weeks' training, and the paramedic training is only another six months. I've had eight *years*' training. They're very impressive.'

Dr Young smiled. 'You're right, they are amazing. It's hardly surprising they need to have these sessions to acknowledge how well they do under such trying circumstances.'

The penny dropped. 'It's that essential belief in themselves that makes it hard for them to accept us,' I realised.

Dr Young nodded enthusiastically. 'Every ambulance officer has learnt how to get the job done in the hardest of circumstances. Succeeding without support is in their blood. Suddenly you doctors have come out of your cosy hospitals and seem to be demanding the right to be on the team. Don't expect it to happen overnight.'

'But in many circumstances we can add to the situation and increase the chances of survival.'

'You're right, of course,' Dr Young agreed. 'But you can't just insist that it happen. You need two things. You need to better the relationship, and you need to speak with authority.' He stopped at the edge of the helipad. 'Is this where you see your career?'

'Yes,' I replied without hesitation.

'Well it's never going to happen like this. You'll need to be a specialist to gain their respect. And as there's no specialist training in emergency medicine in this country as yet, training in anaesthesia and intensive care is the only way you'll get the training you need in advanced care of critically ill and injured patients.' He paused then stared intently at me. 'Are you willing to do that?'

When I got home that evening Amanda and I sat down and discussed our future. I loved the job with the helicopter rescue service just as it was, but I knew it was unsustainable. I needed a lot more medical training if I was going to be able to cope with critically ill patients on long retrieval missions. I needed to make it a long-term career.

I had realised by now that I was not cut out to be an eye surgeon. I would die of boredom. My passion for the helicopter service was where my heart lay. Amanda knew this – she had long ago resigned herself to being a 'helicopter widow' – and she knew, too, how much work was involved in becoming a specialist, how much she would have to sacrifice her own aspirations so I could achieve mine. Yet if she felt any apprehension or resentment, she didn't show it. She told me to go for it.

Three weeks later I was sitting outside the medical superintendent's office at St George Hospital. I had borrowed a starched white medical coat off the rack in the hospital laundry to look the part for my job interview as a specialist trainee registrar. The coat was so stiff I was sure it could stand up by itself.

'You can come in now,' called the secretary.

Inside the office she showed me to my seat. Across the room sat Dr Young, the medical superintendent and one of the other specialist anaesthetists. My application was on the table. Next to it was a stack of identical green sheets of paper. I guessed there were perhaps another thirty applications for this one job. My heart sank.

After five minutes of questioning by the three, Dr Young got to the point. 'As you can see, you are not the only applicant, and we only have one vacancy for next year. You have stiff competition. Have you applied anywhere else?'

'Every other training hospital in Australia and New Zealand,' I replied. I wasn't going to make the same mistake as I had as an RMO.

Dr Young nodded. 'Are you prepared to make the sacrifices and endure the hours and the study required for the next four years to train as a specialist?'

'Yes.'

'Is your wife?'

'Yes.'

'Do you really understand what a career in anaesthesia involves? Your hours are longer than any other specialty, and after-hours emergency work will take its price personally.'

I continued with the cracked record routine. 'Yes, I'm aware of that.' Of course I wasn't. And I wouldn't be until it was much too late.

Dr Young took a deep breath. 'Finally, if perhaps you did get the post, would you promise me not to do any helicopter work from the day you start here till after you pass the final exams in four years' time?'

I looked to the floor. This was the big one. Could I turn my back on my passion for four years so I could make it my career for the rest of my life? I raised my head. 'I'll do whatever it takes.'

The three interviewers looked at each other. 'Could you wait outside? Thank you for coming.' The medical superintendent rose and showed me to the door.

I sat out in the hallway, scratching my neck and wondering whether I could live up to the challenge of being a trainee specialist, assuming I got a posting somewhere. It suddenly seemed impossibly daunting.

The door opened and Dr Young sat down beside me. He looked deadpan. 'I'm prepared to offer you a post starting next January.' Simultaneously we both grinned. 'Congratulations!' He shook my hand enthusiastically. 'You have two years to pass the primary exams. If you haven't done that by then, you're out. Do that and you're on our scheme till you complete your training. I'm serious about the helicopter. And by the way, you've made the right decision.' He patted me on the shoulder. 'Go home and celebrate and we'll see you next January.'

I floated down the hallway and did as I was told.

It was late November and finally the Squirrel was completed, save for a few finishing touches. Before taking official delivery Dan and David both did a type certification course to enable them to fly the new bird. Thereafter the three of us flew sorties around Bankstown Airport to work out how rescue operations would differ from those undertaken in the Jet Ranger.

Capable and faithful as the Jet Ranger was, we felt we had really arrived with the Squirrel. This aircraft was built to last. There was nothing fragile about its appearance or construction, yet its lines were classic French grace. We had seen the crash test results showing how strong the fibreglass cabin was, and a look under the cowlings showed how solid, almost overengineered, this machine was.

The internal layout of the Squirrel was one open cabin, fundamentally different from the Jet Ranger. There were no internal support columns, and immediately we sensed a togetherness amongst us crew members that did not exist in the Jet Ranger. In the Bell cabin there was a central column extending from floor to ceiling, which was quaintly known as the 'broom closet' because it contained all the control rods that operated the aircraft rotor system. The broom closet had the effect of dividing the aircraft into four separate compartments. The two crewmen seated diagonally opposite could not see each other. This divided the team psychologically, and over the years I came to realise how unity amongst the crew was fundamental to success in difficult and dangerous situations.

The Squirrel was a much quieter and more stable platform to work from. The rigid Starflex rotor head and fibreglass blades gave a stability in the hover that the Jet Ranger, with its ageing, teetering head system, couldn't match. For precise hovering, and particularly for winching operations, it was far superior to our present machine.

The winch was the best part of all. It was mounted on a swinging arm that was stowed in the forward position for flying and swung outboard for winch operations. Winching was done outside the line of the left landing skid, making retrieving stretchers far easier. Better still, before commencing a winch down, the crew member was attached to the hook and lifted off the cabin floor and checked for secure attachment before the arm was swung out. If attachment wasn't right the worst that could happen was that you would drop back onto the cabin floor. All those years of worrying about being dropped hundreds of metres to smash on the ground were over.

We practised loading and unloading the stretcher while the aircraft was on the ground. The usual co-pilot's seat had been replaced by a locally designed and built removing folding seat, which could be stored in one of the three rear storage compartments. The stretcher then slid in feet forwards, and I could sit on the low seat in the left rear corner of the cabin, behind the patient's head and with my legs down either side. I was now in a position to provide artificial respiration by bag and mask and was at precisely the right angle to insert a tube down a patient's windpipe should they deteriorate in flight. Along with the monitoring equipment we carried, we could now feel confident to transport the most critically ill patients.

With perfect timing, the lease on the Jet Ranger expired the day before we were expecting to take delivery of the Squirrel. Crew and committee members gathered at the helipad to bid our faithful Bell farewell as it flew back to its home base in northern New South Wales. I admired its beautiful lines as it lifted off and glided out of my life. It was a sad moment for us all as it had served us, and the community of Sydney, so well. Nobody moved a muscle for five minutes till it was a tiny speck disappearing over the horizon.

My sadness turned to excitement as I pondered the next day, when we would receive the Squirrel. Just then our secretary ran down the stairs to the helipad. 'There's bad news from the bank.'

It seemed Westpac had decided the aircraft was not the right colour. Somewhere there had been a miscommunication and the red that had been chosen was not quite the correct shade. The bank was adamant the aircraft would not fly until the colours were perfect.

We were without an aircraft. Aerospatiale told us the repaint would take at least two weeks. Actually it took over a month.

After several days of frantic phone calls we were able to find a temporary aircraft. Far from the bigger, better and more medically able aircraft we had been dreaming of, we were forced to settle on a little yellow bumble bee, a Hughes 500D. There would be no patient carrying capability. However, the generously powered, highly manoeuvrable and nimble aircraft was soon to prove its worth and save several lives, including my own.

12

The raging bushfire marched up the densely wooded ridge towards the three firefighters. There was no escape. Behind them was a two-hundred-metre cliff, and in the unreachable distance, the sight of civilisation, fifteen kilometres north across the valley. David, Bob and I, in our tiny Hughes 500D, were their only means of salvation. As we sped westwards from the city, I prayed that we would reach them in time. I could think of no worse dilemma to be in. I didn't realise that I would soon be in that very situation myself.

Smoke had been spotted the previous day in a remote area of the Blue Mountains National Park, fifteen kilometres south-west of Glenbrook. There was not so much as a dirt track into the area, and so three National Parks and Wildlife Service firefighters had hiked into the wilderness to contain the fire. By nightfall they had managed to isolate the fire to a two-hundred-square-metre area before setting up camp. To their horror, when they awoke, the fire had broken away and was on a two-kilometre front working up the ridge on which they had slept, cutting off all possible exits and leaving them backed up to the cliff edge.

The Blue Mountains, rising to the west of Sydney's coastal basin, get their name from the constant blue haze of eucalyptus oil from the trees that crowd its valleys and line its ridges. The Great Western Highway snakes inland across the central ridge, while on either side lies spectacular bush wilderness protected by impassable cliffs and government legislation.

Today, however, we had little time to enjoy the dramatic scenery. Our task lay to the south of the highway inside the national park boundary. Five kilometres into the park lay Glenbrook clearing. This area was hastily being established as the fire coordination centre. Upon landing we were quickly briefed on the location of the three firefighters, and within minutes we were again speeding further west. The column of smoke ahead led us to the site.

We expected the rescue to be straightforward. In spite of the fact that our temporary aircraft had no hoist, we would land on the ridge, check the firefighters were okay before putting them aboard, and leapfrogging the fire several times to any nearby clearing from which we could arrange their return to safety at our leisure.

As we approached the fire, the folly of our plan became obvious. Below us the trees were so tightly packed that there was no chance we would be able to land. The trees grew right up to the cliff edge, leaving only a metre or two of clearing next to the precipice: enough for the three firefighters to stand on but not enough for us to set the aircraft down.

We described our dilemma to the men below via their radio and then widened our search, but to no avail. The nearest useable clearing appeared to be back at the Glenbrook coordination site. The tiny aircraft could only hold four people so we had only one choice. None of the men below had any helicopter training, so gallantly, or stupidly, Bob and I decided to lower ourselves from the hovering aircraft, create a clearing wide enough for David to place one skid lightly on the cliff edge while remaining in the hover, load the three into the aircraft and then wait till they had been ferried back to Glenbrook for our own escape. We were about to trade places with the men below.

David brought the Hughes as close to the cliff edge as possible, and with the blades snapping at the smaller branches we lowered a chainsaw to the rocks below and then leapt from the skids onto the cliff edge. It was a point of no return. Now there were five in danger where previously there had only been three.

David moved the helicopter to an orbit several kilometres north to allow us some relative peace and quiet in which to create a helipad, check the victims and plan our escape. While Bob proceeded to chop trees, I checked out the three firefighters. All of them were uninjured and displaying incredible calmness in the face of their predicament.

Bob and I discussed the plan with the men. They were reluctant to leave us there knowing the arithmetic was tight. Glenbrook clearing was ten minutes' flying time away. The firefighters estimated the fire would be there in thirty to forty minutes. We briefly considered cutting another landing site upwind of the flames but that would take too long. The original plan would have to do.

Within ten minutes Bob had cleared a large enough area. Without delay we called David back and soon Bob and I were watching the little yellow Hughes disappear to the east with its three extremely relieved passengers. The mad rush was over. There was nothing to do but wait.

The scream of the helicopter was replaced by an eerie silence. There were none of the usual bush sounds, all animal life had fled the danger. The eucalyptus smoke was nauseating, catching in the back of my throat. The sun was blotted out by a thick haze and hung red and ominous in a dark sky. If felt as though the two of us were the only survivors of some terrible apocalypse.

Bob broke the oppressive silence. 'Well, we don't have to light a signal fire for David to find us again,' he commented wryly as we watched the massive smoke plume rising above the bush a few hundred metres upwind of where we stood. 'This is when a Bell 412 would be real handy,' he added. 'Could've just plucked the three off the cliff and been back having a cuppa by now.'

The ensuing twenty-five minutes were the longest in my life. Any number of things could go wrong to prevent David returning to save us. The thought of being burnt to death preyed on us both, and soon we were checking our options along the cliff for an escape route or an area of shelter. There was nothing. Only the fire moving inexorably closer.

We resigned ourselves to sitting, waiting, praying. I thought of Amanda – who might literally become a helicopter widow – of all the hopeful plans we'd made. Staring across the valley to unreachable safety seemed better than watching the approaching smoke column, so we sat down on a large log and chatted calmly, pretending not to be afraid, only the nervous glances over our shoulders betraying our mounting anxiety.

We could hear the faint roar of flames by now, of leaves and tree trunks being incinerated. My throat felt dry and scratchy and each cough was a reminder of how little time we had.

After what seemed an eternity we heard a faint buzz. We scanned the eastern horizon till Bob spotted a tiny black speck coming our way. We barely felt the blast of the rotors or heard the scream of the turbine we were so relieved to see the little Hughes. Using the 'in and out on the hover' technique that Bob had taught me so thoroughly several years before, we boarded the hovering aircraft and flew out of the inferno. Bob and I looked at each other and grinned, giving a silent prayer of thanks to Igor Sikorsky, the inventor of the helicopter.

Soon we were easing our parched throats with a cup of strong tea back at Glenbrook clearing. The National Parks and Wildlife Service's own Gazelle chopper arrived with its water bucket and began water-bombing the flames. Although our aircraft was small, because of its previous duty as a fire chopper in Victoria it had an underbelly cargo pod custom made to carry firefighting tools. Over the next three hours, much to his credit, David ferried over forty firefighters and their equipment into the area to contain the blaze.

A few hours later we were called to Katoomba. We were needed to search for three missing bushwalkers in the Grose Valley, fifteen kilometres north-west of the town. Our flight path took us directly over the ridge where we had waited to be rescued that morning. We silently stared down at the devastated site. The ridge was totally destroyed and the log on which Bob and I had sat was a smouldering pile of charcoal.

As we flew towards Katoomba the extent of the firestorms surrounding this mountain town became appallingly apparent. The Jamieson Valley, renowned for its vistas through the blue haze, was no more than a sea of smoke. Katoomba, sitting on the plateau above the valley, appeared to be floating on dense cloud. Even on the ridge top the visibility over the township was less than one kilometre.

We landed and picked up a National Parks and Wildlife Service ranger, who explained the situation. One of the walkers had been hiking alone. His body had already been found, near Evans Lookout. The other two hikers were thought to be in the lower regions of the Grose Valley, below the lookout. They had had the foresight to sign into the trip diary at Blackheath Police Station with details of their intended journey. They had cited Sweden as their home address. It was unlikely, then, that they would have had the knowledge to escape the firestorm that had raged through the valley in the previous few hours. It seemed as though we would be searching for charred remains.

We flew towards Evans Lookout, the visibility deteriorating considerably. Although this was an area I knew extremely well from high-school hiking and rock-climbing days, it was unrecognisable under these conditions. The ground became all but invisible even two hundred metres below us. Only the tops of electricity towers stood above the smoke and David used these as his guide. The Grose Valley was full to the brim with dense, nauseating eucalyptus smoke.

The ranger advised us this was probably only a surface layer, and the air would be clearer in the base of the valley six hundred metres below us, so we decided to proceed. The cliff face at Evans Lookout drops vertically for nearly three hundred metres; however, the density of the smoke limited our view of that sheer face to perhaps only thirty metres. This was to be the first, but certainly not the last, of my experiences of tight mountain flying.

David positioned the aircraft as far away from the cliff face as possible without losing sight of the rocky wall. If the wall disappeared behind the smoke we would be flying blind, with every chance that the disorientation would prove fatal for all of us. The limit of our visibility appeared to be only a few metres from the cliff and I braced for the inevitable clash and sparks as the fragile blades struck the rock wall. Slowly, metre by metre, we descended into the valley. For a long time I held my breath, too afraid even to think. At last the air became clearer as the valley opened out below us, and we were able to leave the cliff face and start our search for the hapless bushwalkers.

What greeted us was utter desolation. The firestorm had raged right through the valley and signs of the unbelievable heat and destruction were everywhere. Smoking charcoal columns were all that remained of the eucalyptus trees. They stood above a black and grey moonscape.

We slowly tracked down towards Junction Rock in the centre of the valley, and incredibly, only ten minutes into our search, I spotted two people standing on a massive, house-size boulder, waving their trousers in the air.

As we approached, I composed my questions to ask over the external speaker. 'This is the Westpac Rescue Helicopter, are you okay?' They both nodded furiously. 'Do you need medical attention?' They shook their heads. Again we were frustrated by the limitations of our aircraft. We had no way of winching the two men to safety, and no way of getting down to them between the smouldering tree trunks. 'Are you okay for four hours?' Yes, they nodded. 'We will direct a rescue party to your location.' Again they nodded. Even from twenty metres above them the relief on their faces shone clearly. Jubilant with our success, we proceeded north and exited the valley in the clearer skies towards Mount Wilson.

Over the next twenty minutes we circled back to Katoomba and dropped off our ranger friend to coordinate the ground rescue party. We received news that the firefighters were gaining the upper hand at Glenbrook and we were no longer required. Weary but triumphant we headed back to Sydney. By now the pall of smoke had drifted eastwards and the lower Blue Mountains and western regions of Sydney were swimming in the sickly sweet smoke haze.

'I am the greatest helicopter pilot in the world!' shouted David exuberantly, over and over. Bob and I grinned at each other. Jokingly Bob said that it was David's comments, not the eucalyptus smoke, that were making us feel so nauseous. 'I am the greatest helicopter pilot in the world!' David continued, and we had no choice but to agree. All those years of hunting deer in New Zealand had certainly given him considerable close-in flying abilities and we both paid due homage to his brilliance.

After some forty minutes of flying, Bob asked David whether the smoke was making it difficult to navigate. 'No, of course not,' he smiled. 'I am the greatest helicopter pilot in the world!'

'So you do know where we are then?' Neither Bob nor I was quite sure of our direction in the dense smoke haze.

'We are just arriving over the suburb of Hornsby on Sydney's northern outskirts,' replied David confidently.

'Well then, how do you explain the runway and all the military aircraft directly below us?' Bob asked, eyebrow raised.

Our startled pilot looked out both windows. 'Bugger!' he

exclaimed. Far from being over Hornsby, we were actually forty kilometres further north-west, directly over Richmond Air Force base,
and on switching to air force tower frequency, it became obvious that
David was not at all welcome. Rather sheepishly, he apologised and
requested directions back to Sydney, no doubt his task on the radio
made more difficult by the howls of laughter emanating from his two
unsympathetic crewmen. Strangely, he made no more comments
about his unique flying abilities for the remainder of the trip!

The following day, we received a surprise visit from the two
Swedish bushwalkers. They were incredibly grateful for our efforts,
and related their amazing story to us. The two had left home looking
for adventure in Australia's wildest regions. More than anything they
wanted to experience the true Australian bush, its vistas, its harshness
and its wildlife. Top of their list was the desire to see a snake, something extremely rare in Sweden.

They had been camping for some days in blue-gum forest, deep
within the Grose Valley, and on that fateful day were hiking back out
towards Evans Lookout. Fortunately they had prepared well and read
widely about the challenges of the Australian bush. They knew that
Australian bushfires are the hottest in the world and a firestorm can
advance in its own thermal-driven winds at over a hundred kilometres
per hour; any animal caught up in such a storm dies from the intense
radiation in a matter of seconds.

As the two trudged upstream they spotted the fire raging behind
them and realised that it would soon outrun them. At the very same
time that Bob and I had been sitting on the cliff edge awaiting the
return of our helicopter, these two were being run down by the biggest
firestorm ever known to have blown through the Grose Valley.

In desperation they looked for shelter, and adjacent to the nearby
creek found the house-sized boulder on which we had discovered
them. Below this boulder was a narrow crevice, an area perhaps five
metres square and half a metre high. Into this narrow space they slith-
ered, praying there would be enough oxygen to keep them alive as the
storm passed overhead.

As the firestorm approached, it drove all matter of wildlife in its
path up the valley. It was here that the Swedes' wish came true. As the

two lay beneath the boulder, hundreds of snakes, spiders and insects had the same idea and joined them in their refuge. Within seconds they became buried in a mass of creeping, crawling, slithering Australian wildlife. There was nothing they could do but lie very very still, and pray. The firestorm passed over in seconds and continued to rage up the valley. Soon the creatures scattered from their hiding place and to their amazement the two hikers were able to emerge some minutes later, unharmed by their reptilian companions.

They agreed that they had seen enough venomous Australian wildlife to last them many lifetimes!

Finally, on Christmas Eve, 1982, we took delivery of our new Squirrel. David, Bob and I were nervous but excited as we rode in the taxi to Bankstown Airport. David was keen to rack up some flying experience prior to any actual missions and this provided the perfect excuse to fly Bob to his home in Engadine on Sydney's southern outskirts. We dropped into a sports oval near his house, creating quite a sensation among his neighbours.

Neither the aircraft nor its new colours had been seen in public yet. The old colour scheme of white with a diagonal orange stripe had been replaced with fire-engine red and yellow, the colours of both the Westpac Bank and the SLSA. Even we had to admit that this red was far better than the original, and we all felt mighty proud of our new machine.

From Engadine David and I headed east to the coast for a low-level run along the southern beaches before cutting across Botany Bay over Sydney International Airport then back to Royal North Shore Hospital. Under direction of air traffic control we were ordered to pass above the airport at six hundred metres. We were halfway across Botany Bay when, without warning, the aircraft started to shake and buck and roll violently.

We looked at each other in absolute horror; the aircraft was all but uncontrollable. Then, as suddenly as it started, the shaking stopped. At first we thought the aircraft was suffering a terminal disease in its infancy, but then Dave considered the unusually stable weather and total lack of wind and asked air traffic control whether there had been any recent landings from the east. Sure enough a jumbo jet had landed down this glide path some five minutes beforehand. Due to the very stable weather conditions, the wake turbulence of that three-hundred-ton airliner was still swirling through the sky and we had been directed straight through the middle of it.

Sombrely we proceeded over the city and touched down some ten minutes later, 5 pm precisely, Christmas Eve. David would be flying again the next day but I was off duty till the Christmas break was over. Even then I would only be flying for two more weeks; I felt extremely envious of Dr Ian Millar, whom we had chosen as my successor.

I reviewed the cabin to ensure that it was all set for the doctor on duty the next day. Then I closed and locked the door and took a step back to admire the aircraft. We had worked tirelessly for this for six months and finally it was here.

'Merry Christmas, Helicopter Rescue Service,' I said to no one in particular. I picked up my kit bag from the office and headed home.

The birthplace of Australian civilian helicopter rescue services is a little-known beach called Burning Palms in the Royal National Park south of Sydney. The park's eastern limits end abruptly in sheer sandstone cliffs along its entire thirty-kilometre shoreline save for a number of small, pretty beaches.

Burning Palms Beach perches precariously between the Pacific Ocean to the east and a two-hundred-metre cliff to the west. Behind the beach is a steep scree slope dotted with rainforest vegetation. It is the most inaccessible of all beaches in the Sydney region – it can only be reached after an hour's walk from Garie Beach car park or an arduous descent down the cliff face.

There are no amenities at Burning Palms, just a dozen or so fishing shanties condemned many years ago by the Royal National Park. These shanties were scheduled for demolition when the original owners died. Some of these owners would now have been in excess of one hundred and fifty years old!

It was at Burning Palms, in the early 1970s, that Ian Badham, under the auspices of the SLSA, experimented with the concept of using a helicopter to carry out surf rescues. Each year most of the crew members, old and new, would assemble on the beach on New Year's Eve to celebrate in simple and splendid isolation.

Early each New Year's Day the helicopter would divert from its routine patrol to buzz the beach and its hungover inhabitants. The annual flight was known as the Beat Up Of Burning Palms, and it was our only recreational flight of the year.

Traditionally the helicopter would make as much of a nuisance of itself as possible while the crew on the ground demonstrated theatrical annoyance at this rude awakening. Inevitably all the volunteers wanted to be at the party, so it was also traditional that the full-time crew flew on New Year's Day. I managed to score the New Year's Day roster three years in a row, which gave Bob, Dan and me plenty of time to develop our plans from the simple to the purely cunning.

Our first year was unadorned. We zoomed past the cliffs of the Royal National Park, which glowed glorious gold in the sun's early morning rays, then rounded the headland with the siren wailing. Dan descended towards the beach at the optimal rate to induce 'blade slap', the most annoying of the helicopter's noisy repertoire. Below, the sleepy staggering revellers shook fists or saluted us with beer cans.

The following year we added an element of surprise. Rather than the time-honoured tradition of swinging around the headland to the east of Burning Palms, we took a short cut across the neck of the headland separating it from Era Beach. By going directly over the low grassy saddle we arrived without warning, from the north rather than the east, to find our mates looking in the wrong direction. The approach caught them unawares and they all spun around, and some even fell over, in surprise. We were told later that the party-goers had vowed never to be caught out like that again and the following year they were determined to be prepared.

In the New Year of 1983 we decided that something far more sophisticated was required to suit the new helicopter we had received seven days earlier. The three of us planned carefully over several weeks, sworn to strict secrecy. It was barely first light on New Year's

Day when we lifted off from base on one of the clearest Sydney days in my memory.

We again set a course over Sydney airport, then descended over the sea, as we had done the previous two years; but once clear of the southern Sydney suburbia, Dan changed course and flew up Port Hacking. Two minutes later we turned southwards again at treetop level over the Royal National Park, some five kilometres inland.

Dan's idea of flying at treetop level was far more literal than I had anticipated. Being a highly experienced Vietnam helicopter pilot, flying this low was second nature to him. To me in the front left seat it was absolutely terrifying. It was obvious that Dan was in his element and nothing I could have said would have changed his approach; however, he did tell me that the thinnest branches of the trees were always at the top, so touching a few wouldn't impede our progress. I wasn't entirely reassured!

We continued southwards till we were due west of Burning Palms. Dan had insisted on installing a navigation device known as TACAN (Tactical Air Navigation) in the new aircraft. We were probably the only nonmilitary aircraft in the country to have this system, and it allowed us to fly to certain waypoints at low altitude without reference to visible sites. It achieved what is now done by Satellite Global Positioning Systems. None of the crew at the beach knew we had this capability.

There was no need for Dan to rise from the treetops to know when to turn. No one would see or hear us coming. We approached the cliff at breakneck speed then suddenly the earth fell away beneath us as we passed over the cliff edge. At that moment Dan floored the collective control and the aircraft plummeted over the cliff. To our delight there stood half-a-dozen crew members looking east out to sea, and another huddle looking north at the saddle; evidently they were covering all their bases, determined not to be taken by surprise this year. We pulled out of the dive at what seemed to be the very last moment and only touched the sirens as we passed. The unsuspecting revellers scattered like terrified chooks towards the safety of the fishing shanties. Strike one for us!

Now for phase two. Having whooped at our success we slowly returned to a hover some thirty metres above the shacks. Bob slid back the door and lowered six cans of ice-cold Fosters Lager on the winch hook. For over a minute they dangled two metres above the ground while curious eyes peered up, trying to fathom the mystery of our generosity. Then as one they pounced upon the offered gift, and at that very moment our other gifts – some dozen eggs and rotten tomatoes – descended from the skies with several direct hits being scored. Strike two!

We noted that the 'enemy' had also increased the sophistication of their annoyance by placing a large double sheet across the roof of several shanties which read '**** off Helicopter Rescue Service'. That had to go, and phase three was the perfect way to do it.

Having reeled in the winch, we leisurely departed around the headland to the north. No doubt our colleagues were convinced the fun and games were over for another year. They gathered in the clearing to enjoy their morning beers and were caught totally unawares when we reappeared over the saddle carrying a full firefighting bucket containing two hundred litres of sea water. In spite of the cloudless skies the party-goers, the fishing shacks and in particular the makeshift sign were thoroughly drenched over the next few seconds. Strike three!

Jubilant, we headed north to begin our day's patrol. Again the sea was sparkling blue and the cliffs glowed. I gave thanks for the privilege of being alive to experience such fun and mateship in this beautiful landscape.

Passing Port Hacking, we swept in on each of the beaches travelling north: Cronulla, Wanda, Maroubra, Coogee, Clovelly, Bronte and finally Bondi before passing the cliffs of South Head. Already the harbour was alive with pleasure craft heralding in the new year. We flew past the archbishop's palace on North Head, Fairy Bower Beach where I had spent Christmas Day, Manly, South Steyne, North Steyne and along to Dee Why. I could think of no more spectacularly beautiful way to start the new year.

My eyes were subconsciously drawn to something bobbing on the waves, and as we drew nearer I was able to make out the form. 'Body in the water!' I yelled instinctively, and just as quickly thought of all those surf patrols when I had never spotted anything of any significance. There below, several hundred metres off the beach, was a body. It was face down. Our party spirit evaporated and was replaced by a feeling of dread.

Dan wheeled the aircraft around and within seconds Bob was in the water. From the signals he gave, this was a body recovery. He completed the grim task of lifting the corpse to the nearby shore. We radioed the ambulance service during the transfer and spent some minutes on the beach with our victim. She was young, perhaps in her early twenties, very beautiful and very dead. I felt like weeping. This young woman had been robbed of the opportunity that I had been given to experience this glorious day with people who meant so much to me. New Year's Day was supposed to be about celebrating the birth of a new year. It was meant to be about beginnings, not endings.

PART III
Specialist Training

The moment one definitely commits oneself
Then providence moves too.
All sorts of things occur to help one that would
never otherwise have occurred.
Whatever you can do, or dream you can, begin it.
Boldness has genius, power and magic in it.

Goethe

13

I had never seen a blood pressure this high before.

Automatic monitoring of blood pressure during anaesthesia was a thing of the future. Back then, blood pressure was assessed by pumping up an inflatable bulb attached by a tube to a rubber cuff on the upper arm. A second tube led from the cuff to a mercury column to read the cuff pressure. Every few minutes we would note at what pressure the pulse at the wrist disappeared. I had inflated the cuff to its limits and still the pulse remained.

It was my first afternoon as an anaesthetic registrar and it looked as though my patient and I were in serious trouble. The patient was a frail old lady having a metal plate attached to her fractured hip, and I knew she could not tolerate a blood pressure this high for very long.

The morning had been bad enough. My first case was assisting Dr Kelly, the deputy director of anaesthesia, with a patient who had ruptured his aorta. Litres of blood had spilled into his abdomen and we'd fought a desperate but successful battle to save his life.

Now I faced a similarly desperate situation. With the blood pressure this high a catastrophic bleed into the brain could only be moments away. Dr Young re-entered the operating theatre, having been away for just five minutes. I explained the situation and he watched me check the blood pressure again.

'Maybe if you felt the pulse on the same arm as the blood pressure cuff you would find that the blood pressure was quite normal.' His look of dismay pierced me to the core. I felt like a total goose.

To say that my first day had been overwhelming was to put it mildly.

Prior to the emergency case that morning, Dr Young had explained to me what I would be doing for the rest of my training. It seemed that every minute of every day for the next four years was planned.

Days would be spent either in the operating theatre or the intensive care unit. One afternoon a week would be spent at lectures. One day of each week before work I would attend and present at the registrar tutorials. Every fourth night and every fourth weekend I would stay over at the hospital to assist with emergency anaesthetics, running the intensive care unit and heading the resuscitation team.

Every other night and every other weekend would be devoted to studying. The first or primary exams would be early in my second year. My fellowship exams would be in the middle of my fourth year. I had no illusions about how much study this would entail. The primary exams in particular were daunting. These focused on knowledge of normal body functions and drugs related to anaesthesia and intensive care. I was expected to know these subjects in the most minute detail, to perfection. Any gap in my knowledge and I would fail the entire exam. Two-thirds of registrars attempting these exams failed on their first attempt.

As an apprentice, I would be assigned each day to a consultant anaesthetist in a particular operating theatre. Together we would anaesthetise the patients for that particular operating list. Over the next four years, as I became more skilled and knowledgeable (and less overwhelmed and incompetent), I would be allowed to do more and more complex cases by myself. The College of Anaesthetists would receive annual reports on my capabilities, and in the fourth year I would present at the final exams, demonstrating my theoretical and practical knowledge and hopefully proving I was ready to be a specialist.

St George was the smallest of the teaching hospitals in Sydney and did not perform some subspecialties in surgery and intensive care. So, after eighteen months there, I would rotate to St Vincent's Hospital for further training, particularly in anaesthesia for heart and brain surgery. I would also spend six months at Royal Alexandria Hospital learning how to anaesthetise children, including premature babies.

The St George scheme incorporated an opportunity for six months at a teaching hospital of my choice, and I decided to go to the Westmead

Centre. As this was on the other side of Sydney it was a most unusual choice. But I was directing everything towards my long-term career in rescue helicopter work, and working at the busiest trauma centre in the Commonwealth and probably the busiest head-injury centre in the world was an opportunity I didn't want to miss. Then there would be another six months at St Vincent's before I'd finally return to St George for the last six months. By then hopefully I would have passed my final exams and be on the verge of becoming a specialist.

St George might have been small but the more senior anaesthetic registrars told me its anaesthesia training scheme was, in their opinion, the best. It picked the finest available teaching staff from the different hospitals, and this breadth of experience was probably why the hospital's registrars did so well in the final examinations. The scheme was the only one able to guarantee six months at the Children's Hospital, the most sought-after position in anaesthesia training in Sydney. I mused over how lucky I had been since that day I failed to get an ophthalmology registrar post at my first teaching hospital.

For now, however, as Dr Young had told me, my first eighteen months were about learning basic anaesthesia, passing the primary exams and, most importantly, learning the right attitudes towards anaes-thesia and intensive care. By this he meant having all contingencies covered as well as possible in advance, considering the consequences of everything we did, preparing an emergency plan for every case and never being blasé. In all my years since, I have never seen an anaesthesia department that taught these attitudes as well as St George.

My learning curve was nearly vertical for the first three months. I started by assisting the more basic lists. Minor operations usually commenced with injecting a dose of Pentothal through an intravenous cannula till the patient fell asleep. We then had three minutes before the Pentothal wore off to introduce several anaesthetic gases and vapours through the patient's breathing circuit to keep them asleep.

More complex cases required inserting an endotracheal tube past the patient's vocal chords, down into their windpipe. To achieve this we had to paralyse their muscles to prevent their vocal chords going into spasm. This was done by injecting a paralysing agent as soon as they were asleep. While many operations required this technique, the decision to paralyse a patient was never taken lightly. Should there be any malfunction of the anaesthetic machine while the patient was spontaneously breathing, they would wake up. They would be upset, to say the least, but they would be alive. If the malfunction occurred while the patient was paralysed, the patient would not be able to breathe for themselves and they would most likely die.

The need for constant vigilance was hammered home time and again.

The work did not stop there. Once all the 'plumbing' was in place and the operation commenced, continual adjustments were necessary to keep the patient's condition optimal. Over the years anaesthesia drugs had become more potent and had a shorter action time, typically in the order of only five to fifteen minutes, compared to several hours for early anaesthetics. While this allowed us to rapidly increase or decrease the effects of each drug, it also meant that we were continually assessing how the patient was responding and repeatedly topping up the doses. We would usually be administering two to three drugs to keep the patient asleep, a drug to keep them paralysed, and several drugs to prevent pain perception. By the time we checked all the patient's vital signs and drug levels, it was time to start checking them again. There were also numerous requests from the surgeons to administer various drugs such as high-dose antibiotics. All this meant there wasn't much time to stop and relax.

I learnt dozens of variations to these basic techniques over the first few months. Each variation was chosen to suit the patient's and the procedure's particular requirements. There were variations for patients who had heart disease, lung disease, liver disease, and for the myriad surgical procedures. Skills had to be learnt and plans made for patients with short necks, prominent teeth, difficult-to-find veins; the list seemed endless.

On top of this I began my study program, which involved attending lectures, making weekly presentations and reading the prescribed textbooks. I didn't have to know the books well. I had to know them perfectly.

In pharmacology there were dozens of drugs to remember and I had to know how they affected every part of the body, their unwanted or dangerous side effects, duration of action, variations in action, how they were deactivated and their advantages and disadvantages compared to other drugs. Again the list seemed endless. For example, Pentothal was used for most patients. The best description of its effects was an article by J.W. Dundee. It was one hundred and three pages long. I had to know it in its entirety.

Physiology, the study of normal human function, was an even bigger subject. In addition to the main textbooks there were textbooks on the heart, four textbooks on the function of the lungs (one of which was entirely devoted to mathematical models describing lung function), a textbook devoted to kidney function and additional notes from the lectures we attended weekly. Out of curiosity I added up the pages. It came to nearly ten thousand.

One particular day, while I was in the emergency department, one of the junior RMOs told me he had a nine-year-old boy with a part from a plastic toy stuck in his throat. He was about to call the ear, nose and throat specialist and he suspected the boy needed to go to the operating theatre. I disagreed, thinking this was probably a case that merely required a Heimlich manoeuvre. How wrong I was.

An obstructed airway is the deadliest and most urgent of all medical crises. The inexperienced RMO did not realise that an airway obstruction always demands immediate action; for my part, I was about to learn that not all airway obstructions are easily resolved.

A completely obstructed airway can be fatal within two to three minutes. A partially obstructed airway can become completely obstructed at any time. While no longer recommended, the standard practice for relieving such an obstruction in those days was called the Heimlich manoeuvre. This involved standing behind the victim, placing the right fist over the abdomen and the left hand over the fist. Both hands were sharply pushed into the abdomen, which in turn pushed up the diaphragm muscle above the abdomen and below the lungs, pushing air out of the lungs and up the windpipe. Normally this would forcibly expel any object obstructing the airway.

I had used the Heimlich manoeuvre successfully twice before. As a second-year resident I had once come out to the front desk at the hospital's casualty department just as the receptionist was asking a man what his problem was. He wrote on a piece of paper that he had a chop bone stuck in his throat. Amazingly, he also wrote that he had already been to a small inner-suburban hospital where the doctors did not know what to do and suggested he come here by taxi.

I walked up behind the man and briefly explained what I was about to do. Then I reached around and forcibly applied the manoeuvre. The chop bone flew out of his mouth, skipped across the reception counter and landed on the floor. The man immediately took a huge breath then slumped across the counter, croaking, 'Thank you.'

The following year I used the manoeuvre for a patient with a chunk of meat stuck in his throat. This time I hit the assisting sister in the chest with the meaty projectile.

I was not so lucky on this, the third occasion. Although the child was distressed, he was still able to breathe moderately well and appeared well oxygenated, so I had time to ask his anxious father what exactly his son had swallowed. He described the object as a red plastic disc the size of a large coin. The disc had a central spike with a spring mounted on it. The object was part of a plastic jumping frog.

'Here is his X-ray,' said the RMO.

'You sent him to X-ray with a partially obstructed airway?' I chided. 'He doesn't need an X-ray, he needs a Heimlich manoeuvre. What if he had obstructed down at X-ray?'

As the embarrassed resident looked on I quickly explained to the father what needed to be done, then helped the boy off his bed, stood behind him and applied the manoeuvre. I was confident I was about to perform a medical miracle.

It didn't work. I tried it again and it still didn't work. In fact the boy's obstruction became worse. He started fighting for breath and it became obvious that very little air was getting past the obstruction. Something was terribly wrong.

As the resident and the boy's father looked at me in horror I tried to think what to do next. I snatched the X-ray and held it up to the light. The plastic disc naturally did not show up but the spring was evident in his voice box. I guessed that the forcible expulsion of air during the Heimlich manoeuvre had actually made the disc recoil on the spring, exacerbating the situation.

The boy was now severely distressed. He was fighting for breath and his skin was turning blue. I placed an oxygen mask on his face while urgently running through my options. At this rate he only had a few minutes to live.

I turned to the resident. 'Run to theatre and tell them we have a child with an obstructed airway. He needs an immediate anaesthetic.' I figured the only way I would get this object out was with a pair of forceps. Yet the boy was now so panicked, I could barely get near him.

A few seconds later Dr Susan Kelly strode into the emergency ward. She had heard what was happening and had come to my aid. Together we dragged the trolley down the corridor to the operating theatre while I briefly explained to the boy's father what we had to do.

We slammed through the translucent plastic flap doors of the theatre suite, turned right and moved straight into Theatre One.

'Hold him down firmly!' Dr Kelly said to the theatre nurses.

As I placed the anaesthetic mask on the boy's face so that I could deliver one hundred per cent oxygen, I told Dr Kelly, 'It's some sort of plastic disc on a spring. I tried the Heimlich manoeuvre but it only made it worse. I think we'll need forceps to get it out.' Dr Kelly nodded in agreement.

The boy was desperately shaking his head from side to side. I slipped my hand behind his neck and then pushed his face firmly into the anaesthetic mask. Dr Kelly reached over to the anaesthetic machine and started to dial in Halothane, a vapour that would soon have him asleep. What we didn't know was whether, as he became anaesthetised, the change in his breathing pattern and the relaxation of the muscles in his throat would make the obstruction better or worse.

As so little Halothane and oxygen were getting past the obstruction it took five minutes for the boy to settle down. Each of us stayed frozen until his struggling finally subsided. We knew when we took the mask off his face to look down his throat that within moments he would begin to run out of oxygen and the Halothane would start to wear off. We would have only seconds before his oxygen levels dropped to critically low levels and he started to wake.

'Shall I try with the Magill's forceps first?' I suggested. These were specifically shaped for removing objects from the throat. Dr Kelly nodded and held out the forceps, willing to allow me to have the first attempt. She stood on my right side so she would have a clear view of the problem.

I removed the anaesthetic mask and with my left hand inserted a laryngoscope into the boy's mouth to push the tongue away and shine a light down his throat. We saw nothing. There were no features of a normal throat at all, just the red wall of the disc. Using my right hand I inserted the forceps, but there was nothing to grab onto. For twenty seconds I tried to snare the disc without success as it gently pulsed up and down with the boy's struggle for breath.

'Out,' said Dr Kelly, telling me it was time to back off and reapply the mask.

Already the boy was starting to wriggle. The Halothane was wearing off. I hadn't realised that I had been trying to dislodge the disc for nearly a minute. I took out the forceps and laryngoscope and replaced the mask. His skin was again taking on a bluish tinge. We were barely keeping him alive.

After another three minutes of Halothane and oxygen, Dr Kelly repeated my attempts. No success. As we abandoned our second attempt, the boy's pulse slowed and the cardiograph tracing showed runs of abnormal heartbeats in response to his low oxygen levels.

'Get us some other forceps!' Dr Kelly demanded.

'What sort?' asked the nursing sister.

'Any sort!' came the urgent reply.

We tried with several differently shaped forceps, but without success. The heart rhythm was deteriorating.

As we again administered the anaesthetic and oxygen we discussed what else we could use. We agreed the original forceps were as good as any. What was needed was more time and more aggression getting around the side of the object. To further complicate matters, the tissues of the boy's throat were becoming swollen from our pushing around the disc.

We waited an extra few minutes with the oxygen and Halothane. I inserted the laryngoscope from the left while Dr Kelly inserted the forceps. Again we struggled. To time how long we had, I held my own breath. When I needed to take another breath we would again abandon our attempt.

My lungs were about to burst and I was just about to stop our efforts when Dr Kelly managed to get the forceps around the edge of the disc. With a few tugs the disc budged. The monitor in the background was beeping irregularly. We needed to get out, but we continued to press on.

Suddenly the disc popped into the boy's mouth. The spring was still in place on the peg. Dr Kelly removed it and we could see that the airway was clear. I placed the mask back on the boy's face. The bag on the anaesthesia machine filled and collapsed rhythmically, signifying the boy's airway was clear and that he was breathing deeply. Over the next minute his skin colour turned from purple to pink, and his heart rate became regular.

For one final time we looked down his throat. While it was slightly swollen, it otherwise looked normal. We turned off the Halothane, leaving him breathing pure oxygen, until ten minutes later he opened his eyes and started crying.

I had never seen a young child deteriorate so rapidly and come so close to death. My emotions were scrambled. I was proud of having helped this child but embarrassed that I had criticised the RMO in the emergency department and then promptly made things worse. In retrospect the X-ray had helped us understand this highly unusual situation and plan what to do. Once I was satisfied the boy was settled in the recovery ward and his father, pale with shock and relief, was with him, I went looking for the resident. I apologised to him for my arrogance and complacency, and thanked him for his input. I was subdued by my own failings, but inspired by Dr Kelly's actions. No mucking around and unmistakeable leadership under extreme pressure. Hopefully one day I would become that proficient too.

14

During that year I spent three months working in the intensive care unit. The specialty of intensive care was a logical extension of the specialty of anaesthesia. Intensive care units were first created in the 1950s, during the polio epidemics, when the techniques used in anaesthesia to ventilate patients during an operation were used to ventilate polio victims for days, weeks or months as the disease took its course. The specialty had continued to grow and it was in the ICU that all the interventional and life-support skills I was learning in anaesthesia were implemented. Here the fight for peoples' survival continued after initial resuscitation in the casualty department. It was very demanding and draining work. It was also exciting and very satisfying.

Most people were admitted to the ICU because it was considered that they were unlikely to survive without its extensive support facilities. These patients were the sickest of the sick. Most had serious derangement of their bodily systems. Usually they required artificial ventilation and multiple drug infusions to support their heart and kidneys. The longer-term patients also required feeding intravenously with concentrated solutions of carbohydrates, proteins, fats, multivitamins and trace elements. These nutrition drugs, as well as the stronger infusions such as adrenaline, could only be delivered using special intravenous lines placed in the veins adjacent to the heart. One of the first skills I was taught in intensive care was how to place these lines. It wasn't a skill for the faint-hearted; it was risky and required precision and very fine control.

Usually it was done with a fifteen-centimetre needle exploring for one of the larger veins either in the patient's neck or under their collarbone. The target veins lay close to large arteries, nerves and the apex of the lung. While inadvertently piercing these with the needle could have serious consequences, it was a risk that had to be taken in order to deliver the life-saving drugs. Once these needles were correctly placed, soft plastic catheters were inserted through them and the needles withdrawn. The catheters could be used both to deliver drug infusions and measure the pressures in the various chambers of the heart to help finetune the correct rate of delivery of the drugs.

As most of the patients needed to be artificially ventilated, they had to be paralysed in order to place an endotracheal tube into their windpipe. This was the most delicate of all anaesthesia inductions because these patients had little or no reserves to cope with the side effects of the drugs. As such they were a real test of our skills.

I began to wonder how doctors in country hospitals coped with these kinds of situations. Dozens of smaller hospitals were without specialist anaesthetists or registrars. As ever, the helicopter rescue service was not far from my mind; I might be banned from flying, but no one had said I couldn't dream about it! I began to see that the rescue helicopter service could provide a life-saving outreach service for country hospitals.

In the third month of my second year I attempted the primary exams. I had stuck religiously to my study plan and felt quietly confident. Amanda and I had turned our unit into one giant whiteboard. Every available piece of wall and window was plastered with prompt cards ranging from chemical formulas for different drugs to key points describing the control of brain blood flow. Amanda quizzed me incessantly and put up with the fact that when I was at home my head was always buried in a textbook. The result, however, was that all my consultants felt I was well prepared.

The first day was the physiology written exam and I answered all the essays confidently.

The second day I came unstuck. Just prior to the pharmacology written exam I was overwhelmed by the only acute panic attack I have ever experienced. I was driving to the exam site when suddenly I realised I couldn't remember a single thing I had learnt. I started to panic. 'It's all gone blank,' I repeated over and over, feeling the sweat soak into my shirt. Amanda tried to reassure me but I could barely hear her calming words over my loud, chaotic thoughts. I forced myself into the exam room and when I saw the first short question I thought I was going to throw up. It was on a drug that I had never heard of. Considering it was not available in Australia and was not listed in our prescribed textbook, this was hardly surprising. I took a deep breath and looked through the long essay questions. Slowly, as I began to realise that I could answer them all, and if I did so perfectly I might pass, I started to calm down. I picked up my pen and with shaking fingers began to write.

The next day, however, my world fell apart. Discussing the exam with one of my colleagues I realised our answers did not jell. I anxiously reread the paper, only to realise that in my panic I had misread one of the major questions. I knew straightaway that I could not pass. I had no choice but to ring Dr Young immediately and tell him of my mistake. He told me I was a stupid boy and he was right.

It would be another six months before I could resit the exams. All our savings would go in another set of exam fees. If I failed a second time I would be removed from the training scheme. Staying on the boil, so to speak, for another six months was the hardest mind game ever. But I knew that if my dreams were to become reality I had no choice but to press on.

In June I transferred to St Vincent's Hospital in inner Sydney. For the first three months most of my anaesthetic lists were for neurosurgery and the level of complexity of the techniques stepped up several notches. In addition to all the usual anaesthetic skills required for major general surgery, it was often necessary to manipulate the patient's status to make the procedure easier. It was common to have to decrease the patient's blood pressure significantly using cyanide-based solutions and to shrink the brain to provide easier access to the operation site. Neuro-anaesthesia was technically demanding and I loved the challenge.

Fortunately for me several of the consultant specialists at St Vincent's were also examiners for the College of Anaesthetists, and their help proved invaluable when it came to sitting the primary exams again. This time I read and reread every single one of the questions obsessively. Three weeks later I sat the oral examination. The opening question was: In which year was cocaine first used as a local anaesthetic drug? Easy – 1884, precisely one hundred years ago. The questions came thick and fast until the final bell sounded. I felt as though I had been a contestant on *Mastermind*. The examiners thanked me and I walked away from the table. I had barely gone three paces when one of them asked me to come back. A chill ran over my body. What could they possibly want? What had I done wrong?

The head examiner looked at me for a few seconds. I expected the worst.

'Would you mind if we had our pen back, please?' he asked.

I closed my eyes and breathed an enormous sigh of relief, then handed the pen over.

Two hours later I waited patiently on the footpath outside the College of Physicians with the other candidates. I played the exams over and over in my mind and was unable to see how I could have done any better. If my performance this time was not good enough then I didn't know how I could possibly succeed.

Eventually the exam secretary approached the window with the list of results. We crowded around anxiously. Just as she was about to post them she realised she didn't have any sticky tape to attach the paper to the window, so she turned and walked away. We all groaned.

The examiners filed out through the door, surprised to see us still there. I knew one of the specialists but, as was the normal procedure, he had excused himself from being one of my examiners. He knew the results, though.

'What has happened?' he asked sympathetically.

When I told him, he shook his head then glanced from side to side before leaning forward and whispering in my ear, 'You passed!' Immediately he walked away, leaving me dumbstruck but beaming.

The biggest hurdle of my professional life was over. While there were still another two and a half years of training and the fellowship exams to sit, they were considered far more straightforward than the primaries. For the next three months I promised myself I would not read a book that contained an index!

That night Amanda and I attempted to celebrate at one of Sydney's fanciest restaurants. It was a dismal failure. I had taken an anti-adrenaline drug a few hours prior to the exam to ensure I had no further anxiety attacks, but combined with champagne I became as dynamic as a wet tram ticket. Amanda was similarly drained of all emotion. The past two years seemed to catch up with us that night; we had been working towards this moment with every ounce of our energy and now it had arrived we felt deflated. Still, the knowledge that the worst was behind us gave us a little glow despite our exhaustion.

This time I was able to ring Dr Young with good news. He was delighted and generous in his praise.

When I began my cardiac anaesthesia training at St Vincent's I felt a renewed energy and confidence. I considered keeping a patient alive during heart surgery probably the ultimate challenge in anaesthesia, and again I revelled in the work. The hours, however, were horrendous. In addition to my routine weekday lists I was on call every night and every week for three months without a break. I was expected to answer my pager immediately, and once received a 'please explain' memo from the head of the department when I took five minutes to reply while risking a brief swim at the Brighton Baths.

The cardiac unit had recently commenced heart transplants under the direction of Dr Victor Chang, and invariably these occurred in the middle of the night. As such, many of my nights and weekends were spent doing extra cases. Thank God I didn't have to study as well!

Being part of the heart transplant team was an honour. While I was only one of the fifty or so who made up the unit, it was still amazing to be part of such ground-breaking work. We were a very close-knit, dedicated bunch and we all felt that the results of our work compensated for the workload we endured.

Along with the honour of being on the team came the worst possible duty – being involved in the harvesting process. Donors were patients who, for whatever reason, had suffered brain death. This was usually due either to head injuries or ruptured blood vessels in the brain. The diagnosis of brain death is a clinical one, with stringent criteria to prevent even the remotest possibility of the brain injury being reversible. Brain death was only declared after two independent doctors agreed that there was absolutely no brain function.

The rest of the body, however, could continue to function for days or even weeks without the brain. The patient was still warm and pink and there was a pulse and a normal heartbeat. It was hard to convince the relatives and loved ones that the person was truly dead. Occasionally we would take the patient to X-ray and inject dye into the carotid arteries to prove to the next of kin that there was no blood flow to the brain.

In theatre it was torture trying to convince yourself to turn the ventilator off and let oxygen levels drop till the patient arrested, without doing a thing to prevent it. It was my call when the harvesting team could start removing organs. All my training had been focused on preserving life, and the act of turning off the ventilator and doing nothing till the heart gave out went against my most basic instincts. It left a scar that has never healed.

After three months it was time to move on again, this time to the Children's Hospital in Camperdown. Anaesthetising children is another world. It's micro-anaesthesia. Just as the elderly and frail have few reserves to cope with the effects of anaesthetic drugs, so do the young and tiny. It was hard for me to grasp that it was actually possible to give an anaesthetic to a baby who weighed only one to two kilograms. Drug doses were meticulously calculated, intravenous fluids and blood were given by the syringeful rather than by the litre. In newborn children the breathing tubes were one-third the diameter of a drinking straw.

It was, however, the personal element that was the most challenging. In many ways anaesthesia for children is as much about having the right manner as it is about being technically proficient. Young children can't always understand what is happening to them, and learning how to gain their confidence and trust is crucial. Fortunately the consultants in the unit were excellent role models, and more than anywhere else it was there that I learnt how to interact with my patients. I still see inspiring confidence and allaying anxieties prior to an operation as being the greatest challenge and the area of most reward in my specialty. Often this means putting aside my own anxieties and fears so they don't disturb my patient's equanimity. This is doubly important with young children. It is impossible not to be distressed by the terrible afflictions that many brave children have to endure, but as a doctor I had to put my own emotions aside and concentrate on supporting the child.

Still, I found myself unable not to feel pain and to keep from trembling when I was trying to stick a needle into the thin arm of a child with cystic fibrosis to administer his hundredth course of antibiotics. The veins were usually scarred from previous needling, and it would often take several attempts at burrowing through the skin to be successful. I found it even harder to help a young girl paralysed permanently from the neck down and reliant on a ventilator for the rest of her life. It was a struggle not to be overwhelmed by the hopelessness of her affliction. Nothing, though, was worse than dealing with the young burns victims. I knew I was helping them, relieving their long-term suffering, but in the short term what was required caused them so much pain it seemed cruel. The bravest people I have ever met occupied the beds in that hospital.

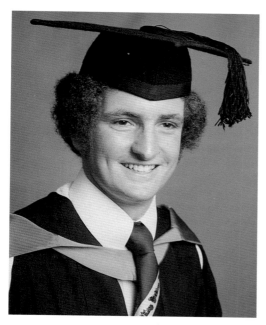

The mortarboard attempts to tame the author's afro on graduation, 1979.

Working as a volunteer for the SLSA in 1981.

Crewman Bob Ford
unloads equipment
from the hovering
Jet Ranger at
Stanwell Park, 1981.

Rescue
demonstration,
National Surf Titles,
1981.

On patrol in the SLSA Squirrel.

Modelling the medical backpack in 1982. (No, it's not a parachute!)

Crew chief Bob Ford (right), chief pilot Dan Tyler (centre) and I take part in a roping exercise from the roof of Royal North Shore Hospital in 1982.

Dan pretends to be stranded (while scratching our initials into the hospital wall) as Bob and I descend to his rescue.

The 'Chickenman' rescue.
I decide the first plan – to jump to the boat's lookout tower from the
helicopter skid – wasn't such a good idea, and instead undertake the
fastest swim of my life!

The inaugural meeting of CareFlight. Back row, left to right: John Hoad, Dr Fran Smith, Ian Badham, Clayton Allison, Sandy O'Meara and friend, Dr Des Bokor and Rick Mailey. Middle row, left to right: Margot Hoad, Peter McCormick, Dr Simon Kinny, Amanda Wishaw and me, with Ben. Front row, left to right: Wayne Vardanega, Dr Luis Gallur, John Cowan and Dr Jenni Saunders.

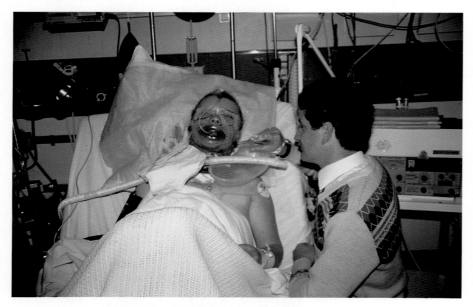

My leech treatment in action during my stay in England.

The original
CareFlight helicopter
base, 1986.

The first CareFlight
aircraft, a single-
engined Squirrel, flies
over Westmead
Hospital.

From left, John Hoad,
myself and Wayne
Vardanega in the early
days of CareFlight.

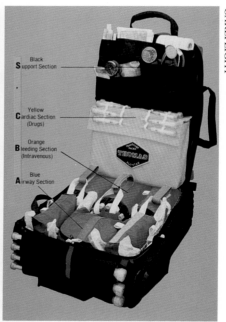

The Thomas medical pack.

Ian Badham OAM,
CareFlight's Executive Director.

An air ambulance at Sydney International Airport.

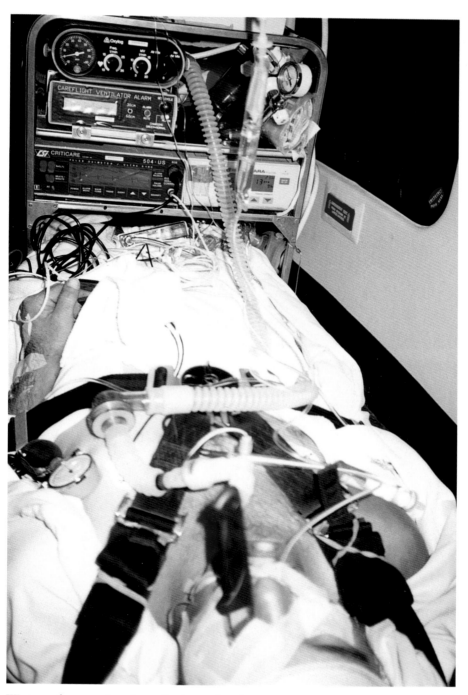

We transfer a patient from Bathurst for the urgent removal of a knife from his eye.

Tina, four weeks after her resuscitation.

Paul Bowdler and me, 2003.

Me and my family, from left to right, Daniel, Christopher, Jackie, Ben, Emma, Jessica and the mystery chicken!

15

After five months I moved to the Westmead Centre in the western suburbs. Over four times the size of St George, with sixteen operating theatres (St George had four) and eighteen intensive care beds (St George had six), it was the largest hospital in Sydney at the time.

I went there to learn trauma management skills, and there were plenty of opportunities to practise. In those days Westmead received more trauma cases than all the other teaching hospitals in Sydney combined. Most were related to motor-vehicle and motorbike accidents, although there was a scattering of knife and gunshot injuries and cliff falls from the nearby Blue Mountains.

In my experience most other hospitals managed their cases well, but at Westmead, probably as a result of the volume of cases received, a lot of thought and effort was put into rapid effective management of critically injured patients. Everyone seemed to know what to do and, probably more importantly, how not to waste time. Time delays are one of the trauma patient's biggest threats to survival and at Westmead things happened fast.

What quickly became very clear was how trauma management could be run by strict protocols and end points; 'If this, do that' sort of thinking. I soon learnt and applied these almost knee-jerk reactions, and wondered why I had never been exposed to them before.

When the media talk about doctors fighting for a patient's life, it is at least as much the anaesthesia team as the surgical team who are frantically doing all that they can. Much of the work centres on coping with massive blood loss and injuries to the heart and lungs, which often make supplying oxygen to the tissues close to impossible. While the surgeons were perhaps setting a fracture or removing a ruptured spleen, we would, in addition to administering anaesthesia drugs, be inserting intravenous lines and central heart lines, giving blood transfusions, inserting drainage tubes through the chest wall to drain blood or air collections around the lungs, repeatedly measuring such things as red blood cell counts, salt balance, clotting capability of the blood, kidney function, heart function, lung function and acid overload. Often there would be four or five of us on the anaesthesia team working flat out trying to keep up with the ever-changing status of the critically ill or injured patient.

More than any other cases it was the management of patients with severe head injuries that interested me. Largely thanks to the director of the ICU, Dr Ian Pearson, I became much more experienced in the initial management of head injuries. Contrary to my previous beliefs, the vast majority of head-injured patients did not require surgery. While some needed urgent operations to remove blood clots that squashed their brains, for most their outcome was, apart from the immediate effects of the initial injury, determined by nonsurgical procedures. These included optimising oxygen flow to the brain, preventing build-up of carbon dioxide in the blood, which might cause the brain to swell if untreated, and minimising pressure changes in the brain, which may occur if fluid leaks from injured brain cells.

The initial brain injury is known as the primary insult. Low oxygen levels, uncorrected shock, blood loss and high carbon dioxide levels in the blood are known as the secondary insults. Nothing can be done to correct the primary insult once it has occurred, but the severity and duration of these secondary insults make the difference between a complete recovery and becoming totally incapacitated. Studies have repeatedly shown that the combination of a severe head injury and prolonged uncorrected secondary insults are always fatal. Some head injuries are mild enough to recover from fully with no treatment at all. Others are bound to have a poor outcome no matter what treatment is received, but many are somewhere in the middle. The outcome depends on timely delivery of very advanced care.

To put it simply, severely head-injured patients benefit greatly from stabilisation through the use of drugs and techniques used in anaesthesia every day, and every effort needs to be made to minimise the time delay between the initial injury and receiving these stabilisation treatments.

In addition to the replacement of lost blood and fluids, inserting an endotracheal tube and artificially ventilating the patient with high-oxygen gas mixtures is the best way to minimise secondary insults. However, without sedating the patient and paralysing all their muscles, intubation can cause extreme irritation of the airway. Coughing and movement or 'fighting the tube' (I would fight a tube, too, if someone put one down my windpipe while I was still awake) only makes things worse. Therefore administration of anaesthetic drugs prior to insertion is essential.

The more I managed these patients, the more I wondered about what happened between the time of accident and the time of definitive care. Often patients would arrive at Westmead Centre with the secondary insults still uncontrolled. Some of these patients had been transferred from other hospitals and had been in an uncontrolled state for several hours. It quickly became apparent that in addition to the superb treatment these patients already received from ambulance officers and country doctors, doctors with anaesthesia and emergency medicine training should be working on them as soon as possible after their accidents. This needed to happen at the first hospital they reached; it should not have to wait until they arrived at a city hospital. Better still, it should be happening at the scene of the accident and, once stabilised, patients should be taken directly to the hospital best equipped to cope with their particular injuries. And what better way to deliver this care than by helicopter?

The more I thought about it, the more it seemed that out here in the western suburbs of Sydney and the surrounding regions there was an epidemic of patients with head injuries that screamed out for a medically staffed rescue helicopter. So it was fortuitous that the Westpac Helicopter Rescue Service now had a spare chopper.

During my absence the service had continued to flourish. Thanks to the negotiating skills of the committee and the generosity of the Westpac

Bank, it had received a massive increase in sponsorship and had realised its dream of owning a twin-engined Squirrel. Most amazingly, there was sufficient money to keep the single-engined Squirrel as a back-up.

While I had kept my promise to Dr Young and not flown any missions (well, only one to cover for a sick duty doctor), I could not resist attending the training day organised for the new aircraft.

The service had a new pilot, John Hoad. John had given up his career as a radiographer and had amassed several thousand hours' piloting experience in just a few years, mustering cattle in the Australian outback and working for mining companies in the New Guinea highlands. Although we were the same age, he looked way too young to have had enough experience for me to trust my life to him. However, any uncertainty I might have harboured disappeared during a high-altitude winching demonstration.

The real mark of a good helicopter pilot is how still he can keep the aircraft while hovering. Helicopters, unlike fixed-wing aircraft, are dynamically unstable; in other words, they do not inherently want to stay upright without constant fine adjustments to the controls. I was once told that hovering a helicopter is about as easy as balancing on a bowling ball while wearing rollerskates, and my few attempts to keep a helicopter even going in a straight line while cruising had shown me how difficult they were to fly.

While most proficient pilots can keep the aircraft relatively still in the hover while close to the ground, as the altitude increases and reference points move further away, the helicopter inevitably tends to wander around its assigned point.

At the Long Reef base we were attempting a new long-line winching technique combining both ropes and the winch. The task was to retrieve a stretcher while the chopper hovered nearly one hundred metres in the air. John brought the helicopter into the hover above the training area and the crewman lowered the rope. It snaked down to the stretcher waiting on the ground, and the ground crew attached the rope's hook.

As John raised the stretcher off the ground, we expected to see it wander around in sync with the shifting position of the helicopter above. It barely moved.

The whole crew looked at each other and then stared back up at the helicopter. The chopper was rock steady against the clouds in the background. Again we watched the stretcher as it ascended. There was no sway at all. It was the first evidence of John's exceptional flying skills.

I came away from that training day more convinced than ever that there was a huge demand for a medical rescue helicopter in the western region of Sydney. At the same time two other doctors who had recently started flying with the service were thinking along the same lines. Dr Fran Smith was a specialist physician who was now completing her second specialist degree in intensive care, and Dr Luis Gallur was an anaesthetic registrar, two years my junior, at Westmead Centre. Along with several other volunteer doctors in the service, many of whom were also training in various acute care specialties, we hatched a plan.

Towards the end of my stay at Westmead I started to talk to the medical administrators about the concept of basing the single-engined Squirrel at Westmead. Slowly, quietly, the plan started to evolve.

After six months at Westmead I spent December at the Children's Hospital, before returning to St Vincent's to start my final year of specialist training.

I had just become a father. Our son Ben was two weeks old, and the sick children I faced every day reminded me how lucky Amanda and I were to have a healthy baby. Like most doctors I had been scared that our child would be born with, or develop, every disease I saw at work, so my first feeling when Ben was born was intense relief. I was optimistic in those joyous early days that I would be a loving, attentive father; I was somehow blind to the obvious fact that I would need to have been Superman to cram in so much study and work and balance that with being a good parent.

The Children's Hospital was sedate compared to Westmead. Everything seemed routine. I enjoyed my interaction with the patients but missed the excitement that Westmead offered. I almost became complacent and started to believe that nothing ever went wrong. That was until the week before Christmas, when I was assigned to help anaesthetise a six-month-old baby boy, who had suffered several epileptic seizures.

Investigations revealed an abnormal tangle of blood vessels at the base of his brain. Surgery would be extremely hazardous, but to leave the vessels there, with possible rupture at any time, would be fatal. There was no time to waste, the tangle had to be cut away, and so the operation was planned for three days before Christmas.

After the consultant and I had prepared the anaesthesia induction room, the mother and child were brought in. Gently we took the baby from his mother's arms and placed him on the trolley. I felt sympathy, as sharp as pain, for the woman; I could not imagine how I would feel if this were Ben I was handing over to such uncertainty. We wrapped the baby in a blanket and held the anaesthetic mask a few centimetres above his face. Confused and disorientated he began to cry, and so did his mother. His crying, however, worked in our favour. The big breaths sucked in the anaesthetic gases and soon he settled. We thanked his mother for being there and gently suggested she give him a kiss before leaving. She knew this might be the last time she saw him alive and sobbed as the nurse led her out of the room.

The surgery was to be performed through the back of the baby's skull, and as such he would be positioned face down on the operating table. Our preparation therefore needed to be meticulous as we would have no access to him once the operation started. We inserted two intravenous lines, a primary line and a spare, then double-strapped them into position. Other tubes and monitors were attached for the three-hour operation.

I inserted an endotracheal tube down his windpipe and listened to all areas of his lungs with a stethoscope to ensure the tube's position was correct. Then the aroma of friar's balsam filled the room as we painted his cheeks. This made his skin sticky. We wrapped two long pieces of adhesive tape around his endotracheal tube and stuck the ends to his painted cheeks. We needed to take all possible precautions to prevent the tube dislodging during the operation. Considering that he would be face down in a frame and paralysed by our drugs, should the tube dislodge it was extremely unlikely we would be able to re-establish an airway fast enough to keep him alive.

The final step in the preparation was to attach a small stethoscope over the boy's left nipple with yet more adhesive tape. This would be a last-resort monitor, to assess the boy should all our other monitors fail once he had disappeared under the massive surgical drapes.

Finally we were satisfied that everything was in place and we disconnected him from the anaesthesia machine in the induction room and reconnected him to the machine in the theatre. Before turning him over onto the theatre table, we disconnected the gas tubes so that they would not dislodge his endotracheal tube while he was positioned in the frame.

His head was suspended over the edge of the table, supported by spikes that were screwed through his scalp into the sides of his skull. He looked so tiny and vulnerable on the theatre table that for a moment I felt a terrible anguish, for him, for his parents, for those of us involved in this risky attempt to save his life.

His wispy baby hair was shaved, then the operation site washed in antiseptic and drapes placed over his entire body. At every step we ensured that nothing dislodged any of our tubes or drips. Eventually the baby had all but disappeared under the drapes and equipment and we were totally reliant on our monitors to assess his wellbeing.

For the next two hours the surgeons worked their way through skin, bone and membranes covering his brain to get at the abnormal blood vessels. We continuously adjusted the drugs to keep his condition optimal.

Suddenly, without warning, his pulse rate dropped. Instead of being a normal one hundred beats per minute, in a matter of seconds it dropped to thirty, then to ten, and then stopped.

We had nothing but a flat line on the monitor screen. Listening through the stethoscope we had taped to his chest earlier we could hear no heart sounds. He had arrested.

The surgeons immediately stopped and looked up at us anaesthetists. A few minutes earlier they had warned us that they were pushing on the brain adjacent to the area that controls the heart. We waited anxiously to see if removing their retractors would reverse the situation. After five seconds the monitor line was still flat.

'Giving Atropine and adrenaline,' my consultant anaesthetist barked. At the same time I changed the gas mixtures to one hundred per cent oxygen.

With the heart not pumping, however, there was little chance the drugs would get to the heart to stimulate it. We all understood that without a word being said.

Normally, external cardiac massage would help the drug delivery, but with the baby face down and buried under frames and multiple coverings, that looked impossible.

'I'll see what I can do,' I said, and quickly threaded myself through all the lines and power cords to the foot of the table. On my hands and knees I crawled under all the drapes that hung down to the floor on each side of the operating table. The monitors were silent as I tunnelled up to the child. It was too dark to see and I could not raise my head to look forwards. I groped with my outstretched arms till I felt the rubber cushions of the table. I was at least under all the covers and in the right layer to find the child's tiny body. The monitors were still silent.

Pushing forwards I felt a tiny foot. But that was as far as I could reach. 'Is everyone clear?' I asked. 'I'll have to climb onto the table to reach him.'

'All clear,' came the reply from the surgeon.

I swung up onto the table and inched forward, infantry style, my outstretched arms feeling the baby's legs, thighs, hips and lower back till I reached his shoulderblades. I pressed my thumbs together over his spine then thrust my fingers between the table mattress and the front of his chest, taking care not to dislodge his monitor leads. My fingers met under his breast bone, and I immediately pushed them up towards his back. With relief I felt his chest compress. It was pitch black and there was little space to breathe, but I pushed on. 'Massaging now,' I yelled.

'Okay, keep going,' my consultant replied.

For twenty seconds nothing happened. Then I heard a beep from the monitor.

'Ectopic!' came the voice of my consultant, telling me it was an abnormal beat. But at least it was a beat. A few seconds later another beat; 'Ectopic!' again.

Beep pause beep beep. 'Ectopic, sinus, sinus!' One abnormal then two normal beats.

Beep, beep-beep beep. The rate was picking up. 'Sinus, ectopic, sinus, sinus!' came through the drapes.

I stopped the massage. The beeps continued. The drugs had reached the baby's heart. The rate picked up and was regular – the rhythm was normal.

Gingerly I extracted myself from under the drapes. I welcomed the feel of the cool airconditioning below the table before crawling back out. While I couldn't see anyone's expression behind their masks, the sense of relief and triumph was obvious. We were still in with a chance.

We all discussed what had happened and why, and decided to proceed, albeit with repeated doses of intravenous Atropine to prevent the heart slowing. Two hours later the last stitch was in place. The operation had been successful and there had been no further incidents.

Soon we had the baby on his side, and as we reversed all the anaesthetic drugs he began to breathe for himself. Vital signs were normal and he was a healthy rosy pink.

Some minutes later, as he showed signs of awakening, I removed the endotracheal tube from his windpipe. Within seconds he was crying. Perhaps that would have been upsetting to his parents but to us it was the sound of victory. Good lung, heart and brain function were necessary to make that noise.

As we wheeled him down to the intensive care unit I silently wished him a Merry Christmas and a long and happy life.

16

My final exams were only four months away. For the previous year I had been studying regularly, now I was into overdrive. There were several other registrars at St Vincent's sitting the fellowship exams at the same time, which, along with the superb tutoring we were receiving from Dr Doug Rigg and other staff specialists, made the task much easier.

I was feeling confident. Confident about the exams and confident about my long-term career. The plan to base the second rescue helicopter, the one I had helped fit out, at Westmead Centre would be the next step in creating a medical helicopter retrieval service in New South Wales. Everything seemed to be coming together.

It took just one phone call to see it all come apart.

It was March 1986, just six weeks before my fellowship exams, when Ian Badham called. 'We need you to come to a meeting of the Sydney branch of the SLSA. The executive of the branch is going to sack Peter MacCormick as general manager of the helicopter service.'

I was stunned. 'Why would they want to do that?'

'They want to have more control, basically. They want all our sponsorship money channelled through them rather than given directly to us.' Ian sounded grim.

We discussed the matter briefly, then Ian moved on to rally support from other crew members. In spite of my study schedule I said I would be there. I found it hard to take the news on board – the very concept on which I had built my career hopes was under threat.

For three and a half years I had forgone sleep, family life and helicopter duties in order to complete my training with the view of returning to the helicopter rescue service and providing it with a higher standard of medical capability and credibility. The rewards for my sacrifices, not to mention Amanda's, and the efforts of the whole team, were tantalisingly close. Now it seemed that everything could fall apart. I felt sick to the stomach.

The days were an anxious blur until the meeting. Finally the night came and at the Coogee Beach Surf Club we heard that the executive of the Sydney SLSA branch was no longer willing to accept the autonomy under which we operated. It was their contention that the helicopter rescue service had been formed and operated as part of their branch and therefore they should control the purse strings. There was also considerable discontent because we were pursuing interests away from the prime objective of beach patrols. While some saw our expanding medical role as having merit, others within the branch executive wanted to keep us restricted to beach and inshore rescue missions.

Peter and Ian attempted to point out that they had been almost totally responsible for securing our corporate sponsorship, with little help from the SLSA, and as such there was no justification for the moneys being directed through the organisation. We voiced our disquiet at having both financial and operational management taken away from us, but to no avail. The vote was taken and Peter was sacked. Ian was spared the same fate only because, in recognition of his services to the SLSA, he was already a life member of the association and so was 'suspended indefinitely' as the Sydney Branch Emergency Services Officer.

I could see their point of view. It was and had always been a SLSA operation, and from where the branch members stood we must have seemed like a bunch of renegades who had forgotten their roots. But our results stood for themselves, and I couldn't understand why they wanted to fix something that wasn't broken.

If the previous hour had been unbelievable, the next few minutes left me agape. In protest, the rest of our committee resigned. Most of the operational crew followed. The service suddenly had only one pilot and one crewman. The helicopter rescue service as I knew it had just ceased to exist.

My dreams were smashed to pieces. Inexplicably, I felt orphaned; self-pitying tears pricked my eyelids.

As we filed out of the room, I realised that all I had worked for was gone. There was no way forwards. Without the key personnel and their experience, capabilities and contacts, it would be years before the helicopter rescue service could rebuild. In any event, the reluctance of key members of the SLSA to pursue medical missions meant that it might never undertake the duties I had been training to perform. There was no doubt that the helicopter rescue service had a valuable role along the beaches and waterways, but that was not where I wanted to go. There was no other option for me, though. My career aspirations were in tatters.

So it came as an absolute shock to reach the footpath outside the club and find Ian, Peter and a few others of the now-defunct executive in an optimistic mood.

In response to my look of disbelief, Ian said, 'We didn't expect to win, but it was worth a try.' That didn't explain why he seemed almost excited. Seeing the defeated faces around him, Ian continued, 'You didn't think we wouldn't have a contingency plan, did you?' He grinned wickedly.

'Let's go find a coffee shop,' he suggested, and soon a dozen of us set off in convoy to Bondi Beach, a few kilometres north. We found a beach cafe, the only one open at that time of night. Ironically it specialised in burgers named after all the terms used in surf life saving.

After our orders had arrived Ian dropped his bombshell. 'We're going to start another service.'

I nearly choked on my hamburger. He made the statement as though creating another helicopter service like the one he had just spent the last fourteen years developing would be as easy as a stroll along the beach across the road from us.

Over the next ten minutes he explained that several weeks ago various members of the committee had realised that the outcome of today's meeting was inevitable. Already preliminary steps had been taken to attempt to form a new service that would be primarily medical with a rescue capability.

Over the next hour as we munched on our 'surf burgers' we brain-stormed what it would take to make this idea a reality. It was all written down on a serviette. I had never been involved in a meeting like this before. There was so much collective expertise firing around the table that this enormous concept seemed almost straightforward.

We needed approval from multiple government departments, an aircraft, crew, training, somewhere to base the service and, most importantly, considerable corporate sponsorship. Ian and Peter would continue in their previous roles as president and manager, and John Hoad would be chief pilot.

A few were already committed to the plan; others decided it was time to retire from flying. The rest of us agreed to let Ian know within a few days what our decision would be.

In closing Ian said, 'We also have a name for the service. It's going to be called CareFlight.'

Most of us thought this sounded a bit corny. It was the most popular name used in the hundred-odd hospital-based medical helicopter services in the United States. Still, we all conceded that this was Ian's project and he had the naming rights. And so it was that CareFlight (with a capital F, insisted Ian) was born in a cafe at Bondi Beach.

Driving home I played the events of the night over and over in my mind. Should I stay with the SLSA helicopter service, which at least existed? Should I sit on the sideline and not commit till I saw what happened?

If I got involved with the CareFlight project it would swallow all my spare time for months. (In reality it turned out to be years.) Amanda and Ben deserved more of my time once the final exams stopped consuming my every waking hour. For their sake I needed to spend more time at home, but if I was to fulfil my dreams, they would have to take a back seat once again. I had no understanding then how the decision I was about to make would impact on my family; selfishly my thoughts were taken up with my own desires and I naively assumed that Amanda would be happy as long as I was.

As I thought it through it became obvious that there was no future with the SLSA, and if anyone could make the dream a reality it was those involved in the CareFlight project. In particular, Ian had suffered a far bigger blow than me and came up more committed than ever to the development of a world-standard medical rescue helicopter service. My loyalties were absolutely to him.

It also became obvious how much was at stake here. More than any other aspect of my life, rescue helicopter work defined who I was. Everything I did in my career was aimed at being a player in providing a service for Sydney. At times in my specialist training it was only this vision that kept me going. I was kidding myself if I thought that I could stay on the sidelines and watch others develop the concept. While I had every confidence in my mates to make it work, I had to be part of the team. Moreover, I wanted to be part of the inner circle again, not just an outsider as I had been for the last three and a half years. I had to be a foundation member.

The next day, with Amanda's agreement, I rang Ian to say I was in. He understood that my support would be minimal until after the exams, but I wanted to be involved with the planning as much as possible. While the others started looking for money to make Care-Flight a reality, I knuckled back down to my study, more than ever wanting to pass first time and move on.

The fellowship exams were divided into several sections and would be both written and oral interview, or 'viva', style. The largest section was clinical anaesthesia techniques. I had to have an answer for dealing with every sort of scenario that might occur, proving I could effectively plan for an anaesthetic regardless of the type of surgery to be performed or the complexity of the patient's underlying diseases. To help with this, I had kept detailed records of every unusual or difficult case I had ever done. The value of rotating to many different hospitals was showing up in my trial exams, as I had experienced many different approaches to similar problems by various consultants at different hospitals. Some of my colleagues struggled on some difficult hypothetical scenarios because they only knew one or two ways to approach a case. Examiners at the trial viva exams I attended every week had a way of derailing an answer by making 'but what if' comments. It seemed to me I had it well covered, partly thanks to the variety in my training and partly thanks to the cautious approach I had been taught by Dr Young and the other consultants at St George.

Applied anatomy was another section of study – in order to block sensation to various regions we had to know intimately the nerve pathways throughout the body. This allowed us to anaesthetise just one area of the body for people too sick or frail to undergo any sort of general anaesthetic and to provide very effective pain relief after operations.

Understanding anaesthesia equipment was yet another section. We not only had to know our equipment in the finest detail, we had to know the standards governing hospital gas pipelines, history of anaesthesia equipment, and hundreds of equipment-related mishaps in order to avoid repeating such disasters.

My weakest section was internal medicine. As most of our patients had underlying medical conditions, we were expected to have a thorough understanding of illnesses, treatment of them and how to vary our techniques accordingly. We could expect numerous questions on this topic in the multiple-choice exams. There would also be a medical clinical exam in which I would be given half an hour to talk to and examine a patient and then fifteen minutes to present my findings to a panel of examiners. There would then be another fifteen minutes of interpreting investigations such as X-rays, electrocardiographs and blood tests to complete the oral exam.

I attended a number of ward rounds and felt woefully inadequate – I was way behind the eight ball in this subject. Dr Fran Smith, bless her, came to my rescue. For several weeks she found interesting cases at Westmead where she was now working as a senior registrar in intensive care, and as she was already a specialist physician she had a vast knowledge of general internal medicine. On my days off Fran and I would see her patients together; they generously let me take a history of their disease, examine them and then present my findings to Fran. Fran refined my skills and added substantially to my knowledge. I am continually grateful for her expertise and generosity.

■ ■ ■

The final exams were upon me.

The multiple-choice exam was hard and I felt sure of perhaps getting twenty per cent of the questions right. But these were very difficult questions and I had been warned that twenty per cent would be a reasonable result. None of my colleagues felt any more confident. So far, so good.

The essays seemed straightforward, and again I took extra care to read the questions several times before planning my answers. Two weeks later came the interviews, to be held at Westmead. The anaesthesia vivas were an hour long, starting at ten o'clock. Six examiners posed all sorts of difficult scenarios, to which I gave my planned course of action and defended my reasoning.

Some questions were equipment related. 'Why does it say Z79 on the side of this endotracheal tube?'

'That means it has met certain standards in its manufacture.'

'But why Z79?'

'Because that was the name of the room where the committee had its meeting.'

The hour was gruelling but finally the bell rang and the examiners politely dismissed me. Making sure I left their pen on the table, I walked out of the room, relieved and fairly satisfied that I had given a good account of myself.

I felt exhausted and headed for the car. Just before I put the key in the door, I stopped. Much as I wanted to rest, I was not going to miss the opportunity to see a few more patients with Fran that afternoon. I turned and went looking for her.

Fran spent her lunch hour discussing her patients with me and then we walked to the car park together. Halfway down the stairs she suddenly stopped. 'We haven't talked about Cushing syndrome,' she said.

Cushing syndrome is related to over-secretion of the multitude of hormones made by the adrenal glands. I had seen a few cases as a medical student. For the next ten minutes Fran described the characteristic clinical appearance of a patient with this illness. She included all the usual blood investigations and how they should be interpreted. It didn't seem a likely sort of case, but it was certainly a disease I had forgotten to study in detail.

The following morning I returned to Westmead Centre. I was verging on panic, knowing how weak I was in the area of internal medicine. I felt sick as the exam secretary led me to the room where my trial patient waited. This patient had given of their time to be part of the exam process. The door opened and I could hardly believe what I saw.

There sat the most florid example of Cushing syndrome I had ever seen. Over the next thirty minutes I listened to the patient's story and examined her. She had all the symptoms and signs: weight gain, ruddy complexion, round 'moon face', muscle wasting and weakness, insomnia, high blood pressure. It was exactly as Fran had described, and I silently thanked her a hundred times during that half-hour.

By the time I went to present my patient to the examiners I was feeling on top of the world. I was so close to completing the exams, and doing well.

I had not counted on the chief examiner's final question. 'Well presented but finally, why do you think she has the syndrome?'

I prattled off several causes.

'How would you figure out which one she has?'

Still feeling confident I outlined the various blood tests. The examiner shook his head. I felt a chill run down my spine.

'Well, she has none of those. What else could it be?'

I ran through all the causes I knew, which, thanks to Fran, was an impressive list, but each time he shook his head. I finally arrived at the answer that every candidate dreads, but I knew it was better to admit it than say something stupid. I took a deep breath, knowing everything now came down to how my answer was received. 'If it isn't any of the things I have listed, then I don't know why she has Cushing syndrome.'

There was complete silence and for a few seconds the examiners stared at me. Was that it? Had I come so close to passing the exams to blow it now? The seconds seemed like hours.

At last the chief examiner broke the silence. 'That's a shame, I was rather hoping that you would.' Oh God, he's going to fail me, I thought. The examiner continued, 'You know the syndrome so well

I was hoping you could tell us, because we don't know either.'

I didn't know whether to laugh or jump across the desk and punch him in the face.

The other examiners took over the questioning, presenting several X-rays and cardiographs before the bell sounded and I was free to leave. I raced to the phone and rang Amanda to tell her how it had gone. I was feeling confident because I just didn't know how I could have done any better. Next I found Fran and related to her the events of the last hour. She was as surprised and delighted as I was. Without her help I would never have passed that exam.

Four hours later Amanda, Fran and I assembled at the main entrance of the hospital where the results were to be posted. I was nervous; perhaps I had misjudged my performance and the exhausting effort of the last few years had been for nothing. The results were on a whiteboard ten metres inside the door. I could barely drag myself over to it; it seemed as though my future was written there, and I was too afraid to look it in the face. Finally I could see the candidate numbers on the board. Mine was there. I had passed!

Relief and exhilaration overwhelmed me. I hugged Amanda and Fran tight and thanked them for their support. I congratulated my successful colleagues and spared a thought for a few others who walked up to the board and then quietly slunk away.

Soon all the successful candidates were ushered downstairs to the hospital boardroom where we were presented to the examiners one by one. Amanda had come to watch and was accidentally presented to the chairman of the board of examiners. She told him it was far easier to receive a fellowship than she had imagined. This confounded the man as no one ever thought the process was easy. Amanda grinned and the faculty secretary, suddenly realising her mistake, ushered her on quickly.

When we had all been presented, we received a glass of wine and a round of applause from the examiners. I needed the drink (though a stiff whiskey would have been better!) and was grateful for the acknowledgements. I could hardly believe there were no more exams. I had only to complete the year to become a specialist or, to give it the full title, which at that moment I felt pleased enough to do, Fellow of the Faculty of Anaesthetists of the Royal Australian College of Surgeons, known as an FFARACS.

What I should have done after this success was take some time out and spend it with my family. What I did was give all my attention to the creation of CareFlight.

PART IV
A Leap of Faith

I learned this, at least, by my experiment; that if one advances confidently in the direction of his dreams, and endeavours to live the life which he has imagined, he will meet with a success unexpected in common hours. If you have built castles in the air, your work need not be lost; that is where they should be. Now put the foundations under them.

Henry David Thoreau

17

I was tired and dirty; my old rugby shorts and gym shoes were covered in dust and flecks of spray paint. While the signwriters were doing their thing, I was helping insert the seats into Care-Flight's newly leased Squirrel. It was a rare quiet Saturday at the heart surgery unit at St Vincent's Hospital, and no operations were scheduled. A day off was a relief from the gruelling three months on call all night every night. I had made my way to Bankstown Airport to help with the helicopter fit-out, something I did whenever I could.

Suddenly my pager went off and a quick phone call told me I was needed urgently back at St Vincent's. Jumping into my old beat-up and badly rusted Holden sedan I headed back towards the city. I had barely gone three blocks when I came over a rise and straight into a police radar trap. I knew I was gone, and sure enough an impressively large and serious police sergeant flagged me down.

'Excuse me, sir, but you were doing seventy-five kilometres an hour in a sixty zone. Do you have a reason for going in such a hurry?' he enquired.

'Yes, officer, I'm on my way to do a heart transplant,' I replied.

He paused for a moment. 'Are you trying to be funny, sir?'

'No, I'm absolutely serious.'

He slowly looked me up and down, then cast a doubtful eye over my rust bucket. 'A heart transplant,' he said dubiously.

'I'm in a hurry. If you would like to ring this number,' I said, scribbling on a piece of paper, 'that will connect you to where Victor

Chang and the rest of his team are preparing. I'm sure they'll tell you that I'm required right away.'

He paused a few seconds, I suppose wondering if this was a ruse to make a bolt for it when he walked away, but eventually he returned grudgingly to his car. A minute later he was back. 'Well, your story checks out,' he said reluctantly, obviously finding it hard to believe this scruffbag in front of him would be part of a heart transplant team. 'You're free to go, but slow it down, okay?'

'Yes, sir, definitely.'

My last view of the policeman was in the rear-view mirror. He was watching me go, one hand on his hip holding his cap, the other scratching his head.

In the past few months CareFlight had evolved rapidly. A major sponsor had been found – the medical insurance company Health Care Fund, better known as HCF. Television station Channel Nine and radio station 2WS had also come on board as supporting sponsors. No doubt there had been an enormous amount of lobbying for this to happen so quickly.

A lease on the Squirrel had been signed, with several members of the organisation giving personal guarantees to secure the deal. There were some misgivings about the aircraft having only one engine, but there was simply no way we could afford anything more sophisticated. One of the first things we had agreed upon was that marine rescue should remain the province of the SLSA, which still flew in spite of the paucity of crew to staff the service, and that we would refer all requests for such work to them. Not only was everyone agreed this was the right thing to do, it was appropriate not to do over-water flights in a single-engined aircraft while the Surf twin-engined aircraft was available. The aircraft was therefore deliberately not being fitted out with a cargo hook or marine rescue equipment.

Two operational philosophies had been adopted. Firstly, the safety of the operation took precedence over all other considerations. Secondly, the service would be developed around the needs of the patient rather than simply creating a service and hoping it would be useful. We knew that most of our work would be either trauma-related scene responses or intensive care inter-hospital transfers. The outcome of trauma patients related critically to the time lapse between the accident and definitive medical care, much of which could start at the scene of the accident if the right doctor and equipment were there. Our philosophy was therefore 'stay and stabilise' as opposed to 'scoop and run'. We intended to use the helicopter as a means of taking teaching-hospital standard medical care to the patient, wherever they might be.

While Ian, Peter and their team had handled the operational, fundraising and political aspects of the project, we doctors had huddled down to plan our equipment, its placement on the aircraft and overall medical philosophy. First point of business had been to appoint Fran as honorary medical director.

The planning of the aircraft fit-out was straightforward. Having fitted out two such aircraft in the past four years, we were clear on what we liked and what changes to make. Most significantly, the right rear seat was replaced with a side-facing seat for use during patient transport, to allow the crewman to take a more active role in assisting the doctor, who would still sit behind the patient in the left rear position. There was no money in the budget for medical consumables, so the doctors donated everything from laryngoscopes to bags of plasma out of our own pockets.

Dr Jenni Saunders, a sports physician who contributed enormously in these embryonic days, had procured a brochure about Thomas Transport Packs from the USA. Frank Thomas MD from Salt Lake City had had the same idea as me in developing a backpack for carrying medical equipment, but he had taken the concept much further. Each compartment was colour coded: blue for airway equipment, yellow for drugs, red for blood replacement equipment. The pack was designed especially for a mobile intensive care team and was perfect for our task. (We not only ordered the pack, we also bought the Australian franchise, selling hundreds of the packs to civilian and military hospitals and organisations over the next few years.)

The noisy environment of the helicopter meant that we could not use the standard electronic alarms to warn of equipment failure or changes in the patient's state. Stethoscopes were useless. Nor could we hear whether a patient was breathing or an automatic ventilator cycling. We were at least able to have the beeping tone of the cardiac monitor routed through to the doctor's flying helmet. Otherwise we had to rely purely on visual cues.

So it was serendipitous that a new medical device became available around this time. The device was called a pulse oximeter. A peg-like clip was placed on the patient's finger and a calibrated red light was shone through the finger to a detector on the other side. The colour of the light revealed how much oxygen was in the bloodstream. Previously this could only be determined by a difficult and expensive blood test, or by waiting till the patient turned blue, by which time it was too late. The pulse oximeter was ten times more sensitive to a change in the patient's oxygen level than the human eye, and could detect a problem with oxygenation well before it became a clinical hazard. To our knowledge we were the first transport service in the world to use one. The most difficult aspect of its use was protecting it from being stolen by just about everyone who saw it!

Westmead had been confirmed as our operations centre following strong support from its founding superintendent, Dr Bernie Amos. The base consisted of a small demountable shed near the hospital oval, where the helicopter would be kept, and a tiny room down the back of the hospital that nobody else wanted. It was a start, and in all other respects the hospital administration was delighted to assist with the project.

There was, however, a real dichotomy of opinion within the New South Wales Health Department and the New South Wales Ambulance Service. Many members of both were highly supportive but some believed that the government should own and control any medical helicopter unit in the state. Even though the government had made no moves to create its own service (largely on the basis that they did not think there was a need), the paperwork to give us the permission to carry patients on behalf of the ambulance service seemed to keep disappearing, and we were powerless to do anything about it.

John Hoad, as chief pilot, was showing that his organisational expertise was every bit as good as his flying ability. Policy and procedure manuals were being developed under his leadership, as was the mountain of paperwork required to have the service approved for operations by the Department of Transport and Communications, which at that time controlled aircraft operations in Australia.

John and I teamed up to analyse the evidence surrounding medical aircraft crashes both here and overseas. There had been an alarmingly high incidence of accidents amongst US medical helicopters and we wanted to learn from their mistakes. Additionally, the Australian Bureau of Air Safety Investigations released to us the data on every adverse incident relating to medical aircraft and helicopter crashes over the previous ten years.

We discovered that human error was the main cause of these accidents, which confirmed the need for obsessive procedural, training and currency standards. Analysis of the data also supported our belief that medical and operational consideration should not be separate. Many aviation rescue services held the philosophy that the medical nature of the mission should not be a factor in determining the conduct of the flying operation, and vice versa. This may have been appropriate for routine medical flying but was a positive hazard in the operations we were planning.

We believed that good communications and a basic appreciation of everyone's, and the aircraft's, capabilities and limitations were fundamental for safety. Only then could the true risk–benefit balance of each mission be assessed. It remains my belief that a number of deaths amongst retrieval teams in Australia can be attributed to poor risk–benefit analysis. For example, our senior doctors, with insight into both the patient's disease process and the operational limitations of the service, could intelligently discuss the options with the pilot and crewman, such as waiting for better weather or daylight, or undertaking the mission by other means of transport. Above all, this meant that everyone respected each other's right to cancel a mission that was not worth the risk.

The first medical helicopter accident in Australia was particularly relevant. A patient being transferred on a Bell 47 in Western Australia had been loaded onto an external litter mounted on the skids. The patient's head rested on a pillow. Some say the patient's pillow dislodged, others say the patient was not happy about the treatment and decided to sabotage the flight. Either way, the pillow ended up in the tail rotor and the aircraft crashed. There had also been a number of accidents in the US attributable to head-injured patients becoming violent or having convulsions and interfering with the aircraft controls.

So it was decided that all but the most minor of head-injured or otherwise medically affected patients would be given a general anaesthetic for the transfer. It was a controversial decision, particularly with some so-called experts outside the service who had never undertaken flying operations, but time has proven the decision to be right. In the first five years nearly two-thirds of our patients were transferred this way.

In early July we were ready to fly. We only needed the paperwork from the health department and ambulance service. But it had mysteriously disappeared for a second time and everything was put on hold. Equally mysteriously it reappeared, after some furious behind-the-scenes political lobbying, and on 12 July 1986, just thirteen weeks after our meeting at Bondi Beach, CareFlight became a reality.

For the first two days Fran was duty doctor and nothing happened. Perhaps nobody really needed us after all, or perhaps we were simply going to be ignored. On the third day, however, Dr Paul O'Connell, our full-time doctor, transported an unconscious child with severe head and neck injuries from Lithgow to Westmead, and by the end of the month we had undertaken eleven medical missions. This was more medical missions than the busiest month ever with the SLSA helicopter rescue service.

A week later I flew my first mission when a teenager jumped off the wharf at Kurnell near the south headland of Botany Bay. It was five metres from the wharf to the water. The water was less than a metre deep.

The teenager suffered a dislocated neck and spinal injuries. The ambulance officers knew that one of Sydney's two spinal units was only ten kilometers away on the bay's northern headland, but a slow trip around the edge of the bay could take over two hours. They requested helicopter assistance and CareFlight was called in to do the transfer.

The boy's spinal injury was around the sixth cervical vertebrae at the bottom of his neck. Three vertebrae higher would have paralysed his breathing muscles and been fatal. He had only partial feeling in his arms and none in his chest or right leg. There was some feeling in his left leg, suggesting only partial damage to his spinal cord. Time was of the essence to correct any malalignment of his vertebral column, lest it still be pressing on his spinal cord. With the help of the ambulance officers we stabilised the teenager's neck and placed him on our spinal transport stretcher.

The lad was an emotional wreck, trying to deal with the implications of his injury. All I could do was reassure him that he might still recover and that, between the ambulance officers and CareFlight, he was in the best hands.

The flight to the spinal unit took just four minutes. The hospital doctors manipulated his spine to reduce the dislocation and relieve the pressure on his spinal cord and he was then transferred to the recompression chamber for high oxygen therapy. CareFlight had shaved nearly two hours off the time between injury and definitive treatment. The patient now stood a far greater chance of partial or complete recovery.

While CareFlight continued to progress from strength to strength, it was time for me to decide what to do with my career. At the end of the year I would finally be a specialist, but I still needed somewhere to work. Ideally I wanted to continue building my medical capabilities while being close to the action at CareFlight, which was why I was delighted when I was offered the job of senior registrar back at Westmead.

It was around this time that the Great Helipad Saga began. In retrospect it was so absurd it seems almost amusing, but at the time it sorely tested the patience of the entire CareFlight team, not to mention that it threatened to put us out of action.

Our nemesis was the Department of Transport and Communications and the story goes back to when Westmead Hospital was first built. Some forward-thinking person had built a helipad outside the front doors of the emergency department on what could otherwise have been a car park, even though at that time there were no services that could use it. A good idea, you'd think. Unfortunately the DOTC didn't agree.

In 1985 new helipad design regulations had come into effect. These required that in the event of a takeoff or landing mishap, reasonable steps had to be taken to ensure any bystanders were not exposed to unnecessary danger. Alternative landing places had to be provided. This might have been common sense but it ignored the incredible mechanical reliability of helicopters.

Worldwide, the type of turbine engine used in the Squirrel had required only two precautionary shutdowns in over 350,000 flights. Our calculations showed that an incident like this might occur at some stage in a flight about once every two hundred years. The chances of an unexpected engine failure in the ten-second period of final approach or initial takeoff without any warning from the highly sophisticated instruments were so remote as to be negligible.

Once every two centuries was too often for the DOTC. Zero risk was the only risk acceptable to them, despite the fact that the rules were nowhere near as stringent for fixed-wing aircraft, whose reliability was no better than that of helicopters. The emergency department helipad at Westmead was closed down.

The effect on CareFlight operations was dramatic. Despite numerous representations to the DOTC outlining our special needs, we were only able to use the pad by citing the mercy flight provision in the regulations. This allowed a pilot to take off and land where he saw fit – even if the area did not meet regulations – if in his opinion and on medical advice it was required to save life or limb and did not expose the crew and passengers to unnecessary danger. It could only be used if no other alternative was available.

Although we could continue to use the emergency pad for the most urgent cases, for everything else we had to land on the oval next to our operations hut and wait for a road ambulance to transport the patient and crew three hundred metres to the emergency department. This required calling the ambulance service by radio while en route in the air and pulling a road ambulance off normal duties. If one was available, the in-hospital transfer could be undertaken in ten minutes, but of course it required an extra loading and unloading of the patient, which was logistically difficult and at times hazardous. Often an ambulance was not immediately available, even if we called for one well in advance.

Nobody was happy with this situation. Each time a mercy flight was declared a written report from both the pilot and the doctor had to be submitted to the DOTC. Each report resulted in a departmental review. The nature of our patients meant that we were doing a couple of mercy flights each week, and the red tape was overwhelming. None of us liked paperwork and we were drowning in it.

John Hoad and our second pilot, Alain Le Lec, put their careers on the line every time they flew. The DOTC thought we were abusing the mercy flight guidelines and took a very dim view of our pilots' actions. John and Alain could have had their commercial helicopter pilot's licences revoked at any time. But as always at CareFlight we supported one another absolutely. John and Alain trusted the clinical judgement of the doctors and were willing to back us, no matter what the consequences.

The hospital understood our dilemma and made a formal request to the DOTC for a review. Westmead offered to clear the adjoining car parks permanently to provide alternative emergency landing areas and thereby comply with the regulations. The DOTC refused point blank to reinspect the pad. We were at a stalemate, and the saga was only just beginning.

Westmead Hospital was the perfect place for a trauma-management-addicted doctor like me. The pace was furious and the work tremendously rewarding.

Under the auspices of Dr Stephen Deane, the hospital was instituting a trauma-team project that allowed ambulance officers or doctors on the CareFlight helicopter to warn the hospital of their impending arrival. If the history of the accident or the condition of the patient met certain criteria, the trauma team would be activated. This meant that senior doctors from the departments of surgery, anaesthesia and emergency medicine, as well as technicians from X-ray and pathology, would be waiting in the trauma room for the patient's arrival. Often it was an overreaction, but many times the prior assembly of the team saved precious minutes in treating the victim's injuries. The false alarms were worth it.

As a senior registrar I had finally graduated to the consultants' after-hours emergency roster. This meant more executive decisions but came with the benefit of not having to remain in the hospital when it was my night on duty. Instead I would stay at home till registrars requested my assistance. It was still busy, but much better than previous years, and at times it almost seemed as though Amanda, Ben and I were a normal family.

There was, however, one more step I had to take before I felt my training was complete. I needed to spend some time overseas. Because the quality of Australian anaesthesia training was – and still is – arguably the best in the world, there was no difficulty finding several offers. The problem was that all of them would involve twelve months overseas. Naturally I didn't want to be away from CareFlight for so long, not while it was in its infancy – somehow I had convinced myself I was essential to its wellbeing. I knocked back several one-year postings in Europe and Canada and eventually accepted a six-month position in England.

I knew I was leaving the service in good hands. Luis Gallur had all but sold his soul to the devil to act as full-time doctor while I was away. He had been granted a year's leave of absence before doing his final year of specialist training. I had absolute respect for his expertise and professionalism; besides, he was as obsessed as I was.

The DOTC declared war two days before Amanda, Ben and I left for the old country. Alain had his licence suspended, and John was asked to show cause as to why he, too, should not be suspended as chief pilot. Without a chief pilot there was no operation. This was becoming a dirty fight; CareFlight was on the verge of being grounded. And amazingly, this time, it was all because Alain had *not* declared a mercy flight!

Alain had undertaken an urgent night flight for a severely head-injured child. It was alleged that he had landed at Nepean Hospital helipad with insufficient lighting and had flown in weather conditions that were below minimum standards. Alain was firm in his conviction that the lighting at the hospital was adequate, and reports from the control tower at nearby Bankstown Airport showed the weather was satisfactory at the time of flight.

CareFlight was willing to back Alain and John all the way, even into court if necessary. The evidence was conclusively on Alain's side, and even if there had been a breach of regulations, suspension for such a minor misdemeanour was without precedent. After lengthy discussion the suspension was lifted, but John and Alain were left in no doubt that this had been an exercise in intimidation. The message was clear: criticise the DOTC and pay the consequences.

I was committed to my job in England and I had to trust that those at CareFlight could handle anything that came their way. Amanda, Ben and I got on the plane and left.

18

Things in England got off to a bad start right from day one. The hospital refused to recognise my Australian specialist qualifications and I was placed on the junior registrar roster. This meant shifts of up to eighty hours were commonplace. I was back to snatching sleep in a room as small as a cupboard, on an old wire bed with a plastic mattress and sheets as thin as fly screens. After hours I single-handedly ran the intensive care unit and performed all the anaesthesia procedures relating to paediatrics and neurosurgery. Often I would be overwhelmed by the workload, not because I didn't know what to do but because I just couldn't do it all myself. On several occasions when I asked consultants for assistance I was rebuked for daring to disturb them. They were happy to remind me that I was a specialist now and should be able to handle it myself; the administration was also happy to pay me only seven pounds an hour because they regarded me as a junior trainee. Several times when requesting help I received the terse response, 'Carry on, colonial.'

It made my blood boil. This was no way to practise medicine. Consultants should lead the medical system, set an example; I vowed never to desert a junior colleague in need when I returned to 'the colonies'. Fortunately major changes occurred in England soon after my stay, which improved the conditions, but back then it was a nightmare. The other registrars had it no better but they never complained. Unlike me, they were totally reliant on these consultants for good references and their future careers. They couldn't afford to rock the boat.

The only consolation was the month I spent working in the intensive care unit; at least there I felt I was learning and contributing. And it was there I came across the most unusual case I have ever managed.

A woman had been admitted from St Elsewhere, the name usually given in medicine when not wanting to identify the real location. Her facelift operation, performed by a doctor who had no specialist qualification in surgery, had gone horribly wrong. After the operation she had bled profusely under all the skin flaps and her face and neck had become horribly swollen. With great difficulty we were able to anaesthetise her and get a small endotracheal tube, one normally suited to a seven-year-old child, down her windpipe. With this in place we took her from the ICU to the operating theatre to have the facelift taken apart, the massive blood clots removed and the bleeding vessels tied off. The skin of her cheeks appeared not to be receiving adequate blood supply and was still blue and dusky at the end of the operation. There was every possibility she would lose substantial amounts of her facial tissue and require disfiguring skin grafts.

I rang the nearby plastic surgery hospital for advice. After hearing my summary of the patient's management to date, the head of the department replied, 'She needs leeches.'

I nearly fell off my chair. 'Leeches?' I replied incredulously.

'Yes, leeches. Put them on the edges of the skin flaps. They will promote circulation and decrease the swelling. I'll send over a box straightaway.'

Sure enough they arrived, two dozen leeches and instructions on what to do and how to care for them.

For the next three days I applied the leeches to the woman's skin flaps. She was still heavily sedated and on a ventilator, but I knew there was a chance she might be aware of what was going on so I explained what we were doing and why, talking gently to her throughout the treatments. It was always a struggle getting the slippery little suckers to bite just where you wanted them to, and they were forever trying to escape and find other prey – namely me. When they were fully engorged they would drop off the woman's face and I would place them in a saline solution until they regurgitated their feed. By the next day the charming little creatures were as ravenous as ever.

Their puncture marks on the face would continue to bleed and ooze for up to a day, relieving the congestion and helping to keep the skin alive. After three days the swelling subsided and we could say farewell to our slimy pets. I can't say I kissed them goodbye.

Eventually the facelift was resutured successfully and a month later the lady returned to the unit. I didn't recognise her until she introduced herself. She thanked me for all my help and in particular for talking to her so reassuringly during the leech treatment. She remembered every moment of it!

The following year she contacted me in Australia to say that she had just won her court case against the doctor. Relating her memories of 'that young Australian doctor putting leeches all over her face for days on end' had made the payout very substantial indeed.

Management of trauma cases in the English hospital was abysmal compared to Westmead. There was no coordination and the task was generally left to the most junior doctors. I was horrified. Trauma victims, whether English, Australian or Outer-Mongolian, needed to be under the care of senior specialist doctors who could make the right executive decisions and make them quickly. I was disgusted by a system that seemed too arrogant to care, and determined to make sure I had a hand in preventing Australia from ever going down the same path. So it was serendipitous that early one morning I received a call from Fran Smith and Peter MacCormick.

'Do you realise what time it is over here?' Amanda asked them sleepily.

'I think about 2 am,' was the reply. Amanda shook her head and passed the phone over to me. I rubbed my eyes and listened groggily.

'A lot is happening here,' said Fran excitedly. 'The helicopter got fogged in one night a few months ago and Luis did the retrieval in an ambulance fixed-wing. As you know, they don't normally have doctors on board, just a flight nurse, but they had no objections to Luis using their aircraft. Now we're thinking we should drop being just a helicopter service and think of ourselves as a medical rescue service that has a helicopter. We've decided that, in addition to the helicopter's role, we want to offer an interhospital retrieval service by whatever means is appropriate. We were wondering if you would work full-time for CareFlight next year and help make this a reality.'

I was instantly wide awake. This seemed incredibly ambitious, but I wouldn't miss it for the world. 'Hell, yes!' I whooped. I wanted to pack my bags on the spot. With a stern look Amanda reminded me I still had six weeks to go here in England; and anyway – she looked blearily at the clock – it was now three in the morning.

As if the English hospital hadn't already taught me how not to manage trauma victims, two weeks after this phone call I experienced a case that would give me nightmares for years to come.

Late one evening, after a relentless day in the neurosurgery theatre, I was in the cafeteria eating a toad in the hole that was about as appetising as those leeches, when my pager went off. I recognised the number as the brain scanner room in the hospital car park. It was an odd place for a brain scanner, but I had long ago given up trying to work out the logic of things in this place.

The neurosurgical registrar explained the situation to me over the phone. 'I've got this woman who came off her motorbike. The brain scan looks normal but she's unresponsive. I don't know why, but she looks awful and I need help.'

'Is she already intubated? Has she got any other injuries?' I asked urgently.

'Well, I haven't examined her yet. The normal protocol for head injuries is for the ambulance to bring the patient to the scan room and when the scan is nearly done they call me to look at it. I called you as soon as I saw her.'

If he said anything else I didn't hear it. I was already running across the cafeteria, leaving the wall phone dangling off the hook.

I knew that other than the neurosurgery registrar there would be only one nurse and the radiographer in the scan room. There was no way of knowing what had been done by the ambulance officers, but their training did not include advanced airway maintenance or administration of intravenous fluids. There were all sorts of reasons why this woman might be unconscious, and many of them could kill her in minutes. It sounded as though the registrar was totally focused on her brain, with no insight into what might be happening elsewhere in her body. The patient was in deep trouble.

From the main part of the hospital to the car park was a long hike. I weaved past patients and beds in the corridors, shouting back the occasional apology to people I hit on the way. I ignored the lift and took the stairs two at a time, dashing out into the pouring rain and across the car park to the scan room. Gasping for breath I flung open the doors and pushed past the radiographer to the woman on the table.

It was immediately obvious that something was terribly wrong. The young woman, who I suppose was in her mid twenties, was as white as a sheet. There was barely any colour even in her lips. I felt for her wrist pulse. Nothing. I felt her carotid artery pulse in the neck; it was barely detectable but extremely rapid. Somewhere she had suffered massive blood loss.

At least by now the nurse had connected the electrocardiograph. The rhythm was normal but at twice the usual rate. Instead of seventy beats per minute, it was over one hundred and forty.

'Call a cardiac arrest!' I shouted at the registrar.

'But she hasn't had a cardiac arrest!' he replied, no doubt confused by my request.

'She's about to,' I hissed between clenched teeth. There was no such thing as a trauma team in this hospital; calling a cardiac arrest was the only way I knew to get help in a hurry.

'Sister, get ready to intubate,' I warned.

As the nurse pushed the trolley over from the corner of the room and fumbled with the equipment, I turned to confirm the woman's level of consciousness. I pushed my thumb hard on the ridge above her eye just below her eyebrow. This is an extremely painful manoeuvre. There was no response. She was profoundly unconscious.

Quickly I intubated her windpipe, having shown the nurse how to stabilise the neck in case of an undiagnosed spinal injury.

Seconds later the radiographer was bagging the patient. He had never done the procedure before but he followed my instructions to perfection. I listened to the patient's chest with my stethoscope to make sure we were ventilating both lungs – we were; her lungs were now being flooded with one hundred per cent oxygen, the first step to getting oxygen to her heart and brain. The next step was to have enough blood and fluid in her circulation system to carry the oxygen from her lungs to her vital organs.

The victim was still wearing her leather jacket and jeans. We got the jacket off but I resisted the temptation to spend time finding where she was losing so much blood from and went about replacing it first.

'Sister, IV normal saline on a pump set.' The nurse began priming a special intravenous line designed to allow large volumes of fluids to be pumped in quickly by hand.

By the time it was prepared I had inserted the largest intravenous cannula I could find into a vein at the woman's left elbow. I turned to the registrar. 'Squeeze this litre in and then another.' Now I had him doing something useful.

At that moment two other doctors and a senior nurse from the coronary care unit rushed through the door in response to the cardiac arrest call. 'Get a line in the right side and start pumping fluid,' I said to one doctor. The other I told to get the blood bank on the line. A quick feel of the carotid pulse showed it was barely palpable.

So far I had covered A for Airway, B for Breathing, C for Circulation and D for disability (meaning an assessment of the patient's mental state). It was time for E – Expose the victim and identify all injuries. With a large pair of scissors I sliced up the centre of the patient's T-shirt. No obvious injuries. The senior nurse looked daggers at me for exposing the woman. Her look changed to outright condemnation as I cut up the left leg of the victim's jeans. 'You can't expose a lady like that!' she cried indignantly. There was no time to explain; I shook my head and moved on to the right trouser leg.

Peeling back the material I stared in horror at the woman's legs. Her thighs were bruised and obscenely swollen. I gingerly moved each leg from side to side and felt the crunching and grating of bone fragments.

I turned to the registrar. 'Did the ambulance officers tell you how the accident happened?'

'Apparently she went over the handlebars of her bike,' he mumbled. 'They said she was conscious at the scene. She hit a lamppost but her helmet was still intact.'

I replied, 'She may not have sustained a severe head injury at all – this is why she's unconscious.' I nodded at her legs. 'Both her femurs are broken. No doubt she did it on the handlebars as she went over. Assuming there are one to two litres of blood loss into the tissues around each of those broken thigh bones, that leaves almost nothing for the rest of her. She's unconscious because there's no blood getting to the brain. She needs a transfusion, fast!'

Just at that moment one of the doctors timidly interrupted to say the blood bank was on the line. I looked around. The registrar was still pumping the saline bag and the radiographer and other doctor were also pumping IV fluid lines. It was clear that everyone was scared of what I might say. 'Keep going, you're doing great,' was all I could manage.

I picked up the phone. 'Blood bank, I need six bags of type O negative blood immediately.' While the saline would start to refill her blood vessels and improve blood flow, she needed red blood cells to transport the oxygen to her vital organs. Most of her red blood cells had been pumped out of the ruptured vessels around her broken bones and were lying useless in the tissues of her thighs. Without more red blood cells she was as good as dead.

I got the usual reply from the blood bank technician. 'I must have a blood specimen from the patient for cross-match before I can release the blood,' he told me primly.

'I know what you need, I'm married to a blood bank technician, but the patient will be dead if I do not get blood in three minutes. I'll get the specimen before I give the blood but send anything red in a bag and send it now!'

The doctor pumping the right-side IV fluid line spoke up. 'I took a blood specimen before I connected the drip.'

'Great thinking, well done!' I replied. At least somebody knew what they were doing.

A rain-drenched orderly flew through the door minutes later. 'Here's the blood for Dr Wisham,' he panted. I ignored the mispronunciation, I was used to it by now – anyone would think they didn't speak English in this country!

'Get it up!' I barked.

Seconds later the blood was running. The room was now packed with nurses and doctors. More resuscitation equipment had arrived. I gave directions on what needed to be done: check for other injuries; insert a catheter into her bladder to monitor urine production, the most sensitive way to measure shock.

It was up to her now. We could only stand by and see whether she would respond. There was no way of telling how long she had been so severely shocked. I felt the carotid pulse again; still weak.

I thought we might be in with a chance until suddenly the woman's heart rate slowed. The electrocardiograph signal went to ventricular fibrillation. The heart, chronically starved of oxygen, had ceased to pump.

'Cardiac arrest!' everyone seemed to shout simultaneously.

I turned to the radiographer. 'Do you know how to do CPR?'

'Yes,' he replied nervously.

'Then do it. Get ready to shock!' I told the others.

For the next ten minutes we ran through the cardiac arrest protocol: massage, defibrillation shocks, heart-starting drugs. But I knew it was hopeless – cardiac arrest due to massive blood loss is almost always irreversible.

Finally her rhythm changed: it deteriorated to a flat line. We gave multiple doses of adrenaline and carried on pumping. Nothing happened, just a flat line and a continuous long tone from the heart monitor. It was futile. The heart had been without oxygen for so long that it had suffered irreversible damage, probably before I had even arrived in the scan room.

'Enough,' I said quietly. 'Everybody stop.' I stepped over and disconnected the breathing bag from the endotracheal tube, then turned the monitors off. With the monitor silent I could have heard a pin drop.

'We did the best we could,' I said despondently. 'Thank you all for the quick response.' I didn't know what else to say.

I walked away. Outside, I sat down next to the garbage bins in the rain and cried.

I endured the next four weeks. I was miserable at work and desperately lonely at home. Amanda and Ben had already returned to

Australia. Amanda was pregnant and I wanted her safely in Australia as soon as possible.

A warm fuzzy feeling came over me as I stepped aboard the aircraft with the big flying kangaroo on the tail. When we crossed the coast to make our descent into Sydney International Airport, Peter Allen's song 'I Still Call Australia Home' came over the cabin speakers and I nearly shouted out with relief.

On our first night back together Amanda and I went to the local Black Stump restaurant. Living on a wage of just seven pounds an hour had been difficult, to put it mildly. Only once during our stay in England had we blown our budget and bought a steak. Over the next month we probably ate several cows between us.

19

I had barely touched down in Australia when I was back in the air, this time for my first fixed-wing retrieval.

Although I still had several weeks of my senior registrar contract to complete, CareFlight was desperately trying not to refuse any request for assistance. Luis had worked every week I'd been away and been back-up every weekend. To say he needed a break was an understatement. His dedication to the service and the people it helped was all-consuming. A recent rescue he had completed with Wayne Vardanega, our crew chief, and Alain, would see him awarded the Queen's Commendation for Brave Conduct. He had even put his plans to marry on hold for the job! My roster at Westmead gave me the occasional day off midweek, and these I spent filling in for him.

Early one evening while covering Luis, CareFlight was requested by Westmead's ICU to retrieve a severely burnt bushfire brigade officer from Wagga Wagga Base Hospital, some four hundred kilometres south-west of Sydney. No sooner had I arrived at the air ambulance base at Sydney International Airport than flight nurse Jenny Parker took me out to the runway apron to board the waiting aircraft. The Super King Air was a twin turbo-prop aircraft originally designed to carry two pilots and up to ten passengers. As one of six full-time air ambulances it was fitted out with two stretcher bays on the starboard side and attendant seats on the port side.

Jenny introduced me to the pilot, Michael Harrington, then she surrendered the co-pilot's seat to me for my first trip. I remembered that twelve-year-old boy full of dreams in Captain Cook's cockpit and smiled at the way his life had turned out.

The two turbo-prop turbines were spooled up and we taxied out to runway 16. To add to my thrill, two Boeing 747s were required to stop and give way to us because of our medical status, allowing us to take off without delay.

We sped down the runway and lifted off over Botany Bay. The last rays of the setting sun bathed the buildings below in an orange glow. As darkness closed in the landscape below faded until it was just a sea of blackness like the sky above. At intervals clusters of fairy lights broke up the night. Looking down at those country towns where people in their cosy homes were settling down for dinner, a sense of isolation and loneliness washed over me. I thought of Ben tucked up in bed in his flannelette pyjamas, and Amanda, so used to nights alone that her evening rituals no longer depended on my presence.

We began our descent an hour after takeoff; ten minutes later two rows of lights, wider down the bottom and narrower up the top, appeared in the inky black. They seemed to freeze in place in the centre of the windscreen, never moving but slowly expanding as we drew closer. I became disorientated; although I knew these were the runway lights, I was fighting the conviction that somehow they were above the plane in the sky, not on the ground. Without any other reference points or a visible horizon, I could make no sense of the view at all. I glanced over at Michael. His eyes were riveted to his instruments. I felt the drag and clunk of the undercarriage lowering and the flaps being extended. The expansion of the lights to either side rapidly accelerated, and finally I could make out the runway between them. A few seconds later we levelled out a metre above the tarmac and Michael throttled back the engines. We floated for several seconds in the narrow layer between sky and ground, and then gently touched down at Wagga Wagga.

Twenty minutes later I was reviewing the patient. The twenty-three-year-old firefighter had received burns to his head, neck and all his limbs. His lungs had also been severely affected and he had required anaesthetising and ventilating soon after arrival to counter-act his precariously low oxygen levels. After initial fluid resuscitation he had been taken to the operating theatre. It was obvious that he would require many days of artificial ventilation and so a tracheostomy had been performed to prevent permanent damage to his voice box.

The patient had also required escharotomies, longitudinal cuts down both arms and legs to release the pressure created by the swelling of his damaged tissues and muscles. Without these the pressure would have become so great it would have cut off the blood supply to his limbs. The soft tissues and muscles were grossly swollen from the heat injury, and there was considerable bleeding where these cuts had been made through unburnt tissue. To make matters worse, his blood-clotting ability was severely impaired. The poor bloke was in a desperate state.

Adequate fluid replacement was now the most critical factor in his survival. Already he had received six litres of saline solution and three litres of plasma in the five hours since the burn, but his urine output was still dangerously low, which suggested that the fluid replacement was inadequate. This was something I had seen before in firefighters, who are often severely dehydrated before their injury. We had to dramatically increase the fluid infusions and begin transfusions of blood and clotting agents.

An hour later, having administered antibiotics and antitetanus injections as well as drugs to promote urine flow, we were back at Wagga Wagga Airport. Before Michael fired the engines, Jenny and I reviewed the firefighter's status. While ventilation and oxygenation were okay, he was starting to ooze blood through his escharotomy dressings and it was clear from his urine production that he was still not getting enough fluid. I was in a quandary. To stop the bleeding would mean taking him to theatre to seal the vessels. Should I return to Wagga Wagga and restabilise, or continue to Sydney? At times like these I felt awfully alone – the fate of this courageous young man was entirely in my hands. A wrong decision could mean the end of a life that had only just begun. I weighed up the options. We were running out of time – he needed Westmead's specialist burns team as soon as humanly possible. We had to make a run for it.

To keep him pumped with fluids Jenny connected one of his IV lines to the automatic infuser and connected the other to a manual pump, and we continued to squeeze bag after bag of blood through the drip. I administered further sedative drugs to keep him anaesthetised and Michael maintained the cabin pressure at sea level throughout the flight to maximise the firefighter's oxygen levels.

The escharotomies were now bleeding profusely. The patient's clotting ability was failing. All his dressings were soaked and the stretcher and his sheets were turning red. We had given him nine bags of blood and clotting solutions, but the fluids were leaking out as fast as we were pouring them in.

As we approached Sydney we used our last bag of blood, so I asked Michael to request the CareFlight chopper to rendezvous with us at the air ambulance base to complete the trip to Westmead. The nine-minute transfer by chopper was far preferable to the one hour it would take by road.

Thirty minutes later I had handed the patient over to the ICU. Without doubt this was the most difficult transfer I had ever done. The adrenaline that had been driving me for the last two hours drained away and I felt wrung out. Still, I was quietly satisfied that what would have been an impossible transfer two years ago had gone reasonably well considering the circumstances. The patient would commence his slow, complicated road to recovery in the very best of hands.

I turned round and headed for home. It was two-thirty in the morning. I was due back at Westmead at seven. What a way to spend my day off!

The health department had not changed its mind. As far as it was concerned there was no need to fund a separate retrieval service. Any money for retrievals was to be taken out of general hospital funding. Apart from the work we were doing at CareFlight, some work being done by a few doctors involved with the SLSA helicopter, and some country hospitals doing retrievals in their areas, there was little other medical retrieval work being undertaken. This was not because it wasn't needed – it was, desperately – but because the hospitals had no money to pay for the work and no spare medical staff to undertake the missions. Critically injured patients were often transferred under the care of a country hospital's most expendable, which usually meant their most junior, doctor. The flight nurses coped with the rest.

This was about to change. CareFlight's plan was as simple as it was ambitious. Using the money we raised we would provide a retrieval service for the whole state, offering to work for any hospital for free. We knew how great the demand was, and eventually the health department and ambulance service would not be able to ignore the evidence. They would be forced to fund a retrieval operation properly. Till then we would have to pay for the service ourselves.

This meant that CareFlight needed another full-time doctor to work with me. None of the existing doctors was in a position to take up the offer as they were either still completing their specialist training or already involved in their own specialist careers. Or perhaps they were just too smart!

A senior registrar from Waikato Hospital in Hamilton, New Zealand, applied for the job. His references, both professional and personal, were impeccable.

'The job's yours!' we told Dr Blair Munford. 'The hours will be long; the pay will be low; and by the way, there's no guarantee we'll even exist in six months. Congratulations!'

We impressed upon this lanky, dark-haired New Zealander how his references and credentials had stood out from all the other applicants. We didn't have the heart to tell him he was the only applicant! Nevertheless, he turned out to be one of the most capable and dedicated doctors ever to work with the service. In Blair we had hit the jackpot. Within two weeks he had completed his operational training. He had even managed to escape from the equipment shed after Wayne had padlocked him inside before departing on a mission. Wayne claimed it was a mistake but we all suspected it was his final test to check out Blair's resourcefulness.

The Great Helipad Saga continued, becoming more melodramatic by the minute. While I'd been in England the DOTC had employed an overseas consultant to review the whole issue. This investigator interviewed CareFlight personnel at length and was astounded that the

Westmead helipad could not be used. He agreed that, over the long term, rooftop helipads should be available at all major hospitals. Such pads were the norm overseas, affording direct lift access from the helipad to the emergency ward and an ideal landing site away from the public and the turbulence around the base of large buildings.

In his report the investigator recommended that our helipad be reopened. We were delighted, but the DOTC soon put an end to our celebrations. Their response was beyond belief. Not only were the findings not accepted, it was stated that the report actually *supported* the DOTC's decision to ban all flights, including mercy flights from the Westmead Emergency Department Helipad! It became illegal to use the pad under any circumstances.

There was no logic to the ruling. The DOTC, backed into a corner, was just not willing to admit that it had been unreasonable all along. The absurdity was that a mercy flight could still legally land on the road next to the helipad, or hover above the pad and winch the patient to the ground; it was only *landing* on the helipad that was not permitted. No other piece of ground anywhere in Australia was subject to such a restriction. All our patients would now have to be transported by road ambulance from the back oval. It might have been funny had the consequences not been so deadly serious. Sooner or later the situation was going to contribute to a patient's death.

It was early morning in the new year of 1988. This was my first day as Australia's first full-time rescue helicopter specialist.

I had spent the previous night in CareFlight's three-bedroom unit in the hospital residential complex, which the service had been using since becoming a twenty-four-hour operation six months previously. Amanda, Ben and I were living about twenty minutes from the hospital, which was just too far when I was on call. The unit was spartan but adequate, with bare brick walls and royal blue camel-hair carpet tiles. It was freezing cold in winter and boiling hot in summer. The office phones had parallel lines to the 'Bat Phone' in the unit and there was a twenty-five-metre pool next door. Before breakfast we usually had swim training. Alain was the undoubted champion, always starting his day with eighty laps before tucking into one of his unusual and disgustingly healthy breakfasts comprised of various nuts, vegetables and fruit, not all of which we could identify.

Early that morning we were called by ambulance control to a head-injured man in the Royal National Park, south of Sydney. It turned out that he'd been drinking and in his drunken state had gone wandering into the night. This would not have been a problem if he hadn't camped next to a twenty-metre waterfall and fallen over it. It had taken some hours for his mates to find him and then raise the alarm.

He had been unconscious for several hours during the night but had since regained consciousness. Examination revealed he was moderately shocked; more worrying, though, was the persistent weakness in his left arm. I was afraid that, together with his period of unconsciousness, this indicated he had an expanding blood clot on his brain. I decided it would be better to fly directly to a neurosurgical hospital rather than the closest regional hospital. After the ambulance rescue officers and I had stabilised and prepared the man, we winched him into the chopper. Leaving him in the rescue stretcher, we made the nine-minute flight to the nearest neurosurgical unit, a trip that would have taken over two hours by road.

Brain scans ruled out a blood clot and the left-arm weakness slowly resolved over the next few days. He was a very lucky man.

We were just sitting down to lunch when we were interrupted by a request to transfer an eleven-year-old girl from Nepean Hospital in Penrith to the Children's Hospital in Camperdown. She had run out in front of a car and sustained severe head injuries. Resuscitation was underway and, having been given authorisation by the ambulance service, we were in the air within minutes.

The child had been unconscious on arrival at hospital. The tendency of her eyes to gaze to one side and the presence of blood behind her eardrums pointed to significant brain injury and a possible need for urgent neurosurgery.

The excellent doctors at the Nepean had, as usual, predicted our need to intubate and anaesthetise for the transfer, and things were well prepared by the time we arrived. My main duties were to check that nothing had been missed and we had all the equipment prepared if any change in her condition occurred during flight. We drew up further doses of the anaesthetic drugs, checked we had all the airway support equipment laid out and working normally, and adequate oxygen supplies for the trip. Soon we had her loaded, and twenty minutes later were landing at the Children's Hospital. We had completed another urgent retrieval of the sort that didn't need funding according to the health department. In fact this was our three hundred and sixty-fifth such 'unnecessary' medical mission.

Later we learned that the girl's recovery had been without mishap and she appeared to have no ongoing problems. It was expected that she would make a complete recovery and would be home within a week. It was the opinion of the neurosurgeon and intensive care specialists at the Children's Hospital that this good outcome was in large part due to the effective stabilisation at Penrith and the continuity of that care during her transfer.

The following morning we transferred a young man with a possible neck fracture. He had dived into a shallow pool, and in addition to severe bleeding from a scalp laceration, X-rays suggested a possible fractured vertebrae. Full spinal injury precautions were taken and we transferred him to Westmead. Numerous X-rays and scans later, the radiologists made their conclusion. The fracture line was an artifact due to faulty X-ray film. The patient was free to go home. He was jubilant.

The case I did in the afternoon was just the opposite. I travelled to Tamworth with the air ambulance to a burns victim. This time the injury was self-inflicted. The woman had doused herself with kerosene and set herself alight. Essentially, she had burns to one hundred per cent of her body.

Although the correct procedures had been undertaken, she was not responding to fluid therapy. A careful review of her status, blood tests and X-rays confirmed that her lungs were severely burnt and she was not going to respond, no matter what we did. Along with the local doctors and her family we decided that transferring her would serve no purpose and everyone's efforts should be directed at making her comfortable in her final hours.

It was a sombre flight back to Sydney. We sat in silence, haunted by what awful tragedies this woman must have suffered to want to take her own life in such a violent way.

On a brighter note, just two weeks after starting at CareFlight, I received a call of a very different kind. Amanda was in labour. I rushed home and brought her back to Westmead Hospital, where our second son, Daniel, was born. Other doctors took over the roster and I managed a week off. It was far too short and I had to rely heavily on my mother and mother-in-law to help Amanda as I waded back into clinical work and the politics of keeping CareFlight a reality. I didn't want to be an absent father, especially not when our son was so newly born, but this was a crucial time at work.

There is an urban myth about a patient with a blood clot on the brain. The story goes like this: a doctor, on his way to work, comes upon an accident scene. He rushes over to the head-injured patient and diagnoses a blood clot, identifying exactly where in the brain it is. Using his trusty Black and Decker drill – which he just happens to have with him, as you do! – he drills a hole and releases the blood, upon which the patient immediately wakes up and the doctor continues on his merry way. Along with the story about waking up in a bath of ice water with a message on the wall saying, 'Both your kidneys have been stolen', it is a load of rubbish. That is probably why a Black and Decker drill is not part of the equipment in the CareFlight medical pack.

Blood clotting around the brain following trauma is, however, a management dilemma if the patient is a long way from a neurosurgical centre. As the clot swells it increases the pressure on the brain till the blood supply is so impaired the patient dies. While the clot needs removing, it is most definitely not a job for part-time players. The clot requires a brain scan to accurately locate it and instruments much more sophisticated than a drill to remove it. Performing the operation without adequate facilities and training may sometimes be justified but it is fraught with danger. That was why, with the advent of Care-Flight, country hospitals with such patients were tending more and more to move them to neurosurgical centres, concentrating instead on nonsurgical means of keeping brain pressure down prior to and during the transfer.

Early one morning I was dragged out of my warm bed for another trip to Wagga Wagga. A nineteen-year-old woman had wrapped her car around a power pole. In addition to a serious head injury, she had suffered facial and jaw fractures as a consequence of being thrown through the windscreen. A brain scan had demonstrated a clot on the left side of her brain and early evidence of rising intracranial pressure. Wagga Wagga Hospital, perhaps all out of Black and Decker hand drills, preferred to transfer her rather than operate themselves.

I was called at five-thirty; we were in the air before seven and at the patient's bedside by eight-thirty. The girl had been well prepared, and was already anaesthetised for her trip. I inserted a second intravenous line in case the one the hospital doctors had put in place became dislodged. Inserting lines during transfer can be extremely difficult because the aircraft vibrates so much, and it is always better to have a spare already in place. In view of the rising pressure in the patient's brain, we decided to give an infusion of Mannitol, a drug that would suck out some of the water from her brain cells. It would buy us some more time. I reviewed all the X-rays and blood tests to ensure nothing had been missed, and then we were ready to go. The whole team had worked quickly and we were back in the air by nine-thirty. The patient was being personally assessed by the neurosurgeon and prepared for the operating theatre by eleven-thirty. The clot was successfully removed within an hour.

What a way to start the day! This was the part of the job I loved – everyone working together efficiently and professionally to make a very real difference to a patient's outcome.

A few days later saw me doing a fixed-wing transfer from Bathurst to Westmead which didn't run quite so smoothly and highlighted a problem with other services' adaptation to CareFlight's capabilities. The thirty-three-year-old patient was suffering from a progressive but usually not permanent paralysing disorder called Guillain-Barré Syndrome. He was at the stage where his swallowing and breathing were impaired. There was every possibility he would need to be on a ventilator for days or weeks till the paralysis resolved.

Bathurst, some one hundred and seventy kilometres west of Sydney, had always been a fixed-wing retrieval area. From the Care-Flight base, however, it was about three-quarters of an hour flying time, as long as it would take me to get a taxi across town to the air ambulance base at Sydney airport. There was no doubt the patient needed urgent assessment, but the air ambulance insisted that the retrieval be done by fixed-wing air ambulance as per tradition, and so I had to take that forty-five-minute taxi ride to their base.

To make matters worse I arrived at the airport to be informed that the takeoff could not proceed. The policy was that air ambulances could not depart till one hour after the mission had been formally authorised. This was intended to prevent undue pressure being put on the pilot to fly before he was fully prepared. While it was a reason-able idea, and part of the contract the ambulance service had with East West Airlines which supplied the pilots, in this case it seemed ridiculous. After the situation was explained to me and it was evident that nothing I could say would make any difference, I resigned myself to sitting in the tea room and having a cuppa.

Finally we were given permission to go. Forty minutes later we touched down at Bathurst. It took another thirty minutes for the ambulance to drive us to the hospital. Fortunately the patient's condition had not deteriorated, and I decided that we did not have to ventilate him for the return journey. It was a hard call, but transport-ing a patient sedated, paralysed and dependent on a ventilator is not without its risks, and I never like to do it unless absolutely necessary. Thirty minutes back to Bathurst Airport, thirty-five minutes in the air, another hour in the back of an ambulance and the patient finally arrived at Westmead ICU. All in all the mission had taken four and a half hours. The patient was outside the hospital environment with all its support for two hours. Had we been given permission to do the transfer by helicopter, the mission time would have been two hours and thirty minutes and the patient would have been outside a hospital for less than an hour.

It was incredibly frustrating to know that CareFlight had the capabilities to make a real difference but, for reasons that could only be political, was being sidelined. The machinations reminded me of the English television show *Yes, Minister*. Except they weren't funny. Especially not when Fran and I found ourselves under fire for a Care-Flight rescue – and a successful one at that.

Some months earlier our helicopter had been dispatched to some very isolated mountainous countryside fifty kilometres north-west of Sydney. A schoolgirl had fallen over a cliff. Her injuries were unknown. Our doctor found the young girl twenty metres below the ledge she'd fallen from. She was profoundly unconscious but still breathing. She appeared bluish from lack of oxygen and examination revealed that this was due to a collapsed lung. As no other emergency personnel were on the scene yet, our doctor inserted a chest drain to stabilise the punctured lung and then placed an endotracheal tube down the girl's windpipe to protect her lungs should she vomit, and to allow her to receive one hundred per cent oxygen.

The dilemma was what to do next. The aircraft winch could not carry the girl on the stretcher and the doctor at the same time. It would take over an hour for another chopper with a larger winch to arrive. The delay could prove fatal. Our doctor decided to winch the girl out; she would be unattended for the thirty seconds the lift would take. He would give her one hundred per cent oxygen beforehand and the rescue crewman would place her back on one hundred per cent oxygen as soon as she was in the aircraft. The doctor would easily be able to climb up a pathway next to the ledge and rejoin the chopper on the hover at the top of the cliff.

Before agreeing to the plan it was decided that in the unlikely event that the winch malfunctioned and the lift could not be completed, the helicopter would sling the stretcher over to the road ambulance that had just arrived in the nearest clearing five hundred metres away.

The winch operation went smoothly. In all, the girl was unattended for less than thirty seconds – about the same amount of time patients were unattended on the hydra lift while being loaded onto an air ambulance. Seconds later the doctor was at the top of the cliff, and he reboarded the helicopter. The girl's condition was further stabilised with the help of the ambulance officers after landing in the clearing, then she was flown to Westmead where she underwent emergency neurosurgery. Her recovery was slow but eventually complete.

The case, however, led to a complaint, the source of which was never revealed. The health department had formed several committees to review retrieval matters; it had one main retrieval committee and two subcommittees, one each for operational and medical matters. All it needed now was a committee to oversee the committees. I was reminded of the saying that 'committees are cul-de-sacs down which good ideas are lured and buried'!

'You should never leave an intubated patient unattended!' was the criticism Fran and I were fending off from the medical retrieval committee, which included senior intensive care specialists who had no helicopter experience whatsoever. We felt more like the accused in an inquisition than equals trying to learn from the case. Step by step Fran and I led the committee through the retrieval. We said that under those conditions we would have done exactly the same thing. That raised a few eyebrows! We asked how they would have done it better, but they avoided answering the question. Their hostility was palpable.

We suggested that if the health department wished to increase our funding we would gladly buy a larger chopper with a two-person winch. This was met with stony silence. Fran and I knew the whole exercise had more to do with a desire to discredit CareFlight than any clinical or operational concerns. Together we also suspected they were using our dedication against us.

Answering each criticism was no simple matter. Every single one required an internal investigation to ensure we had done everything just right. Every response had to be perfect; there could be no gaps in our defence. Our determination to prove we were squeaky clean was wearing us out.

The health department's next ploy was to contract an external consultant to review all medical retrieval services; no doubt he was briefed on CareFlight's poor operational standards. In his interviews with us, however, he gave the impression he was convinced by our explanations and arguments. A month later his report recommended that the CareFlight and SLSA helicopters be closed down. I couldn't help feeling we'd been set up.

It was suggested that CareFlight become wholly integrated into the health department and that the ambulance service purchase our helicopters and base them at Sydney airport. The appropriate crew would be determined by an overseeing board on a case-by-case basis.

To us, this was a disastrous idea. Helicopters had to be hospital-based to integrate with medical staff, as well as equipment maintenance and supply. Further, close ties between hospital and medical retrieval personnel were vital to good communication and planning. The only thing operationally wrong with our service was that we did not have the finances to afford a larger helicopter. Even so, because of our sponsorship funds, we could operate a larger helicopter at the necessary standard far more cheaply than the ambulance service.

This was the message we took to every politician, journalist and high-profile person we could think of. We were fighting for survival.

20

In March 1988 both the SLSA and CareFlight were called to the Health Minister's office. The minister announced that the report's recommendations would not be accepted and our services would be allowed to continue. In addition, both services would receive a grant. The amount was fairly small but it was better than the kick in the teeth we'd been half expecting.

This political battle was won, but another was brewing. The ambulance union was threatening to blackban our service in the Wollongong area. The union accused CareFlight and SLSA of encroaching on the area of operation covered by the National Safety Council chopper that flew with their paramedics. The aviation division of the Victorian branch of the NSC had, some time prior to this, begun operating from Albion Park near Wollongong. The NSC was not interested in providing a retrieval service, just making helicopters available to any government service that wished to pay for its aircraft. The whole operation was clouded in some mystery. There was no doubt that its Bell 412 aircraft and aerial operation were run to the highest possible standard, but from what source the council received sufficient funds to pay for it all, no one had any idea.

There wasn't one shred of evidence that we had encroached on anyone's turf, unless at the request of the New South Wales Ambulance Service. The matter was raised at yet another Health Department Retrieval Committee meeting and we were able to produce all the evidence required to substantiate our defence.

We decided to use the opportunity to ask why we were being called to so few accident scenes. We strongly believed that many of the trauma cases would be better managed if we were called to the accident site itself rather than left to wait till we were called to a small hospital that was unable to cope with the incoming injuries. We wanted the opportunity to educate, to devise protocols as to when the helicopter should be called to an accident scene, and eventually it was agreed that this was a subject that needed to be investigated.

Finally we reminded the committee that we were not, nor would we ever want to be, in competition with the ambulance service; and in fact, since day one we had been lobbying to have ambulance service officers on our crew. The request was deemed not possible. The issue seemed to fizzle, and we were left wondering why people couldn't see that we were all on the same side.

'Let's get a bigger helicopter,' said Ian quietly.

By now I was used to him raising the stakes just when it was least expected, but this time even I nearly choked on my coffee. It was May 1988 and to say that our financial situation was precarious was a severe understatement.

We were in the middle of a committee meeting in the little central office CareFlight maintained at 79½ George Street. The building stood in The Rocks, the site of Australia's first European settlement. What better place to face impossible odds?

In ten minutes we had drawn up plans for a massive expansion. We left the meeting bursting with enthusiasm. Stuff the detractors. We'd just keep pushing ahead till no one could possibly believe we weren't the right service for the job.

Already we were the only rescue helicopter service in the state that staffed its base twenty-four hours a day. No other service came even close to our medical capability. Our weakest area was the aircraft we flew, but we were going to see if we could become the gold standard there too.

Blair summed up the plan succinctly. 'In six months I've learnt that you guys have a habit of biting off more than you can chew; and then chewing it!' I couldn't have put it better myself.

Some cases seemed to happen in threes, and this was the season for motorbike riders to run into power poles or trees. We were on our way to Bowral to retrieve an injured rider. Bowral is some one hundred kilometres south-west of Westmead; at least the air ambulance service was beginning to accept that they could not compete with our response times to areas within this distance from our base. So when a good clinical argument could be made for rapid transfer, they were starting to authorise helicopter retrievals from sites that six months ago had been strictly fixed-wing territory.

We arrived in Bowral at three-thirty in the morning, some forty-five minutes after being called out. The man had hit a power pole at high speed and had been found twenty metres from his motorbike. His left lower leg was still attached to the bike. In addition to the traumatic amputation, he had sustained fractures to both thighs, right kneecap, left arm and face. He was unconscious on arrival, and only superb resuscitation by the local ambulance officers, doctors and nurses had kept him alive this far. Despite such severe injuries, it was just a standard transfer for us: continue the anaesthesia, pump in the blood and fluids, maintain oxygen levels, and get him to the hospital best suited to his condition.

Mission accomplished, aircraft sponged out and ready for the next mission, and we were home by sunrise.

In the second case a twenty-year-old lad had suffered a massive skull facture, cleaving open his skull and leaving part of his brain exposed. Once again it was a 3 am call-out, this time to Orange, and the patient was well stabilised prior to our arrival. Time was of the essence and we were on the ground for only twenty minutes. The normally furnace-like cabin heater failed on the return trip, which was no fun at high altitude over the mountains in midwinter. The temperature was so low that all the monitors failed because their batteries could no longer function. At least the ventilator was oxygen powered, and I could still check the patient's colour and feel his pulse – if I stopped shivering long enough. Still, the low temperature was probably good for his brain.

In spite of these challenges, his condition remained stable, and by 6 am a brain scan had been completed. He had a significant haematoma on the brain. The pressure of this blood clot was pushing his brain out through the skull fractures. The clot was removed and the bone fragments resited to their correct positions. Four days later the man was awake and transferred from the ICU to the general ward. He was alert and orientated. Like nearly all our patients, he remembered nothing about the ride of his life.

A week later the third victim's case was not so routine. The patient deteriorated from fully conscious to deeply unconscious as we flew out to Campbelltown Hospital to collect her. No sooner were we on the ground than we proceeded to anaesthetise her in an attempt to lower her brain pressure. Everything ran smoothly until just after takeoff.

The woman's left pupil dilated over the course of a few minutes. This was an ominous sign. The compressed brain was trying to squeeze down through its supporting membranes in the base of the skull, pressing so hard on the nerves to the eye that they were deprived of oxygen, hence the dilated pupil. The brainstem, next to the optical nerves, might also be deprived of oxygen and this would very likely prove fatal. I increased the ventilator settings and administered two hundred millilitres of Mannitol. There was no change.

The only thing left was to further dehydrate her with diuretics and induce deep barbiturate anaesthesia. I administered the drugs and by the time we were on the ground the pupil was returning to a normal size. We had radioed ahead to warn of our precarious situation and the Westmead trauma team was waiting for us. There was no blood clot and the management I had begun was the definitive treatment for her condition. Eight days later she was discharged from the ICU, well on her way to recovery.

I remembered that young doctor on the railway platform, desperate to help the head-injured boy but without a clue as to where to begin. I wished I could go back in time and give that young man the knowledge I had now. No matter how many lives I saved, it was those I hadn't been able to save that stayed with me.

■ ■ ■

Being an obsessive perfectionist is not always a good thing in life, but it is essential in operating a rescue helicopter. At the beginning of each duty shift it would take the crew over an hour to complete all the required checks to ensure that we were prepared for any possible mission. As the crew doctor this involved me checking my own state of readiness, selecting and adjusting rescue harnesses and, with the crewman, checking all rescue equipment including stretchers, winches, roping gear and radios. Once this was done I would start the long and arduous task of checking the medical equipment. There were several hundred items to run through, from on-board oxygen supplies down to the expiry dates of every single ampoule in the medical pack. While we were able to devise ways of streamlining the procedure, it was never a task that anybody looked forward to.

Sometimes missions were called at the beginning of the shift before the checks had been completed. In these cases it was necessary to rely on the crew from the previous shift to have done their job thoroughly. However, it was all too easy after the completion of a rescue for the crew to be so exhausted that restocking the aircraft did not receive the attention it required. On one occasion these two circumstances – an early mission and weary crew – combined with disastrous consequences.

We were tasked to a mountain rescue minutes after our shift began one Sunday evening. The rescue was completed without incident but no sooner had we touched down at Westmead than a medical transfer was required, and it seemed only a few minutes later that we were dispatched to Katoomba Hospital to transfer a multiple trauma patient. We departed for the mountain town around midnight, cold and exhausted.

The motor-vehicle accident victim had received severe head and chest injuries, and a tube had been inserted into his chest to reinflate his collapsed lung. I commenced a general anaesthetic to be continued throughout the return to Westmead. This involved giving further sedation, paralysing all his muscles and inserting a tube into his windpipe prior to placing him on an automatic ventilator. We had all done this many, many times before and were well rehearsed for any possible in-flight emergencies. We were not, however, prepared for what would unfold during this flight.

The temperature had dropped well below freezing when the ambulance arrived back at Katoomba oval and the waiting helicopter. I had wrapped the patient well to avoid hypothermia and we hurriedly transferred him to the aircraft. I sat in the left rear on the floor, my legs straddling the stretcher, which had replaced the left-hand seat. From this position I could watch the regular rise and fall of the patient's chest and ensure the ventilator was working normally and sufficient oxygen was being delivered. There was little else to do during the transfer as all the anaesthesia drugs were being delivered automatically via an electronic syringe pump.

Five minutes into the flight things started to go drastically wrong. I noticed that the left side of the patient's chest was no longer moving. This could mean one of two things: either his left lung had collapsed again or the tube down his windpipe had shifted down too far and was in the main bronchus tube supplying his right lung and therefore robbing his left lung of any ventilation. The normal procedure in this case is to have a look down the back of the patient's throat with a laryngoscope, withdraw the tube back to the windpipe opening and then reposition it just far enough into the windpipe to allow ventilation.

I ran through the procedure with Wayne, our crew chief, then inserted the laryngoscope into the patient's mouth. I could easily see where the tube entered his windpipe. I asked Wayne to decrease the pressure inside the balloon around the end of the tube, which sealed the tube in the patient's windpipe and helped maintain its position. What I had not realised was that the head of the ventilator connected to the tube was actually pulling at the tube. No sooner had Wayne deflated the balloon than the tube flipped out of the patient's windpipe into the back of his throat. While this was annoying, it was not particularly hazardous; I simply had to withdraw the tube from the mouth and reinsert it back down the windpipe.

'Pass me the scissors,' I asked Wayne, intending to untie the tape that held the external part of the tube around the patient's mouth.

Wayne quickly inspected the medical equipment. 'They're not here!' We scoured around for them frantically, but to no avail.

Our rescue knives would have done the job just as well, but they were stowed with our harnesses in the unreachable rear compartment of the Squirrel. Unless we did something fast, our paralysed patient, his lungs already extensively damaged, would not survive long.

'Pass me the ventilation bag!' I shouted.

'That's not here either,' replied Wayne desperately.

We looked at each other in horror. We knew straightaway what had happened. There had been no time for us to check the equipment before the start of our shift and the previous crew had not completed their checks at the end of their busy day.

Our patient's pulse rate had started to increase. A glance at the monitor showed that we had very little time to spare – his oxygen levels had already dropped significantly and the cardiograph tracing was showing signs of oxygen starvation to his heart. John had increased the flight speed to maximum but we all knew that we were ten minutes from the nearest helipad, where we would be able to retrieve our rescue knives. At this rate the crisis would be over well before that.

Exhaustion and adrenaline were battling each other as I tried to think straight. 'Pass me the Magill's forceps,' I told Wayne. These curved forceps allowed me to manipulate the breathing tube, but I was unable to insert it back down the man's windpipe. The best I could do was to hold the tip of the tube near the windpipe, turn the ventilator to maximum and hope that some oxygen would get to his lungs.

'I'll hold the tube here; see if you can undo the knot holding it in place.' It was all I could think of.

Thankfully some oxygen must have been getting to the man's lungs because although his oxygen levels were dangerously low, they did not continue to deteriorate. For five minutes I held myself frozen so that the tube would not move, and slowly, as I counted each passing second, Wayne picked away at the knot. The instant it was untied I repositioned the tube correctly in his windpipe and resumed the ventilation. Oxygen levels improved marginally but the left side of his chest remained still.

It was then I realised my error. If I hadn't been so anxious to hurry the loading of the patient into the helicopter in the freezing weather, I might not have made such a simple mistake. In my cold and exhausted state I had inadvertently concealed under a blanket the reservoir bag to the tube draining his lung; unmonitored, this had become blocked. I wrenched the connector of the bag away from the chest tube. Bloodstained gas gushed out and within seconds the left side of the patient's chest was moving again. As we touched down at Westmead, his vital signs had returned to normal.

While we waited for the rotor system to stop so we could unload, the three of us stared wordlessly at each other. We had come this close to an in-flight death due to a failure in our protocols. The sun was peering over the eastern horizon when we returned from the casualty department. Without a word being said, we placed a spare ventilation bag and scissors in the cabin of the aircraft. Each was attached to a cable and screwed to the rear bulkhead so that it could never be removed.

21

Our expansion plans had begun. The first task was to decide which aircraft to purchase. We knew that the Aerospatiale Dauphin N was our preferred model. Ian, John and I had examined services that flew these aircraft in the United States and were convinced they were the best compromise medium helicopter for our work. A Dauphin N would give us triple the cabin space of the Squirrel, have twin engines, carry a two-person winch and have the potential for all-weather flights.

The following day John and I met with the Australian Aerospatiale representatives and, after some discussions, were shattered to find that the aircraft of our dreams was millions of dollars beyond our reach. Ain't that always the way! However, second-hand aircraft of the earlier Dauphin C model might be available and within our budget. The older model had the same internal dimensions; the differences lay mainly in construction technology, airspeed and appearance.

A few days later John and I were flown to Melbourne by Aerospatiale to visit the Victorian Police air wing. They flew three of the Dauphin Cs, both as police observation and ambulance helicopters. For two days we discussed the aircraft with the pilots, crewmen and ambulance officers. We stripped the aircraft down, made hundreds of measurements, weighed equipment and pored over every flight and procedure manual they possessed. I was flabbergasted by the amount of equipment the ambulance considered essential – their medical equipment weighed ninety kilos more than we presently carried in our single-engined Squirrel.

When I told John this, his reply was: 'Don't even think about it, the equipment you carry is too heavy already!' I don't think he was joking.

We returned to Sydney full of enthusiasm. As luck would have it, a Dauphin identical to one used by the Victorian Police but with more powerful C2 engines became available in Kuching, Malaysia. It was used for VIP transport and was in mint condition. I was spared the incredible financial dealings and responsibilities required to raise the money for this aircraft, but within a few weeks a deal had been made and before long the aircraft would be winging its way to Sydney.

My main concern at this stage was how to install our medical equipment. I knew that anything involving aviation or medical design was expensive. When it involved both, the cost was astronomical. Moreover, none of the fancy medical fit-outs I had seen on a reconnaissance trip to the USA were compatible with our rescue role. We needed to have flat, clear floor space for performing winch rescues and for winching rescue stretchers on board. All the medical stretcher fits in the USA would take over half an hour to be removed by a licensed aircraft engineer. By that time the patient could have died of natural causes!

Even if we could solve all our logistical difficulties, we were continually challenged with the problem of how to maintain life support between the hospital and the aircraft at either end of the retrieval. Presently we had no choice but to remove the equipment and place it ad hoc on top of the patient. The process was haphazard, time consuming and presented a real risk to the whole crew in the event of an accident – a ten-kilo monitor could become a lethal missile in a crash.

I was starting to get the glimmer of an idea. One redeeming factor of my time in England was to have worked on perfecting a system for transporting patients from the ICU to the brain scanner or operating theatres. A trolley had been designed with several shelves containing all the necessary life-support equipment, which could easily be wheeled up to and attached to a patient's bed to form a single unit. Once the patient had been attached to all the equipment, the bed could be wheeled anywhere in the hospital with the trolley attached.

I started to wonder whether there was a way to adapt the English concept to our needs, and I knew one of our former doctors, Howard Roby, was working on a similar idea at the hospital in Griffith. Using our existing stretchers as a base, I drew up a box with two shelves and four legs that could fit over the patient and carry all our life-support and monitoring equipment. I made a crude cardboard mock-up using boxes I pinched from the hospital rubbish bins. I was beginning to think that the thing might have potential.

What I needed now was an engineer, but I wanted to keep this away from aircraft companies or I would never stay within budget. Our office was in the most isolated corner of Westmead, two floors above the Biomedical Engineering Department, which serviced all the hospital's equipment. I thought they might know who could help with the project; they knew just the person – their own engineer, Rob Wilkins. Everything I needed to make the concept a reality was on site at Westmead!

After a few weeks of discussions Rob and I decided the idea was feasible and I took it to the CareFlight committee. I explained how the bridge would work. We would slide our standard stretcher under the patient as soon as we arrived on scene, then place the stretcher bridge, as I called it, over the patient and attach it to our stretcher. Then we could transfer the patient from the hospital life support equipment to our equipment on the bridge. Once complete, we could commence the transfer. The only thing we would have to disconnect throughout the transfer would be the oxygen supply.

I told the committee that minimal modifications were needed in the Dauphin fit-out, which got the pilots and bean-counters on side. To this I added that in a rescue situation we could fly with the stretcher on the opposite side of the aircraft to the winch, leaving free floor space. If necessary the stretcher and bridge could be removed in seconds at a staging site near the rescue, providing a clear floor and removing thirty-seven kilos of weight from the chopper. The pilots and rescue crewmen were very happy!

Finally, Rob, John and I had done the measurements and the equipment would fit inside the Squirrel, so we could build it and start using it before the Dauphin was ready to fly.

Everyone thought it sounded great. I was given the go-ahead. This was the beauty of not being a government department. If anybody had a good idea, the whole organisation became stepping stones, not stumbling blocks, to making the idea a reality.

Working with the police was a continual part of the job. Without exception they were a fantastic support. One day, however, I overstepped the mark with them.

I was called to assist at a truck accident in the northern suburbs. The helicopter was on another mission so I was taken by ambulance control car to the crash site, complete with my medical pack and four units of O negative universal donor blood in case a transfusion was required.

The site was one of devastation. Nearly two hundred dead bodies lay scattered around the truck where it had driven off the embankment – pig carcasses. Fortunately the two men driving the vehicle from the abattoir to the wholesale butchers were still alive, but they were buried in the cabin under all the pigs.

It was a bizarre scene: police scratching their heads at what to do; fire-brigade officers carting the pig carcasses up the steep incline one by one to gain access to the two men; ambulance officers trying to make contact with the victims and continually slipping over on the pork grease that covered everything.

'I haven't seen this many pigs at a crash for years!' I exclaimed without thinking.

If looks could kill, the police superintendent would have been guilty of murder. The fire chief and ambulance controller doubled up laughing as the superintendent lectured me about respect for his fellow officers.

It took nearly an hour to reach the two men; one was lying face down outside the truck with the truck cabin resting on top of him; the other was squashed under the dashboard. It was obvious that it would be some time before either of them could be cut free, and both were in extreme pain.

Compression syndrome was a real threat. As areas of the body that had been compressed were released, massive amounts of metabolic wastes and potassium could pour into the bloodstream, causing the heart to stop. We prepared for this eventuality by inserting in intravenous lines and making sure that the men received adequate fluid replacements prior to any attempts to remove them. We also prepared infusions of dextrose and insulin and sodium bicarbonate to treat any abnormal heart rhythms.

I gave both men repeated doses of intravenous morphine as the painstakingly slow process of extricating them continued. The fellow under the truck was freed first. Amazingly his injuries were minimal and he was transported to hospital while we stayed with his partner. It was another two hours before he could be released. As the pressure of the crushed dashboard came off his abdomen, his heart rate slowed. He demonstrated the characteristic changes on his cardiograph consistent with compression syndrome, but just as we were about to administer the drugs, the changes resolved spontaneously. Although he had a dislocated hip, a fractured skull and multiple bruising and abrasions, the man was remarkably unscathed.

And what happened to the pig carcasses? I don't know, except that in the coming weeks there were rumours of numerous barbecues at fire stations across the city.

Blair was doing a larger share of the missions to give me more time to complete my managerial and political duties, and to work on the stretcher bridge. The feedback I was getting about Blair from the hospitals was excellent and that matched my assessment of his performance. However, somewhere in the ambulance service there were people who just didn't get along with him, and several complaints were made to the relevant committees about his work.

I was appointed to a working group that examined all such complaints, and we could not fault his work. What we did realise, however, was that complaints were more likely when Blair deviated from standard ambulance service protocol, as was his right as a senior physician. One complaint consisted of whether in a resuscitation he should have put in a chest drain before intubating the patient as per ambulance protocol, rather than doing it the other way around as he had. Blair was nothing if not thorough. His written reply to the allegation of mismanagement was a fifty-six-page treatise on options in the treatment of severe chest injuries, giving a detailed account of the pros and cons of his decision. The report contained numerous references to textbooks and journal articles, most of which he knew off the top of his head. Somehow the complaints rapidly diminished after that.

Our feeling was that if ambulance officers were allowed to fly with us they would be able to spread the word that we didn't have horns growing out of our heads!

Despite the pressure he was under, Blair never lost his sense of humour. He was always looking at ways to contribute more to the service and he decided to start a newsletter called 'Idle Torque'. It was a terrific way of looking at the organisation's lighter side – we needed a few laughs; we certainly weren't getting many from all the committees we were constantly asked to front up to. Apart from briefing people on goings-on, both professional and personal, it became an antidote to the seriousness of our work. No effort was spared by the contributors to have a dig at each other. Blair was an accomplished cartoonist and his quick wit and pen were never slow to see the funny side of any event. The effect on morale was enormous and each issue was eagerly awaited – the organisation would all but grind to a halt for half an hour after its distribution.

The Dauphin touched down at Bankstown Airport while we were out there for a routine service of the Squirrel. Aerospatiale had flown it from Kuching, with a three-week stopover in the Celebes Islands for a mechanical problem. Or so they said – we thought they just fancied a holiday! The chopper came complete with a walnut drinks cabinet, large swivelling lounge chairs and illuminated signs in Arabic reading, 'In Allah We Trust'. The chairs and cabinet went but the signs stayed.

Two foam cushions would attach to the rear bulkheads and serve as the attendants' seats. As usual the comfy pilot seat would remain. We jokingly argued for keeping the executive armchairs, but for some reason no one was convinced. Without doubt the radio gear would make this the most sophisticated communications aircraft in the country, allowing it to be an airborne command and control centre.

Meanwhile a prototype shell was completed for the stretcher bridge project. The system seemed to slip on and off the stretcher easily and it was large enough to accommodate the necessary equipment. All that remained was to see whether it was strong enough to meet the requirements of the Civil Aviation Authority, as the DOTC was now known.

We had to determine whether it would survive a ten g's crash – deceleration at ten times the force of gravity. Would it hold up under such massive acceleration loads or would it buckle or disintegrate? To test it, the aircraft stretcher was bolted vertically to one of the hospital walls with the bridge attached. We placed a large metal plate on the front of the bridge and proceeded to load twenty-five-kilo bags of cement onto the plate. One by one we continued, each time expecting something to give way. We needed it to support ten bags. As the tenth bag was lowered, Blair and I could barely watch; even Rob, Peter and Murray, who had built the thing, were rigid. Only the aircraft engineer looked confident. The tenth bag was lowered on. It held! Similar tests were done on the sides and the aircraft engineer approved the design for aircraft use. The stretcher bridge concept was a reality.

22

'Drowning near Camden!' John yelled as he ran from the equipment shed. Terry Mortimer, John and I had barely finished checking the aircraft on this frosty winter morning when the emergency phone had rung. John had rushed inside to answer it.

What crazy person would go swimming in this weather, I wondered. And how do you drown in Camden? There are no rivers there and it was forty kilometres inland from our base in western Sydney.

I hated drowning cases. It seemed we were always too late and they all died. In the past eight years it had been the same story again and again: if we didn't arrive early enough to rescue a relieved and exhausted swimmer, we performed a body recovery.

I had learnt to cope with deaths from trauma. After so many crash victims I was numb to it all. It had become almost easy to accept death when there was blood, broken bones and bandages to explain it. But drownings left no blood, no marks; it was as though the victim had just fallen asleep. Each time I dealt with a drowning victim I felt angry and frustrated at my helplessness. So close to life, yet so far.

I experienced the usual sense of futility as we followed ambulance directions south-west through the mist to the outskirts of Sydney. Do the best you can, I told myself. Make sure the bystanders realise we tried our hardest.

Luckily, we spotted the rotating beacons of the ambulance shining through the murk directly on the track we were following. This saved precious time. Below we saw the vehicle parked between a caravan and a small dam on a farm miles from anywhere. We were on the ground fifteen minutes after receiving the call.

As the rotors wound down I raced over to the two paramedics and general duties ambulance officers who were kneeling near the dam, while John and Terry unloaded the medical pack and stretcher. The officers were performing basic life support on a little girl, aided by a stricken-looking man who could only be her father.

'We've been going for twenty minutes, the cardiograph tracings are on the machine,' gasped one of the paramedics. In spite of the cold they were flushed and sweaty with exertion. Terry took over the heart massage and the man walked over to a distraught woman who was shivering severely in dripping clothing and sodden woollen boots. Mum and Dad, I thought.

'Her name is Tina, she's four years old,' one of the paramedics told me. 'She and a friend left the caravan to pick flowers about an hour ago. Fifteen minutes later her mum found her face down in the dam and dived in to rescue her. A friend and her parents started resuscitation straightaway.'

I couldn't imagine how I would feel trying to resuscitate my own child. I'm not sure I could have done it. I looked down at Tina's frail, pretty face, her long black curls, the ventilation tube sticking out between her blue lips. She was as cold and pale as marble. No pulse; worse, no response from her widely dilated pupils. That invariably meant the end of the road. There were reams of heart monitor tracings that told of Tina's struggle to live, and the hopelessness of that struggle.

As usual the paramedics' and ambulance officers' resuscitation techniques had been done to perfection, but in spite of numerous attempts with both drugs and the defibrillator to restart her heart, she was presently in ventricular fibrillation. For brief moments her heart had restarted but each time her rhythm had failed and she had arrested again.

With the parents standing beside us we had to rely on nonverbal communication with the paramedics. Their expressions were grim and one of them gave a subtle shake of his head. I thought I sensed the message, 'This is hopeless, she's dead.' I wondered whether the paramedics had called us because they thought there was a chance or because they wanted a doctor to make the decision to stop resuscitation. And who could blame them – it was not a decision I wanted to make either. At the very least I decided we were going to fly Tina's body to Westmead to make it clear that everything possible had been done.

It was usual to discontinue resuscitation attempts after a cardiac arrest if we couldn't restart the heart within twenty minutes. We were over forty minutes into this case. It was time to call this arrest. Time to say 'enough'. I scanned back through all the cardiogram tracings one last time before making my decision. I knew that if I did, we would continue the masquerade of resuscitation into the aircraft but cease once we were in the air and out of sight of the parents. It was then I realised what the first tracing was. I felt the adrenaline surge through my system as I checked and rechecked the waveform.

Yes! Oh yes!

Had it not been for a chance tutorial about rare ECG tracings just prior to my specialist exams the previous year I would have missed it. I had never seen it anywhere except in the textbooks. On first glance I had thought it was an idioventricular rhythm or IVR. The paramedics had drawn the same conclusion. IVR is the last sigh of a dying heart and is usually irreversible. It was the sort of tracing you would expect to see when thirty minutes had elapsed between the immersion and the arrival of the paramedics. IVR means 'too late'. But the shape wasn't quite right for IVR. There was an unusual little notch on the first tracing. It wasn't IVR at all.

'J waves!' I shouted. 'She's got J waves!'

They all looked at me blankly as Terry continued the heart massage.

'Look at this first strip,' I said excitedly as I stretched the paper tracing out in front of the two paramedics. 'That's not IVR; it's an extremely slow but normal rhythm that looks like IVR. It looks that way because she has severe hypothermia. She's extremely cold. The heart monitor tracings show she didn't really have a cardiac arrest till after you arrived. There's still a chance!'

The teaching of 'They're not dead till they're warm and dead' sounded in my brain. 'Never declare someone dead if they are extremely cold,' my old boss Bob Wright used to say. 'Don't underestimate the preservative powers of cold.' Having worked as an anaesthetist on a heart surgery team I was familiar with deliberately cooling patients to protect them while they were on heart–lung bypass machines. In England I had heard of successful resuscitation attempts after prolonged immersions in the North Sea. Paradoxically, the colder the water, the more likely one could survive a lengthy immersion. People had lived long after they should have been dead due to their cold body temperature. No wonder the girl had not responded to the usual treatment. Normal resuscitation regimes only make things worse if the patient is extremely cold. Although her low body temperature was blocking the resuscitation attempts, it was preserving her vital organs. It also explained the fixed dilated pupils. Perhaps the part of her brain that controlled her eyes was still okay but was just too cold to respond. The chances were slim and without precedent in the warm climate of Sydney, but in an instant my whole body was energised with hope.

We were never going to improve things with her lying half naked on the ground on this chilly morning and there was nothing I could do to warm her up except wrap her in a foil blanket. She needed rewarming in a hospital, and intensive care support as she did so. It was a good decision by the paramedics to call us.

'Another dose of Atropine!' I barked. 'Get ready to load and go!'

As John and Terry unfolded the stretcher I had the paramedic stop his heart compressions. 'There's a pulse!' I whispered. I wanted the others to know there was a chance but I knew it was a slim one. I didn't want to fill the parents with false hope.

I left John, Terry and the paramedics to start loading Tina into the chopper so that I could have a quick word to her parents. I was never one to use euphemisms and always preferred to play it straight. I told them her chances were slim but whatever happened they were to know that the initial resuscitation they had given was superb, as had been the treatment by the paramedics. I told them we would do everything we could on the way to Westmead, and there she would get the best care in the world. Not knowing what else to say I gave them a quick hug and turned back to the aircraft, which was now winding up for our dash back to hospital.

'Great job,' I said to the paramedics, and I meant it. 'Could you organise an ambulance to meet us at the Westmead oval?' They nodded, not daring to hope, and closed the door of the chopper.

As I took my position behind Tina's head I prayed that this would be like one of those North Sea miracles. But I knew Sydney's climate was way too warm for a miracle. I could not remember anyone surviving such an ordeal in our mild climate. But a hundred coincidences and a chain of expertise had come together to give this little girl a glimmer of hope and I decided she was just going to have to be the first.

'Don't you dare give up on me now, little princess!' I whispered as we lifted off.

Barely two hundred metres into the initial climb I lost the pulse. It had been feeble on the ground and perhaps the movement of the aircraft was masking it. The heart rhythm still looked okay, but I wasn't going to take any risks. It could be that the heart wasn't pumping and the heart rhythm would cease any moment.

'I think we've lost output!' I told Terry and John, and lengthened my lap belt to the limit so I could lean over her tiny body and continue pumping her chest.

As the ventilator continued to breathe for her, Terry and I shared the task of pumping her heart, desperately hoping we would not become too exhausted to continue. I remember focusing on Tina's face, pale and delicate, framed by matted muddy hair. I remember my radio calls; the rest is a blank.

Come on, come on! Go faster! I urged. From where I knelt I could see the engine gauges and knew John was pushing the Squirrel as hard as it would go. No change. Come on, princess, you and I are going to do this! I don't know whether I said these words aloud, but they ran round and round inside my head like a mantra.

The door of the helicopter burst open. I was so intent on Tina's treatment I hadn't even noticed the final approach and landing. The ambulance officers helped us to unload while the aircraft was still running. As soon as we got into the ambulance I asked them not to turn the engine on till I felt her pulse. It was there. Feeble but present. I slumped into my seat in the back of the vehicle, exhausted. Thank God, I thought. I just couldn't pump any longer.

Ten agonising minutes later Tina was in the emergency room and the arrest team took over. Looking haggard with fatigue and worry, I related events to the team. Drips, tubes, blood tests, X-rays, everything became a blur. The blood results were all wildly abnormal; but just what would be expected from severe hypothermia.

'Don't get your hopes up, we're in Australia, not Iceland,' some well-meaning person said behind me as I wrote up the case records at the central desk. I glared at her and walked wearily away. There was nothing more I could do. I took one final look at Tina half buried in a sea of medical equipment. I thought I saw her make a feeble attempt to gasp, but it didn't happen again.

For the rest of the day I just couldn't stop thinking about how I could have done a better job. I analysed the mission until I thought my head would burst. I should have done this; I should have done that; I should have picked those J waves straightaway. I nearly stopped a resuscitation on a patient with hypothermia. Damn it, I rebuked myself, I was an anaesthesia and intensive care specialist, I shouldn't make mistakes like that.

Rage finally submitted to hopelessness. No one had survived a scenario like this in Sydney before. I eventually conceded that if Tina didn't make it, at least she had had the best help the world could offer. Now she was under Fran's care, and if Fran and the ICU team couldn't save her, no one could. I decided that would be my consoling message to her parents. I was so sick of saying that to people.

Events of the next two days took over and we seemed to fly nonstop with only brief hours of sleep in between. All through the days and nights I replayed the events of Tina's retrieval in an endless loop. I completed my last flight of the shift around late morning on Monday. It was over forty-eight hours since the shift had begun, and I was beyond exhaustion. After handing over our last patient to the emergency room, I went straight to the ICU. I felt like a man walking to his own execution. I took a breath, braced myself for the inevitable news, and pushed through the heavy flap doors.

In the first bay were eight beds. Each was occupied by a shape barely recognisable as a human being buried under miles of plastic tubing. Ventilators sighed in a regular but uncoordinated rhythm, and each of the bedside monitors tried to outbeep its neighbours. The nursing staff sombrely adjusted dials and recorded every alteration on large spreadsheets attached to boards at the base of every bed.

My heart was pounding as I forced my way to the second bay where Tina's bed lay. When I had worked in intensive care, we had started the morning ward round informally by noting which beds were empty. We used this euphemism rather than enquiring who had died. It was a way of coping. Logically we knew that patients were admitted to the ICU to increase the prospect of certain death to an eighty-per-cent chance of survival, but it was still hard to bear the fact that one-fifth of our patients did not leave alive.

Every bed had a white plate with the patient's name written in black marker pen. I looked at each one till I found the bed with Tina's name. The ventilator lay silent and the monitors were blank. The bed was empty.

My worst fears were confirmed. And my heart ripped. Once again, as had happened with so many of our patients, the die was cast before we even arrived on the scene. What a terrible waste of a young life. I felt my capable, controlled persona begin to disintegrate.

Then someone behind me said hello.

I spun around. It was the ICU's nurse manager. The significance of that was not lost on me. Here comes the explanation. For a moment I was consumed by an upwelling of anger and grief.

Then I realised that it wasn't the nurse who had said hello. It had been a child's voice. I looked down to see who was in the wheelchair the nurse was pushing.

It was a gorgeous little girl in a ridiculously large hospital gown. She had long black hair, pink cheeks and red lips. 'Debbie said that you are the doctor who saved my life. Is that true?'

Real men don't cry, I know, but I suppose at that moment I must have forgotten to be a real man. Tears of joy rolled down my cheeks as I stared in amazement at the girl before me. Trembling, I knelt down and hugged her. 'Just one of many,' I replied, and thought of the hundreds of people linked to her miraculous survival.

I held Tina at arm's length and stared. 'We've just been out shampooing her hair,' the nurse explained. It was hard to recognise her. Saturday's vacant stare and blue-white skin were gone; the tangled dirty hair was clean and shiny; her cheeks were rosy and her sky blue eyes full of life. Only the telltale marks extending from the corner of each lip across her cheeks, where the ventilator tube had been tightly tied in, identified her as the same girl we had fought so hard for.

Once in intensive care, Tina's heart had continued to beat spontaneously as she had slowly warmed up. Gradually her blood tests had become more normal and her brain had started to function. She'd begun to breathe spontaneously and from there she recovered rapidly. While she would require several more days of heart monitoring in the children's ward, her condition and all her tests had essentially returned to normal. She was to be discharged from the ICU that morning.

Just then Tina's parents arrived. The fatigue of their weekend vigil was barely visible through the beaming smiles and gratefulness they expressed to us all. I couldn't wait to get back to the hangar to break the good news. This was why CareFlight existed. This seemed to make all our personal sacrifices worthwhile.

That night I lay in a happy, self-satisfied state, musing over the mission. As usual I had written to the paramedics to tell them of the outcome. The fact that Tina was going to be okay was a shining example of cooperation between emergency services with all politics left aside.

I tried to imagine how many thousands of people had contributed in some way to Tina's survival. The inner circle might have been the paramedics, the CareFlight team and the hospital staff, but it rippled outwards from there. Thinking not only of who was involved in the CareFlight contribution, it extended to the ambulance control room that called us in, to the maintenance staff who ensured the aircraft could get us to the accident scene, to the administrators like Ian Badham and all the other support staff who kept CareFlight flying but never got to fly themselves. This victory also belonged to the companies that sponsored CareFlight, putting contribution to society ahead of dividends. There were hundreds of community clubs that ran sausage sizzles and raffles and sports days to fundraise for us, and thousands of private donors who supported us from their hard-earned wages. They, and many more, were all part of the team that had kept Tina alive.

Soon Tina returned home under the careful eye of the children's rehabilitation specialists. There appeared to be no lasting effects from her ordeal. John, Terry and I were guests of honour at her next birthday party.

In my final days working for CareFlight the Health Minister, Peter Collins, opened our new operations base. He used Tina's story to illustrate why New South Wales needed CareFlight and why the government had boosted our funding. He held Tina's hand as she cut the ribbon. It made great press.

23

My measured and calm actions concealed the frustration and rage I felt inside as we desperately tried to keep the young man alive. He was going to die while we sat stranded just three hundred metres from the Westmead emergency room. There was nothing we could do except continue the resuscitation procedures and wait for help to arrive.

Starved of blood and oxygen the man's exhausted heart had abruptly slowed as we approached to land at Westmead. We weren't keeping up with the blood loss from his ruptured spleen and liver. He was receiving one hundred per cent oxygen from the ventilator; there was just too little blood to get it from his lungs to the rest of his body. His pulse was down to twenty beats per minute and any moment it would stop. Cardiac arrest due to blood loss is almost always irreversible.

I injected a dose of adrenaline and turned to Col Robshaw, the ambulance officer who was unofficially moonlighting as one of our volunteer rescue crewmen on his day off. 'Another ampoule of Atropine!' I demanded urgently.

While Col complied, I reviewed how Ken Vote, the pilot, was doing. As soon as we had landed he had abandoned his seat and raced around to our side of the chopper to help pump blood into the man's veins. He was still pumping two drips as fast as he could.

For over ten minutes we had been sitting on the ground at the sports oval, waiting for an ambulance to drive us up to the emergency receiving room where the trauma team was assembled and waiting. The helipad adjacent to the emergency room was clear but we were forbidden to use it.

The ambulance arrived, bouncing over the gutter and rapidly backing up to the aircraft door. Central District Ambulance knew of our dilemma and had done well to provide us with transport on this frantic Friday night.

We bundled our man into the ambulance and jumped aboard. Ten minutes later we were in the emergency room. Extra lines were inserted and blood was pumped in furiously. Slowly the heart rate picked up. Five minutes later the patient was on his way to theatre. He survived, but only just.

I could handle the clinical stresses of the case but I was incensed at the Civil Aviation Authority rules that, while professing to protect the public, were in fact putting lives at risk. What was the point of us all working ourselves ragged to help save people's lives, only to have crazy bureaucratic regulations undermine us?

The helipad ban almost caused the death of another of my patients. The extra time getting into hospital was, for him, crucial. Thankfully, luck was on his side, but I knew it was only a matter of time before a patient didn't make it. That patient turned out to be Blair's.

The middle-aged man had been admitted to Liverpool Hospital with chest pain. In addition to all the textbook symptoms of a heart attack, he had no pulse in his left arm. This suggested that his aorta was slowly rupturing, preventing blood from reaching the vessels that supplied his heart muscle and arm. A chest X-ray confirmed this diagnosis and his only chance of survival was immediate cardiac surgery.

CareFlight was called at 11.30 pm. By 12.35 am Blair had flown to Liverpool and was in the air on the way back to Westmead. The patient's condition had deteriorated further and just after takeoff he had arrested.

Blair and the crewman applied CPR and one minute later the man's heart rhythm was restored. But as the aircraft landed, his heart rate abruptly slowed again. Blair resuscitated him and continued with the CPR as the ambulance transferred them to the hospital's emergency department. The flight had taken ten minutes, the in-hospital ground transfer twelve.

By the time Blair and the ambulance officers wheeled the patient into the emergency room it was all over – the man's heart had stopped. Resuscitation attempts were continued for only a few more minutes before it was decided to abandon them. Blair was devastated. No matter how hopeless the case, the fact was, the man had died in his care. We tried to tell Blair that it wasn't his fault, but he still felt a terrible sense of responsibility, as did the whole team whenever a patient didn't make it.

The latest request for re-opening the pad had been knocked back. John and the Helicopter Association of Australia had been pushing as hard as they dared, but still the CAA refused, because – and this was the crazy part – people's lives would be put at risk if helicopters were to use the pad. This was insane. How many more bodies did the authorities want to be presented with before they came to their senses? A line had been drawn in the sand. It was time to step up the pressure.

Fran and I worked into the night, preparing yet another submission, making phone calls, writing reports. The next day we talked to the deceased man's wife, who bravely consented to our proposed course of action. We were interviewed by the police that afternoon and the wheels were set in motion.

Finding somewhere to land was not just a problem on helicopter retrievals. One day I found myself stuck above cloud in an air ambulance with our options running out as fast as the fuel.

I had been dispatched to Moree, six hundred kilometres north-west of Sydney, to retrieve a patient with a ruptured aneurysm in the base of his brain. The clinical picture I had been given suggested that he had suffered a significant bleed and required urgent neurosurgical management.

The weather report had not been good but we had taken off in the hope that we would be able to get through. Conditions deteriorated as we approached Moree. Flying in cloud was not a problem but we needed at least some visibility to land. On the final approach to the runway we could see nothing so the pilot applied full throttle and climbed away. I had the briefest glimpse of planes parked on the runway apron as we abandoned our landing. Opinion from the ground was that the weather was unlikely to improve. We had no choice but to abandon the retrieval for the time being.

As we were returning to Sydney we were ordered to land at Quirindi, which was halfway home. A routine transfer was scheduled for the next day but it made sense to pick the patient up on the way.

We lined up at Quirindi and were five seconds from touchdown when the ambulance radio bleared, 'Abandon Quirindi and return to Moree! Weather has cleared.'

For the second time that morning the throttles were opened, the undercarriage retracted and we set off for Moree, two hundred kilometres away.

The second approach was as bad as the first. The weather had closed in again and landing was impossible. Via the ambulance controller I contacted Fran. Fifteen minutes later the message came back that the patient's condition had deteriorated; there was no hope for him. Wearily, we turned for home. The only problem was that by now we did not have enough fuel to get back to Sydney. Plans were made to land at Tamworth on the way south, but as we came nearer, the weather deteriorated across the whole region and Tamworth airport was closed to all traffic.

We had been in the air for nearly five hours and our fuel supplies were getting critical. There were no airports open within reach. For the first time I saw an air ambulance pilot look worried. I knew we were in serious trouble.

Suddenly there was a break in the clouds below, the first I had seen for over an hour. I could see all the way through to the ground. To my amazement I was looking directly at a tarmac strip! 'There's a runway down there!' I shouted, and the pilot immediately banked hard left to see for himself. He could hardly believe it, but I was right.

The hole in the cloud was narrow and he wasn't going to let that runway out of his sight. He throttled back and spiralled straight down the hole for a thousand metres, eventually coming out under the cloud base with barely six hundred metres to spare. Cloud was fast approaching from the west, so he cut short the landing circuit and had us down before the clouds could drift back over the field.

'I'm guessing this is Gunnedah,' the pilot said as we taxied over to the refuelling bowser.

'I don't care where it is, it's solid ground!' was my reply.

We shut down the engines and climbed out of the plane. A local who had watched our landing stared at us open-mouthed.

'No jet fuel here, mate,' the fuel attendant told us. 'Nearest jet fuel is Tamworth.'

'We know,' we replied in unison. The attendant couldn't figure out why, in spite of the bad news, we thought this was funny.

'The coroner's inquest is tomorrow,' said the policeman.

How on earth was I meant to prepare the case in just twenty-four hours? Following the death of Blair's patient, Fran and I had lodged a complaint with the coroner in the hope that the CAA would be forced to reopen the helipad and patients in the future would have a better chance of survival. It was the only way we knew to make up for the man's death. We had received support from everyone from the Health Minister down, but still the CAA stubbornly refused to have the helipad reopened, coming up instead with the brilliant suggestion that we build a three-hundred-metre underground trolley tunnel from the oval to the emergency department!

Fran and I had been interviewed at length by the police, as had John as chief pilot. After that we heard nothing for five months. Until now. We had been summoned to the coroner's court with no time to prepare. I was beginning to worry that we were being set up.

The first thing I needed was legal representation. There was no time to find a lawyer so I made a frantic call to my old mate Dan Tyler. Dan was now acting as a relief pilot for CareFlight after several years working as chief pilot of Child Flight. In one of his previous incarnations, however, he had been a barrister, and he was as knowledgeable about aviation law as anyone I knew. But considering what had happened to Alain and John when they had challenged the CAA, was he ready to risk his career and challenge their authority in court? I rang him and without a moment's hesitation he gave me his answer: you betcha!

The next day, exhausted after having spent much of the night running through the case, Dan and I staggered into the coroner's court under the weight of mountains of notes, files and charts. I didn't have a clue what would be needed, so I'd brought everything I had.

Several representatives of the CAA and their legal team arrived looking slick and unharried. They were obviously well prepared. I felt intimidated and anxious; it seemed I had finally bitten off more than I could chew.

We stood as the coroner arrived and the legal representatives of the CAA immediately moved to make some comment. They were cut short by the coroner, who stated that he had already reached his conclusion and would be taking no further evidence or opinion.

Was this good news or bad news? I asked Dan. He shrugged and said he didn't know.

The coroner told a hushed court that he had found the care the deceased had received to have been exemplary at all times and that the death was probably inevitable regardless of the helipad situation. When he said there was no blame to be apportioned to the CAA, my heart sank. The whole exercise had been a waste of time.

However, he continued, it was in the public's best interest that a helipad be established near Westmead's emergency department and that a solution to the present impasse be found as a matter of urgency. My hopes soared.

After concluding, he looked sternly at the CAA representatives. 'Off the record, I don't ever want to see you or this problem in my court again.'

I could hardly believe my ears. The CAA representatives were obviously stunned. Dan and I grinned at each other, hopeful that now things would have to change.

Fran and I had argued hard and long for a single centralised retrieval service run by CareFlight. The service had undertaken medical retrieval services for the state without a cent of assistance from the government. We had been repeatedly told by the health department that there was no demonstrated need and we were now able to prove them wrong. In twenty-two months CareFlight had undertaken five hundred and forty-four retrievals. We presented graphs analysing our cases by location, time, medical classification and level of intervention. The vast majority were intensive care cases, two-thirds of them requiring general anaesthesia techniques to ensure stability during transport. Our case for a dedicated medical retrieval service using anaesthesia and emergency medicine specialists or supervised trainees was compelling.

The SLSA agreed; they had realised medical operations were the way of the future and had started to rebuild their medical capabilities. We were primarily a medical operation and our medical capability was far greater than theirs. This often led to disputes as to who was most suited to undertake particular retrievals. The problem of which form of transport was most appropriate was a complex issue as it required consideration of logistic, clinical and financial matters.

Finally the Health Minister, Peter Collins, agreed to formalise the use of CareFlight and SLSA as medical retrieval and medical helicopter services. Medical officers would be funded for 1989 on a trial basis; after two years of intense lobbying we were finally seeing our goals achieved. New South Wales was the first state to have a dedicated full-time medical retrieval service.

As always we were left wondering what the catch was. We were yet to realise that moves were again being made to cut CareFlight out of the equation.

Once the long-awaited Dauphin came on line – and what an amazing machine it was – we had an aircraft that met the aviation standards the health department operations committee had deemed necessary. Somewhere within that department and the ambulance service, however, there were people who just would not accept that we were able not only to provide the appropriate helicopter but also to determine who should staff it. CareFlight would never budge from the position that a senior doctor should always be on board, and we would not separate the medical and operational aspects of the service. We were absolutely convinced that integration was the key to our success.

It was quickly apparent that the Dauphin would work best with a four-person team. We had already decided that all the rescue crew should be employed full-time, as volunteers could no longer keep up-to-date with the complexity of the new aircraft. The pilot needed the crew's assistance on all legs of the flight, and the aircraft could comfortably accommodate four crew. We approached the ambulance service and offered them a full-time position on the helicopter. They told us they'd think about it.

As we now met every standard in the book, those who did not like our autonomy decided to make life difficult by insisting that the whole medical helicopter system for New South Wales be put out to tender. Only organisations that were able to meet the tender requirements straightaway could apply, even if the successful candidate would not be decided for several months. There was no way either CareFlight or SLSA could meet those requirements without guaranteed funds and several months lead time to expand operations. Once again we were fighting for our existence.

I started to wonder why I was doing this. It seemed every time we took a step forwards someone pulled the rug from under our feet. Between the helipad saga and the ambulance and health department politics, I was spending thirty or more hours a week in meetings. Blair was shouldering the burden of my clinical workload – he was a trooper and played a fundamental role in the service's survival at this time – but he was doing the work I had spent so long training for. If I'd wanted to be a politician, I certainly wouldn't have spent half my life qualifying as an anaesthetist.

One day a senior ambulance administrator took me aside. He told me we were wasting our time. The ambulance service wanted the National Safety Council's Victorian Aviation Division to supply them with helicopters. He was confident that the NSC would win the tender and assured me that when it did, doctors would only be invited on missions at the discretion of the ambulance controllers.

Members of the NSC operation at Albion Park made it clear that they were in the business of supplying helicopters to whoever could afford to hire them; how they were used was none of their business. We knew their operation was second to none. No one else in the country could match it for size or facilities. We were also told the rates they were charging the health department for the use of its aircraft, and there was no way we could compete with their prices. They were obviously making a substantial loss on the deal. How on earth were they funding their operation?

The party line was that the NSC had other lucrative government contracts that paid for the operation and allowed them to supply to the health department at cost. However, theories in the aviation industry were rife. The most popular involved the use of a NSC helicopter to help control protesters at Pine Gap, a US military installation in Central Australia. It was surmised, and nobody ever denied it, that the NSC Victorian Aviation Division was heavily funded by the CIA.

Dr Ian Millar, my successor at SLSA and a good friend, was working for the National Safety Council, so I took the opportunity to visit him in Morwell, Victoria, to catch up and get a perspective on their operation. Did they really have all the equipment they boasted of? If they won the tender, would CareFlight still have a role?

It was one of the most amazing experiences of my life. It took two days just to see all the aircraft and equipment they had on line. There were over ten aircraft and more rescue equipment than I had ever seen, including remote-sensing and infra-red equipment. There was a massive recompression chamber, boats and even a submarine. There were several rescue teams that could parachute any expert into any location in Australia within hours of the request. The para rescue shed alone contained millions of dollars of equipment. By comparison CareFlight's operation was miniscule.

Finally I was shown a field filled with dozens of cargo containers. One was opened to reveal masses of rescue equipment, which was said to be worth over half a million dollars. Looking at the contents, it seemed a fair estimate. I left for Sydney feeling that we didn't have a chance.

Still, I couldn't get past the fact that in terms of actual rescues around Australia, the NSC's figures were far smaller than Care-Flight's. Who was paying such enormous amounts of money to have such an operation on standby just in case? Try as we might we were unable to get any answers.

24

In January 1989 I took over from Fran as medical director for Care-Flight, and was at the same time appointed part-time staff specialist at Westmead. Fran had decided to add an anaesthetic fellowship to the intensive care and physician's fellowships she already possessed; she needed to surrender some of her duties to concentrate on her training and exams for the next year and a half. Somehow she still made the time to lend her support and accompany me to all the Health Department committee meetings.

The increased funding from the government saw us expanding to six part-time positions. Blair and I were joined by Luis, Dr Rod Bishop, and another two kiwis, Dr Mark Duncan and Dr Sean Beehan. We rotated between CareFlight and hospital duties, thereby keeping current with mainstream hospital practice while still providing a considerably improved roster compared to the previous year.

As medical director my mission workload was decreased to give me time to cope with the administrative duties and political wrangling. I no more wanted to fly a desk than any of the pilots or doctors. But that was where my expertise was needed and I was a driven man. Looking back on this time I am not sure whether Amanda ever complained about my continual absence from home and the lives of our two small sons. Perhaps after so many years living like this, she was used to it. In my heart I knew that Ben and Daniel needed me around more, but I kept thinking that eventually, when CareFlight had overcome all these hurdles, things would settle down and I would have more time to devote to being a father. Instead, things only got more frantic.

The emergency phone woke us all in the unit one morning. 'The ambulance service has asked us to send a doctor to a motor-vehicle accident. Can you do it for us?' asked Westmead's emergency room registrar.

'Of course I can, who do I contact?' I asked. For over a year we had repeatedly stated that we would provide medical services by any appropriate means of transport, so I was wondering why the ambulance service hadn't rung us direct, but there was no time to worry about that now.

I rang the ambulance controller. 'We have a man trapped in a car in Blacktown,' he told me. 'He has severe head injuries and lacerations to his scalp. We don't know what injuries exist below his neck as we can't reach him. So far the paramedics have given eight bottles of Haemaccel to compensate for his blood loss, but they are requesting permission for a doctor to give blood while they are trying to extricate him.'

'Can you have a vehicle pick me up in five minutes?' I said.

'We'll be there.'

While I pulled on my uniform I organised the blood bank to send over our 'blood bucket', namely an esky containing four bags of O negative universal blood. Ten minutes later I was speeding through the western suburbs to the accident scene.

Once again someone had proven that cars and power poles don't mix. The vehicle was almost unrecognisable; the engine had been forced through the passenger seat and the bonnet was a mangled crush of metal. It seemed impossible that anyone would still be alive beneath the wreck.

The paramedics briefed me. 'His girlfriend is dead in the seat beside him. We've got two drips in and so far have given seventeen bottles of Haemaccel to keep his blood pressure up. We've put a tube down his airway. He gave no response to us doing that. He's still bleeding from his scalp and we don't know where else.'

'Did you say seventeen bottles?' I asked incredulously.

'That's right; we just can't stop the scalp from bleeding.'

Climbing onto the bonnet I quickly confirmed their assessment. The victim was indeed profoundly unconscious, and as white as a sheet where his skin was visible beneath the bloodstained bandages the paramedics had put in place. His pupils were widely dilated and did not react to light. His breathing was severely laboured so I paralysed him. Hopefully with easier ventilation his oxygenation would be optimised. Statistically he had no chance of survival, but this was hardly the time to worry about statistics.

'We'll need to take a blood sample for cross-matching, which has to go straight to Westmead, and then we'll give him all the blood we have. While that's happening we'll see if we can stop the blood loss.'

By now the fire officers had access to one of the man's legs. I took a blood sample from the femoral vein in his groin. Because of the IV drips in his arms I didn't want to contaminate the sample by taking the blood from there.

As the police sped the sample to Westmead we commenced the blood transfusion. The paramedics took it in turn to squeeze the IV sets while I climbed further into the vehicle to look at the man's scalp. As I removed the bandages I was hit in the face by blood spurting from arteries that had been sliced open. Oddly enough I was pleased by this because it meant the man's heart was still pumping strongly.

There was no way that direct pressure or bandaging was going to control this bleeding; thankfully I had come prepared. Over the next five minutes I clamped half-a-dozen artery forceps onto the worst bleeders, and then tied off the vessels with black silk suture material. The clamps were then released and several other bleeders identified and clamped. To save time I just left these clamps in place once the bleeding was largely under control.

My mobile rang. 'This is the blood bank. You've taken this blood sample out of the man's IV line. We need another sample.'

'No I haven't, the lines are in his arms and the sample came from his leg. That's his real blood.'

'But I can nearly see straight through it!'

He was right – it was amazing the man was still alive with barely any red blood cells to carry oxygen to his vital organs. Ten minutes later the blood arrived, and not a moment too soon – we had used every single one of the O negative bags.

While waiting for him to be freed I rang the emergency department and explained the situation. The trauma team was on standby and I asked them to notify the brain scanner staff that we'd need them in the next hour.

Eventually the dashboard was lifted away just enough for us to reach the victim. We put a cervical collar in place before moving him and I was able to make a quick assessment of his other injuries. He had obvious fractures to his left thigh and foot, and evidence of bleeding into his abdomen. We gingerly extracted him from the vehicle onto a spine board before loading him into the ambulance.

'Let's hold off detailed assessment till we get to hospital,' I suggested, and the paramedics agreed. The only priority was blood transfusion – any other injuries were of secondary importance at this stage.

The police, sirens blaring, drove ahead of us to Westmead, clearing the traffic. The ambulance screeched to a halt at the emergency entrance. The trauma team was waiting for us. Further blood was ready and soon it was pouring in.

The man's initial blood count on arrival had his red blood cell levels at eighty per cent below normal, despite the three litres of blood he had already received at the accident site. How there had been enough oxygen being transported to keep his heart beating was a mystery.

Slowly his blood pressure rose and he could be fully assessed and scanned. X-rays revealed injuries to his lungs, skull fractures, facial fractures, severe bruising of his brain, a ruptured spleen, injured kidneys and multiple leg fractures. A splenectomy was performed before he was admitted to the intensive care unit.

Four days later he woke up. Eight weeks later he walked out of hospital. By sheer coincidence I was standing at the front doors as he left. I smiled at him, but he didn't have a clue who I was. He probably thought I was just another visitor.

It was March and we had been told that the decision on the tender was only two weeks away. The Health Department had softened and allowed us to apply. The SLSA and CareFlight had put in a joint proposal but again I had been told that NSC would get the nod. We could do nothing but wait.

Just when it seemed hopeless the National Safety Council of Victoria's Aviation Division self-destructed. The answer to where the money had come from was finally revealed. There never had been any government bodies – Australian or American – paying huge standing charges to underwrite the organisation. Banks had been lending the council money on the strength of the arguments put forward by the head of the operation, John Friedrich. All the banks around that time were falling over themselves to lend money to anybody who would pay the high interest rates.

Everyone had been misled into thinking that the equipment the NSC had was owned, when in reality it was all leased. Everyone had been duped, as I had been by the cargo containers. In fact, all but two of them were empty. The proceeds of each bank loan were needed to pay lease fees and the interest on the previous loans. Initial estimates put the organisation in debt to over one hundred million dollars. The unofficial figure was far higher.

The demise of the NSC operation saw the Health Minister award the ambulance operations contracts and an increase in government funding to CareFlight and SLSA almost immediately. A week later the ambulance service agreed to second paramedics to CareFlight. The ambulance service had recently created the Special Casualty Access Team (SCAT); in addition to being experienced paramedics its team members were trained in caving, abseiling, mining and other difficult-access rescues. On 27 May 1989 five SCAT paramedics presented for training.

We booked a meeting room in the hospital and all the CareFlight directors were there to welcome them on board. To say we were anxious was a great understatement. We had no idea how this was going to work but we continued to believe that integration, not confrontation, was the key to our acceptance.

As medical director I made the welcoming comments to the five paramedics and the State Superintendent of Ambulance who accompanied them. The superintendent replied with the usual pleasantries and then left us to our training. No sooner had he gone than the paramedics stopped the proceedings.

'We know there are a lot of politics surrounding CareFlight,' one of them said.

We all held our breath, wondering where this was going.

'We just want to make something clear. We don't want anything to do with the politics. We're here to do the best we can for our patients and, while always remaining ambulance officers, to become part of the CareFlight team.'

Suddenly the whole mood of the room lightened. That first day was the start of a great relationship. Every one of those five paramedics adapted to helicopter work extremely well. Ground and flight training progressed quickly and they all became a terrific asset to the operation. Without exception they were a great bunch of blokes to work with.

Should I classify this mission as an interhospital transfer or a rescue? I mused as I sat in front of the computer. While the mission had been a transfer, we had responded with all the speed of a rescue mission. Several hours earlier, just after midnight, I had been woken in the unit by a call from the air ambulance centre. 'Would you please ring the doctor at Lithgow Hospital regarding the transfer to Westmead of an injured truck driver?' he asked.

A few seconds later the Lithgow doctor was describing how the middle-aged driver had run off the road, been ejected from his truck and had a number of the logs from his truck roll over him and down the embankment. There was no doubt that this patient was seriously injured and required urgent transfer. By now the crew had appeared bleary-eyed from their bedrooms and were waiting for some hint from me as to whether to return to sleep or prepare for flight.

Lithgow Hospital was one of many tiny hospitals about a hundred kilometres from Sydney. The town was trapped in the conundrum of being too close to Sydney and too small to receive base-hospital funding and status, yet far enough away to be dangerously isolated from expert medical attention. It was just such hospitals for which CareFlight filled an emergency response void.

As I listened to the story of the unfortunate truck driver it became more and more apparent that his injuries were well beyond the capabilities of the hospital in general and the attending doctor in particular, although he was without doubt doing the very best he could.

'Are you giving oxygen?' I asked him.

'Ah, no,' he replied sheepishly.

'Well go and do that right now.'

Shortly he returned. 'Are you giving intravenous fluids?' I demanded.

'He's nearly through the first bag of saline. One arm has fractures and I've only been able to get a small line into his other arm.'

'He's going to need more, a lot more. Do you know how to put in central lines?'

'No.'

'How much urine is he putting out?'

'I don't know.'

'Well, have you put in a urinary catheter?'

'Um, no,' he replied hesitantly.

'That's going to help you a lot in assessing how much fluid to give; I suggest you organise to do that immediately.'

'Um . . . I don't know how to.'

Now I knew this poor doctor was way out of his depth. Inserting a urinary catheter is a fairly basic procedure and if this was beyond his expertise, I needed to get up there fast. At that point I put my hand above my head, my finger pointing to the ceiling, and gave the wind-up signal; John and Wayne bolted back to their bedrooms – we were going flying and there was little time to spare. Within seconds they were sitting in the lounge, flying suits on, lacing up their boots. Meanwhile, in the most encouraging and supportive way I could, I described over the phone the simplest steps that could be done to keep this patient alive until we arrived.

Once I knew from John that the mission was flyable, I returned the call to the air ambulance, who had heard my assessment, and then hung up. The ambulance service had a strict protocol for authorising interhospital transfers which required that once a clinical request had been made, no further dialogue would be entered into until a formal request to the pilot to check for the safety and flying conditions was made. Some controllers took this literally, and even though we might all be in the same room, would hang up the phone and ring us back on the correct telephone number to formally give the mission the go-ahead.

It seemed as though minutes were ticking by as the three of us sat watching the Bat Phone, but in fact it was probably only twenty seconds before it rang. 'This is the ambulance centre; may I talk to the duty pilot please?'

'Speaking,' John replied.

'We have a request from a Dr Wishaw for an interhospital transfer from Lithgow to Westmead, are you available?'

John's serious tone was at odds with the ironic smile on his face. 'Yes, we are,' he replied.

'Would you please check for weather conditions and contact us with regards to the suitability of flight.'

'I've already checked the weather and it's all okay; flight plan is lodged, we can launch in ten minutes,' John stated.

'Ah, well, okay then.' The ambulance controller was caught off guard by John's preparedness. He gave us our authorisation number and finally we were officially permitted to depart.

While John and I played out this little pantomime Wayne was speeding across the hospital grounds to prepare the Dauphin for flight. This would save precious minutes in our response time. We had no doubt that the mission would be authorised and proceed for two reasons. First, there was no other way to reach Lithgow in time to save this man's life: the clinical parameters were undeniable. Secondly, if the air ambulance controller had felt the transfer should be done some other way, or by some other service, we could require that he refer the decision to one of the four Health-Department-appointed medical retrieval consultants, who would impartially decide on the best way to complete the mission. We were sure that if it came to this the retrieval consultant on duty would support our calls. This was simple, because the retrieval consultant on duty that night was me!

Within ten minutes the aircraft had been prepped, and thirty minutes after takeoff we walked through the doors of Lithgow's casualty department. The referring doctor had followed my instructions to the letter, but there was not much improvement in the man's condition. They were trying to pump blood through the tiny cannula in his arm, but his vital signs still showed he needed a lot more blood and quickly.

I turned to Wayne and told him to open the pack and prepare for insertion of central lines. Meanwhile I snatched the few seconds while this was happening to review the man's X-rays. In addition to the fractured pelvis and forearm there was severe bruising of the lungs and five broken ribs. At least his cervical spine X-rays were normal.

I felt his abdomen. It was rigid – he had lost a significant amount of blood. Intravenous access was the highest priority. Normally, to gain fast access, a large cannula would be put into his thigh veins, but the fractured pelvis and rigid abdomen meant those veins might be damaged closer to the heart and transfusing through them would just spill the fluids into his abdomen. The jugular veins of his neck were the only other choice.

By now Wayne and the nurses had opened up our central line pack as well as several trays of sterile drapes. I briefly described to the patient what needed to be done and did a quick sterile scrub before donning gown and gloves. Standing behind the patient's head I swabbed antiseptic over his throat then injected local anaesthetic over his external jugular veins on either side of his neck. After piercing the skin I inserted the largest cannula we had into the vein on the right side. This small pipe would allow us to infuse blood over thirty times faster than the line in his arm.

Blood gushed back, confirming it was in the right position, then I pressed on the vein to stop the leak till I could connect up a drip. This was a lifeline, so I painted his neck with sticky friar's balsam before securely taping the line in place. I simply could not afford to lose it.

While Wayne pumped fluid through the right side of the neck line, I turned the man's head and repeated the procedure on the left side. Now we had plenty of access.

Within ten minutes we had infused nearly two litres of blood and plasma and the man's vital signs had improved dramatically. There was no doubt he needed urgent surgery for his abdominal bleeding, but we were at least able to keep up with the blood loss.

I took a closer look at the X-rays. I was a little puzzled by the appearance of a metal ring on the lower border of his pelvis X-ray but I assumed that this must have been in one of his pockets when the pictures were taken. I examined the patient for other injuries. It was obvious that this man was a typical, swarthy, tough-as-nails truckie. His skin was like dark tanned leather and his eyes seemed to watch my every move with suspicion. I explained to him that we needed to insert a catheter; he objected strongly but with a little persuasion resigned himself to the procedure.

The nursing staff had already undressed him and placed him in a white gown, but when I lifted the gown to prepare for the catheter insertion, my eyes fell on . . . frilly pink silk knickers! I glanced up at him. His eyes were a cold, hard blue; he set his jaw and hissed fiercely, 'Don't you say a f*** thing, Doc.'

'We'll look after them for you,' I promised, trying my hardest to remain clinically detached. I gently removed the ladies' knickers, and the mystery of the metal ring was solved. Skin piercing was extremely unusual in those days, but this gentleman had had a large metal ring inserted through the tip of his penis. For what reason, your guess is as good as mine. Still, it proved to be very useful because pulling on the ring made insertion of the catheter far easier. Over the next thirty minutes we continued stabilisation and then we flew the truckie back to Westmead.

The following afternoon I returned to intensive care to see how he was progressing. The surgeons had removed his ruptured spleen and he was shortly to be transferred from intensive care to the general ward. Fran was on duty and she came with me. The nurses introduced us to the man's wife, a delightful but very anxious lady who had flown from interstate to be by her husband's bedside.

She turned to us and said emotionally, 'Thank you so much. Last night I received the phone call that every truckie's wife dreads.'

I glanced at Fran and could tell she had read my mind. You mean the call with the news that your husband wears frilly knickers?

25

As the year progressed CareFlight became busier and busier. The team performed each mission with utmost professionalism.

Halfway through the year I was chosen to attend the first course of a new national trauma training scheme run by the College of Surgeons. In time this would become a compulsory part of training for all specialists in surgery, anaesthesia and emergency medicine. The course had its teething problems but nothing beat the dramatic events of day two.

No amount of theory can replace hands-on skills, so, after obtaining ethical approval, we were going to practise resuscitation techniques on anaesthetised sheep. A new procedure had been devised to provide an airway in cases where intubation of the windpipe was impossible or inappropriate. Some people have anatomy that makes visualisation of the windpipe with a laryngoscope impossible. Severe facial injuries can rule out windpipe intubation, as can the possibility of a broken neck because moving the neck around might damage the spinal cord further.

A simple but difficult-to-pronounce procedure called a crico-thyroidotomy had been developed, in which a cut was made into the front of the neck in the small depression just below the Adam's apple and a breathing tube inserted directly into the windpipe. One of the sheep had been anaesthetised and the instructor was inserting the laryngoscope to begin intubation. To his horror he found that there was only a dog laryngoscope on hand. It was thirty centimeters too short for a sheep. Nothing he did corrected the situation and the sheep arrested due to lack of oxygen. Thinking quickly, the instructor took the opportunity to demonstrate the cricothyroidotomy. He grabbed a scalpel, cut into the neck and inserted the endotracheal tube. When he connected a resuscitation bag to the tube and gave one hundred per cent oxygen, the sheep sprang back to life. There could be no better demonstration of the value of the technique than that!

Two weeks later I was in western New South Wales preparing to retrieve a motorbike rider. While he had suffered multiple severe injuries, it should have been a survivable accident. However, he had arrested while being intubated. The local doctor had struggled for forty-five minutes to intubate him and in the process the man's heart had stopped. The heart had been restarted but his cardiograph showed signs of permanent injury.

The victim's neck was long and thin and a cricothyroidotomy would have been simple for someone who knew the technique. But it was too late now. I transferred the patient to Sydney, knowing that if his heart was severely damaged due to lack of oxygen, then in all probability his brain had suffered even worse damage. He died seven days later. What a waste, and all for want of a simple skill. The futility of his death affected me deeply.

It was serendipitous, then, that a few days later I was approached by the head of the new trauma training course to see if I wanted to become an instructor. I was delighted, not just because it was a great honour – I would be only the second Australian anaesthetist trained to instructor level – but it would give me the opportunity to pass on my skills to country doctors who bravely coped with trauma patients with far fewer resources than we had at Westmead. Hopefully I would contribute to saving lives by teaching these doctors simple and effective ways to deal with severely injured patients.

The handle of the knife protruding from the man's left eye twitched ominously with each heartbeat. It was a shocking sight. The thirty-year-old had slipped while trying to prize the cap off a beer bottle, with horrific results.

Awful as the implications were, it wasn't the eye injury that worried me so much as the twitching. It implied that somewhere an artery was touching the knife blade. Looking carefully from all angles I realised that the tip of the knife was probably resting against the man's left internal carotid artery at the base of his brain. This artery carries one-third of the volume of blood the brain receives. If it were ruptured, the man would be dead within a minute. No surgery would be fast enough to save him. He was literally living on a knife edge.

The patient was panic-stricken, jerking around in pain, and his terrified words indicated that he knew just how precarious his situation was. I talked to him gently but rapidly, asking him to trust me and let me anaesthetise him. He was petrified but desperately wanted the pain to go away, so he consented.

While the local doctors prepared the drugs and equipment I looked at the knife from different angles. I visualised the intubating procedure and it was obvious that we could easily knock the knife handle as we inserted the endotracheal tube. I placed a protective cover over the knife which I fashioned from a Styrofoam cup from the drinking fountain. I then quickly discussed the procedure with the local doctors. I suggested that I inject the drugs but leave the intubation to the local anaesthetist so that I could watch the procedure and warn him if he was about to knock the cup.

I talked confidently to the patient as he drifted off to sleep. Soon he was paralysed. The local anaesthetist gingerly inserted the tube and skillfully avoided knocking the cup. We all breathed a great sigh of relief when the tube was in place without mishap. We placed an extra intravenous line and prepared the drugs he would need for his transfer.

Eventually I was happy that the knife guard was securely in place and we lined up on one side to lift him up and slide our stretcher underneath him. Four people lifted him from one side while I held his head and called out instructions on how fast and far to move him. Once he was on our stretcher the bridge was placed over the top and we began to transfer him to our life-support systems. The stretcher bridge had been an outstanding success right from the start, and this was one of the many retrievals it made very much easier. Once I was satisfied that the patient was secure, we started to wheel him down to the chopper at a painstakingly slow pace. Any sudden jolt might be enough to rupture his carotid artery.

Eventually we had him beside the aircraft and, our hearts in our mouths, we lifted him inch by inch inside. Once we were all secure we were ready to start up. Invariably this is the roughest part of the flight. Ever so gently I clamped the man's head between my hands and lifted it off the pillow just enough to keep it stable. The helicopter rocked on its landing skids slightly as the rotors wound up to flight speed. As we took off I couldn't help thinking what would happen if the knife actually severed the carotid artery. First there would be a sudden rise in blood pressure, followed by a slowing of the heart as the pressure inside the skull cut off all blood flow to the brain. It would be over in seconds and there would be absolutely nothing I could do.

It took us fifty long minutes to get back to Sydney. I felt as though I held my breath the whole way. At Westmead, John set the aircraft down as lightly as a feather and the patient was transferred, again with agonising caution, to the emergency room. Brain and artery scans confirmed the knife was against his carotid artery. The artery was up against the flat of the blade but the edge was precariously close to the ophthalmic artery.

I accompanied the man to theatre where he was scrubbed and draped for surgery. Slowly, millimeter by millimeter, the neurosurgeon withdrew the knife. Thank God he had steady hands. There was no bleeding. For ten minutes we watched anxiously for signs of increasing intra-cranial pressure, before really believing that there had been no mishap inside his skull.

The ophthalmic surgeons had no choice but to remove the punctured eye. By the next day the man was sitting up in bed, sorry for the loss of his eye but grateful that he was still alive.

If the true test of how well a team is working together is in its members' ability to laugh at one another, then the paramedics and the CareFlight crew were working together brilliantly.

The paramedics referred to us doctors as the 'SPIT Team' because we only knew one approach: 'Sedate, Paralyse, Intubate and Transport'.

We reminded them that paramedics were still known as 'frogs', because everyone they touched croaked. They accepted this with a laugh and the 'Fantom Frog' became a regular contributor to the Care-Flight newsletter.

Humour was essential in dealing with the day-to-day hurdles the service faced, though sometimes it was an effort to raise a laugh. For several months we all lived on our own knife edge, not knowing whether we would find another corporate sponsor – we had lost HCF. Once again Ian, Peter and the finance team were tireless in their lobbying, and finally the motoring and insurance company, NRMA, came on board. The paramedics told us that NRMA would replace SPIT as the term for the doctors. It stood for 'No Real Medical Ability'! Blair had the final word with a cartoon saying SCAT stood for 'silly clots acting tough'.

Despite their questionable sense of humour, the paramedics' incorporation in the team had huge effects within the ambulance service. No doubt word was leaking out about our capabilities and philosophies, and our acceptance was growing every day.

We also became an accredited training post for the College of Anaesthetists and College of Physicians. Now trainees could work for us for six months and have this count towards their specialist training. We were the first non-hospital organisation to achieve such status and it was a recognition of the high standards of operation, training and supervision we were able to provide.

The politics and departmental committees were less impressive. The helipad saga was never-ending, and we continued to cop criticism from a small number of the old guard within the ambulance service, Health Department and a number of doctors with no experience in the field. I spent hours lobbying over the most petty matters, always trying my best, along with the other CareFlight founders, to shield the rest of the team from such negative judgements. I was too busy to realise how burnt out I was becoming.

One night I slumped into the lounge chair after barely acknowledging Amanda and the boys. I was exhausted beyond belief. The effort of keeping people alive and the slow crumbling of my pride under the barrage of constant criticism by armchair experts was wearing me out. I was unable to separate criticism of the service from criticism of myself. I thought the legacy of what we did would make me happy. Instead I was miserable.

I sat staring vacantly at the TV screen, trying to take my mind off the events of the last few days, weeks, years. On the screen a helicopter was skimming along a long golden beach. I had seen this insurance ad many times before. Eventually the camera zoomed in on a group of people on the sand. It was a young dad playing cricket with his kids, and suddenly somewhere in my brain a switch was thrown.

I looked at Ben. He was sitting on the sofa, his blond hair rumpled after his bath, his big brown eyes glued to the TV. Daniel was wearing the little blue flight suit he had been given for Christmas. He had just finished mowing the carpet again with his plastic mower. As usual he was sucking the middle and ring finger of his left hand, his little finger resting on his right cheek and his index finger on the left. They were the two most lovable, gorgeous kids in the world. They were also strangers.

Amanda looked frazzled; my lack of support, her third pregnancy and the constant demands of bringing up the two boys with little help from me was making her life just as hard and frustrating as mine. We were drifting apart.

It suddenly struck me that working so obsessively for CareFlight was never going to let me be like that father on the TV. All I was doing was recreating for my kids what I had experienced as a child. I didn't want them growing up seeing their dad one afternoon a fortnight. I realised that more than anything else I wanted to be a big part of their lives and for them to be a big part of mine. In four months' time we would have three children, and all of them needed a dad.

CareFlight was an addiction. I felt incredibly good being part of a team that made such a tangible difference. But at what price? It was hard for me to admit to myself – so much of my self-worth was tied up in my career – that CareFlight would continue to grow with or without me. The service would face many battles in the future but there were plenty of other talented, driven people to continue the fight. In that moment I understood I couldn't continue to work for CareFlight and be a good husband and father too. And I wanted to be a good father more than I wanted to be a CareFlight hero.

Amanda and I talked long into the night. I think she was relieved that I had finally come to the conclusion she had reached some years ago. But if I were to leave, where would I go, what would I do? The CareFlight job was who I was; without it I would be a nobody. But without it I also had the chance to dream up a new life. We wanted to move somewhere warmer and on the coast, not too big, not too small, a great place for the kids to grow up. Over the next few days we looked at all the possibilities in New South Wales but for one reason or another they just didn't cut it.

'Well if you could live anywhere in Australia, where would you live?' asked Amanda. I guess I should have been asking her that question, but old habits die hard.

'Noosa would be nice,' I replied, almost without thinking.

I arrived home the next afternoon to find Amanda looking like the proverbial cat that had caught the canary. There was an ad for a staff anaesthetist at the base hospital in Nambour in the *Australian Medical Association Journal*.

'Where's Nambour?'

'It's the main town just south of Noosa!'

I grabbed the magazine and read the ad. It sounded perfect. I applied. Six weeks later we had heard nothing. Phone enquiries had elicited no response. I was not a believer in coincidence any more. That job was meant for me. We had a week's holiday due and so we drove to Nambour. As soon as we arrived I went straight to the office of the medical superintendent. He saw me there and then.

'I'm Ken Wishaw,' I told him breathlessly, 'and I applied for the staff anaesthetist job six weeks ago. Nobody is answering my calls and I would like to know what's going on.'

He stared blankly at me for several long seconds. Then he picked up his phone. 'Cancel my afternoon appointments, I'm going to look at real estate,' he told his assistant. For the next three hours we traipsed around the coast while the medical superintendent showed us nice places to live.

'Does that mean I've got the job?'

'I can't tell you that,' he replied.

'Then why are we doing this?'

'Be patient.'

No amount of probing got us any further, but it was mighty strange behaviour if the job wasn't as good as mine. We returned to Sydney and heard absolutely nothing for another four weeks. Then the medical superintendent rang one afternoon.

'The job is yours but we need to know now.'

I was stunned. 'Let me think about it.'

'I need your answer.'

'How about tomorrow?' I offered.

'How about this afternoon?'

'Okay,' I replied. I already knew the answer but wanted to check in with Amanda first. An hour later I accepted the job. Now all I had to do was say goodbye to CareFlight.

26

As the year wound to a close, so did the Great Helipad Saga. The coroner's case, combined with the pressure we exerted through the Helicopter Association of Australia and the medical retrieval committee, forced the Civil Aviation Authority to send a fact-finding mission around the world to review helipads.

The findings were no surprise, but the CAA's response was. The regulations regarding the helipads were dropped completely. From the new year they would become advisory only. Put simply, it would still be recommended that pilots keep safety factors in mind, and be responsible for negligence leading to damage to people or property, but otherwise they could land – subject to the property owner's approval – wherever they saw fit.

Most importantly for us, the Westmead emergency pad would reopen. Furthermore, rooftop helipads would be permissible. This represented a quantum leap in medical helicopter access to hospitals around the country. Our persistence had finally paid off.

Fran and I also achieved a major victory with the medical retrieval committee. We had helped formulate criteria by which ambulance officers should request a medical helicopter directly to an accident scene. They were now accepted and were soon to be distributed throughout the state. Finally it appeared that more and more often, instead of being called to country hospitals we would be called directly to the accident sites and be able to introduce intensive care management at the earliest possible instant.

The most beautiful Christmas present I received, however, was two hours and two minutes late. Emma was born, in the same room as Ben and Daniel, and I vowed not to fly for a week. Nothing short of an earthquake would move me from my family's side.

And that's exactly what happened.

The popular misconception that Australia was geologically inactive was disproven on 27 December 1989 when an earthquake shook the town of Newcastle.

I was at home, having spent the night welcoming my beautiful daughter into the world, when the news arrived. CareFlight had been tasked to travel to Newcastle and as the New South Wales duty retrieval consultant the ambulance had recommended that I coordinate the retrieval effort of the possible injured.

During the earthquake all communication links between Newcastle and Sydney had been severed and no news was available as to the state of the city. As the flight path from Westmead to Newcastle lay roughly over my house, I donned my flight uniform and sprinted five hundred metres to the nearest school oval. Bemused bystanders wondered what this man was doing standing on the oval by himself in a flight suit, until the high-pitch scream of a Fenestron tail rotor heralded the Dauphin's appearance in the skies above. Within minutes I was aboard and we were heading north. I was briefed that there was still no information whatsoever available as to conditions in Newcastle.

Our first view of the city revealed several fires in the central business district and billowing smoke on the western horizon; we noted the collapsed workers' club, but other buildings seemed intact. I directed the helicopter to Royal Newcastle Hospital, as that was the most likely place injured patients would be taken. We were not prepared for the amazing sight that awaited us there.

The hospital, while intact, had developed signs of structural stress and had been completely evacuated to the adjacent park and surf beach. Hundreds of patients lay on mattresses on the grass or sand, while staff hurried between them. We were briefed by the duty disaster commander, who then showed us through the deserted hospital; as yet they had not received major casualties, but due to total communications failure were unaware of what still lay out in the rest of the city. It was apparent that no messages had arrived in Sydney to inform the disaster coordinators of what support was needed.

It was then that I devised a solution that would be beneficial to those Newcastle emergency resources and CareFlight. We climbed to three hundred metres and I punched some numbers into our mobile phone to contact Sydney. Triple 0, the standard emergency number, was engaged. After several unsuccessful attempts I decided to ring 2GB, one of Sydney's radio stations. The phone was answered by the news editor and I was unceremoniously told to get off the line, there'd been an earthquake in Newcastle. Before the man could hang up on me, I blurted, 'I'm in Newcastle, don't you want to know the story?' That got his attention! I then proceeded to introduce myself and suggest that we use the radio station to describe to all emergency services the situation on the ground. He enthusiastically agreed and said that he would contact the emergency services and have them tune to 2GB. I would be able to brief them all simultaneously. The news editor saw the obvious coup in this concept and of course it was not lost on me that 2GB was one of CareFlight's new sponsors.

During the next half-hour we cruised over Newcastle describing the situation. The town appeared largely intact, and while moderate numbers of minor injuries had been presented to both Royal Newcastle and Wallsend Hospitals, there had so far been only a few major casualties, which were well cared for. Wallsend, the second-largest hospital in Newcastle, was still intact and fully functional, and along with the local scene commanders it was decided to make it the primary triage hospital. Unknown to us, major rescue efforts were underway at the Newcastle Workers' Club, which had collapsed. We soon landed at Wallsend and were joined by the helicopters from Sydney and Newcastle SLSA and also the Child Flight retrieval helicopter from the Children's Hospital in Camperdown. Fifty patients had already arrived, but only two had been seriously injured; rumours were filtering through, however, of a major mine disaster to the west.

I recommended that all but the most stable patients be transferred to Sydney. All hospital staff had been called in and I knew that ten hours from now there would be nobody left awake to look after patients if there continued to be an influx of casualties. We took off again so that I could re-establish the phone lines and discuss casualty transfers with Sydney. For the first time in memory there appeared to be numerous vacant ICU beds available in the capital and I was confident that we could handle reasonable numbers of injured. We returned to the ground and I pleaded that we shouldn't wait to see how many more came in but start moving patients south right this minute.

I was ignored. No one could see the importance of using Sydney's resources to help spread the load. Even the staff still stuck on the beach outside the Royal Newcastle did not comply. After hours of trying I gave up and just started praying that the casualties stayed at a minimum, because if they didn't we would be in big trouble that night. Fortunately, the casualties never arrived.

Incredibly, the collapse of the workers' club was the only major catastrophe. The residents of Newcastle had largely been spared.

To lighten our mood word got around that the loss of electricity meant unlimited free ice creams to all staff of Wallsend Hospital. We spent several hours waiting, hoping and getting progressively sicker on the ice creams. Slowly communications were re-established, and by late afternoon it became clear that Newcastle was once again self-sufficient. The Royal Newcastle was declared safe and the patients returned to their wards. Early that evening we flew back to Sydney, extremely grateful that the earthquake had not extracted a greater human toll. Fifteen people had died, but for the grace of God it could have been far worse.

The next week I was visited by the manager of 2GB. It appeared that my live report from Newcastle had earned the news report of the year for the Macquarie network and he pledged continuing sponsorship to the service for the ensuing years.

Personally, I was frustrated that CareFlight's potential in a disaster was not recognised. While Fran at least had more success the same month working from the ambulance control centre to co-coordinate the transfer of numerous patients after the Kempsey bus crash, it would be many years before our capabilities in disaster management were truly appreciated.

Thirteen years later, after the Bali bombing in 2002, CareFlight's disaster coordination role finally received the recognition it deserved.

27

'Contact!' I yelled into the microphone. Leaning out from the left rear door I had glimpsed, one hundred metres below, the glint of a silver rescue blanket spread on the rocks, two people frantically waving and a third lying still.

Tempted as he must have been, John did not look down. Even a brief glance at the people stranded below could disorientate him, and in these tight circumstances that could mean a brush with the nearby trees and an abrupt fiery end. John's job was to keep the chopper safe and in control, secure in the knowledge that the rest of us knew our jobs and would perform them professionally. Sitting opposite me, Peter Cribbs, our SCAT paramedic, was doing what every 'down the wire' crewman does at this stage: checking and rechecking that his rescue harness was tight and secure.

This was my last mission with CareFlight and for the past twenty minutes we had been steadily making our way down the Wollamgambie Canyon, peering down into this geological masterpiece. A party of five had decided to explore the hidden canyons, wading, rappelling and scrambling through icy water and over slippery boulders. They had been travelling for four hours and it would be another three by foot before they could exit this world. This was not the place to sustain a significant head injury.

The victim had fallen while traversing a waterfall and had lost consciousness. The group had elected to send two members downstream for help while the other two had remained with their unconscious mate.

It was a mere twenty-minute flight from the metropolitan comfort of the CareFlight base to this freezing wilderness. I marvelled, as I always did, at the ability of a helicopter to transfer us to such different vistas so quickly. There's no doubt they are the ultimate off-road vehicle.

'Winch height?' John enquired.

What he wanted to know was how low he would need to hover to be within access via the ninety-metre winch cable. In addition he wanted an opinion on how high above the canyon section he should fly to be clear of the gum trees on either side of the steep lower part of the main valley.

Mark Cruse, the crewman sitting in the front left seat, had sighted the stranded party and gave his assessment. 'Thirty metres in the canyon and forty metres above the canyon. There's a four-metre-square rock platform fifty metres upstream of their position, which will have you adjacent to that large blue gum on the canyon left.' All this he had determined in a two-second glimpse.

Canyon winching is tight stuff. The helicopter must hover with pinpoint accuracy to drop the cable and the rescuer – affectionately referred to as 'the dope on the rope' – down the narrow canyon slot without him touching the sides. 'Touching' the sides would not necessarily be gentle if we figured it wrong. We intended to fly as low as possible in the main valley so the reference points John could sight were close, very close. This made preventing drift easier but left very little margin for error. If anyone could do it, it was John. Recently he had been awarded the Golden Hour Award in the USA as international rescue helicopter pilot of the year.

We climbed out of the lower valley, circled, and noted the references for the rescue so we could find the location again. In the space of a few seconds we determined wind direction, obstructions to our descent path, best approach angle and contingencies for any problems. Few words were spoken, but nothing was missed.

Mark, in the rear left of the cabin, would have the task of guiding John in. Squatting in the doorway and leaning out, with just a safety harness to keep him secure, he would be providing John with a constant flow of information. John would integrate this with what he could see from the front. My job would be to look behind us and check for tail clearance of trees, and if necessary be winched down after Peter had assessed the patient.

'We'll reconfigure – it's hot and high.' John was happy with our plan but wanted to lighten the aircraft prior to the winch. High altitude and high air temperature required more engine power, and every kilo less helped.

Three minutes later we were unloading our nonessential equipment at the quaint picnic ground at Mount Wilson. Without a word spoken, we then took our new positions inside the chopper. John remained in the front by himself. With the sliding door open, Mark was now in the rear left on the floor, secured by his 'monkey strap' to an anchor point. He flashed me one of his devilish 'this is sooo much fun!' grins before zipping his navy blue flight suit up to his chin, flipping the green-black visor on his helmet down, and positioning the boom microphone as close to his lips as possible without swallowing it. I took my position opposite him, facing backwards, while Peter secured himself to the seat between Mark and me.

I glanced at Peter. Like all of us he was well trained, experienced and very capable. He looked calm and relaxed. His fingers were flitting from buckle to buckle on his harness; checking, rechecking. We exchanged quick smiles, his more tentative than mine. Seventy metres is a long way for a winch and Peter was going to have a lot of time to think about the consequences of any mishap in the procedure as he rode the wire.

Two minutes later we were lining up for the approach to the valley floor. While John flew the approach he would receive our description of the view and amalgamate this information with his own perspective. It was a process of skill, knowledge and, most importantly, trust.

Mark's patter began. 'Two hundred metres to run, line good, increase descent rate; one hundred and fifty metres to run, come left on line two metres, descent rate good . . . Twenty metres to run, passing over gum tree ten metres below, line good; maintain present descent rate.'

'Tail five metres clear of trees,' I informed him from my vantage point.

'Increase descent rate, ten metres to run; come left on line; five metres, three metres, standby, steady. Position good, move back two metres, standby; steady, this is the winch position. Gum tree on left clear of rotor ten metres.'

'Tail clear ten metres with treetop five metres above present height,' I added. The dialogue was seamless, as though it flowed from one mind.

Now John would be triangulating his own reference points to maintain this position. Perhaps the fork of a tree lined up with a mark on a rock to his left, or a small boulder among the dry grass with the windscreen frame on his right.

The pleasant little dry sclerophyll valley was now a maelstrom of wind as the rotor downdraft whipped the air into a frenzy. Helicopters don't fly, I remembered, they beat the air into submission.

Mark lowered the winch hook two metres and passed it inside to Peter. Once hooked on, Peter unclipped his seatbelt and donned the medical backpack, then bum-shuffled to the open door. To the un-initiated it would seem that the way Mark grabbed Peter's harness was excessive, but I knew how reassuring it was to receive that message, 'I have you safely'.

'Crew at the door ready to winch; come left one metre, forwards two metres, standby, steady.' Mark was now standing outside the helicopter on the left-hand skid, leaning back against the door sill. His left hand above his head held the ceiling-mounted winch control handle, his right hand firmly grasped Peter. Using his fingers to toggle the winch control buttons, Mark took up the slack and Peter was dangling just outside the door. I knew the feeling so well at this significant moment. It's one of relief. The cable and harness have taken the weight and everything is okay. It doesn't matter how many times you go down the wire, that first moment is always the worst.

Slowly at first, then accelerating, Peter started the journey down. The patter never stopped. 'Clear of the skids and descending, position good, five metres below the skids; come forwards two metres, standby, steady; ten metres below the skids, position good, entering the canyon, thirty metres to run.'

I envied Peter his descent into the canyon. Such rapid entry to another world is an awesome experience and only possible on the end of an abseiling rope or a winch cable. While our standard routine in these rescues was to send the SCAT paramedic down first and the doctor only if required, I wished I could experience this unique journey one last time.

Peter had thrust his hand out to the side with his thumb up. At this signal Mark stopped unwinding the cable and let John gently lower the helicopter, and Peter, the last two metres. This prevented John receiving any surprises as the weight came off the winch cable and the helicopter's centre of gravity changed.

'Down and unclipped,' Mark stated. 'Retrieving cable.'

I sensed a collective release of tension now Peter had been delivered to the exact centre of the rock platform. What a team, I thought. We radioed Peter that we would depart and give him some peace and quiet in which to assess the situation. 'You make sure you come back!' he replied, only half joking.

'CareFlight One from Portable,' we heard five minutes later.

'Go ahead,' I replied. This would be the clinical assessment.

'Pulse 100, BP 120 on 80, he's conscious Glasgow Coma Scale 13 and able to stand with assistance. Apparent loss of consciousness was estimated to be twenty minutes. Lacerated forehead but no other significant injuries. Suggest lower patient strop and we'll both come out.'

'Roger,' I confirmed. I trusted Peter's assessment implicitly. It looked like he wouldn't need me down there. I was disappointed, but it was good news for the victim.

The extraction of Peter and the victim went as smoothly as the insertion. Ten minutes later we were shutting down the chopper at Mount Wilson Park. Now it was my turn to do my bit. While the middle-aged man seemed alert and orientated, given the fact that he had been unconscious for twenty minutes, there was the possibility that he had suffered a bleed inside his skull, which could have dire consequences. I proceeded to thoroughly check his condition and make a detailed neurological assessment. Systematically I checked for normal power, sensation, reflexes and position sense in his limbs and face. His pupils were okay and after ten minutes I was satisfied that he had suffered concussion but the chance of anything more sinister evolving was minimal. He did not need to come to Sydney with us and I dispatched him by road ambulance to the nearby hospital for overnight observation.

Another very grateful patient. Another mission superbly executed. 'Synergy' was the word that came to mind as we discussed the rescue afterwards. The individuals in the team had worked as a unit, and although few words had been spoken, there had been an extraordinary amount of communication going on. No one person was more or less important than the others. Peter may have been the one to go down the wire, but the whole team had performed the rescue.

Egos were noticeably absent at CareFlight. No one was there for his or her own glorification. The service didn't attract narcissistic mavericks of the kind portrayed in *Top Gun*. Sometimes they came but they never lasted long. They quickly realised they didn't belong. Everyone was with the service to do a vital job to the best of their ability, to strive for constant improvement and serve the people of the region. Through this there developed a unique bond, and a synergy.

When a team of people move beyond self-serving, ego-driven action to one of dedicated service and cooperation, they act as a single entity rather than a collection of individuals. They become more than the sum of their parts. Synergy sizzles between them and suddenly the team becomes electric, it 'clicks' together and is unstoppable. Synergy is elusive. It appears and just as quickly disappears.

Synergy is one of the peaks of human experience. CareFlight seemed to have it all the time.

I stood alone in the centre of the hospital sports oval, staring back at the brand-new CareFlight hangar. My fists were stuffed in my pockets and tears trickled down my cheeks.

After three and a half years and hundreds of missions my last shift was over. I would never again scramble to the shrill call of the Bat Phone. I would never again experience the glow of a team rescue well done.

My passion for what CareFlight stood for was as strong as ever but I no longer had the energy for the never-ending struggle of keeping the service alive. Since its inception I, along with so many others, had fought for its very existence. I could not remember a moment when CareFlight was not fighting to survive. That was not going to change, not yet. We weren't totally controlled by the government and a small number of powerful bureaucrats would never accept that. The politics was constant, exhausting and demoralising. I had had enough.

Thankfully, though, the tide of opinion, even in the government, seemed to be slowly flowing our way. With every rescue and life saved – and these now numbered in the thousands – the groundswell of public support grew, and it would be a brave politician who moved against us. But I could no longer maintain the fight. My family deserved more. My daughter was two weeks old and I was determined to see more of her first few years than I had of the boys'. Stronger, braver, cleverer people would continue to work for what CareFlight stood for; it was time for me to nurture my marriage, my family and myself.

Standing alone I ruminated over what I was leaving. The adventure, the action, the feeling that we made big differences to the quality and often the continuance of so many lives. Hardest of all was saying goodbye to my workmates. Our bonds and friendships were based on sharing challenges, adversity, danger and triumph together, and they would be terribly difficult to leave.

I walked back to my car and sat watching the aircraft silhouetted against the last light of my last day. The high-pitched scream of the turbines gave way to the throbbing beat of the rotors. Delicately the aircraft lifted a metre off the ground and sidled over to the very spot in the middle of the oval where I had been standing, the point that marked the beginning of each flight, and the point where my service with CareFlight ended. The Dauphin turned into the wind, hovered, and then ascended into the night sky.

A slow smile appeared on my salt-streaked face. God knows, I was going to miss this.

Epilogue

The voyage of discovery lies not in seeking new vistas,
but in having new eyes.

Proust

The Bell 47 floats just above the meandering Noosa River as it snakes through the hinterland on its way out over the vast ocean. Even the grey clouds cannot detract from the thrill of taking flight again in one of these magical birds; it's a familiar thrill but one that never fades.

It seems apt that this is a joy-flight, because that's exactly the emotion I feel. Joy settles in my heart, uplifting, peaceful, unexpected. For a long time, though, joy, or any other light-filled emotion, was a stranger to me. I might have landed a job in paradise, but the move to the Sunshine Coast turned out to be a descent into darkness.

The workload in my new job was challenging, to say the least, and I spent many evenings and weekends at the hospital. Quitting Care-Flight had left an enormous hole in my life and my identity, so when word leaked out about my past I found it impossible to say no. Soon I was being requested to do helicopter and road retrievals for both the local and Brisbane hospitals. All these were done on top of my already hectic roster. The RAAF had discovered my expertise and called on me more and more. During these missions I faced even greater challenges than I had faced at CareFlight and was involved in some thrilling adventures. Before long I had forgotten why I had left Care-Flight in the first place, and was carrying on just as I always had.

I felt morally obliged to help others, but by putting patients first, family a distant second, and ignoring self-care altogether, I was heading for disaster. I was pretending again that the personal and family costs could be ignored. I felt trapped but I didn't know how to change. Understandably, Amanda felt more deserted than ever now that the dream had turned sour, but neither of us had the knowledge to change the course the marriage was taking.

Our family's disintegration seemed to happen overnight. In reality it had been leading this way for many years, I had just been too absorbed in my career to notice. By the time I finally realised what was most important to me, it had slipped through my fingers. Amanda left for a new life and she took the children with her. Three years after moving to Queensland I found myself in the depths of despair.

Far from having created a better life, I was divorced, deeply in debt and suffering severe depression. I saw my children only a few days a fortnight, just as it had been with my own father. Hardest of all was realising that they were experiencing exactly the pain I had felt when my parents divorced. Nothing hurt me more than to see them living through a similar experience and to know that I must accept most of the responsibility for the way our lives had turned out. I found it impossible to forgive myself for creating my children and then failing them.

I did the best I could to be a good dad when Ben, Daniel and Emma were with me. When they weren't I distracted myself with numerous adventures, from learning to fly to becoming a dive master. But no matter how beautiful or amazing these experiences were, nothing gave me any lasting happiness. Without human connection it all seemed meaningless.

Outwardly I looked successful – I had resigned from work as a full-time hospital specialist and started in private practice. I was always busy, always in a rush. Being overworked is a status symbol among medical practitioners and I was as good as any at achieving that foolhardy goal.

The depression became deeper and deeper. I could not eat or sleep; I lost seventeen kilos, and I am not a heavily built man. Although it must have been clear to my colleagues that I was in trouble, no one asked me if I needed support. Our medical training had instilled in all of us a belief that we needed to be self-sufficient, to deal with any illness, including our own, with detached concern. So used to presenting a controlled, professional front to the world, doctors find it almost impossible to admit their vulnerability and ask for help. I was no exception. Until one day I was so desperate that I rang a colleague. 'I'm lost,' I told him in despair. He cancelled his afternoon's patients – a big deal for a specialist – and met with me straightaway. He didn't give me any answers, he simply listened, and by doing so gave me permission to acknowledge my anguish, to speak it aloud. His simple act of human compassion lifted the veil of loneliness that separated me from others and from my own inner strength.

It was a long and painful journey to recovery, in many ways the hardest challenge I have ever faced. I had built up a kind of survival personality – detached, driven, controlled – in order to cope with the stresses of the profession I had chosen. I had to break this persona down to find out who lay beneath.

After five years of self-development books, courses and spiritual forays I emerged battered but a little wiser. I knew then that I was ready to be in a long-term relationship but I just couldn't find the right person. One day I sat down and wrote in fine detail everything I could think of to describe the partner I was looking for. I carried that piece of paper with me everywhere. I don't think it was a coincidence that it was soon after this that I met and fell in love with Jackie. She fitted my description almost to the letter.

Jackie helped me slow down, create time to think about what I wanted for my life. Inside this quiet, undisturbed place I gained the clarity to rediscover the world that had been around me all the time. And I wanted to share that world with my children. To do that I needed to cut back on my working hours so that I would have the time to become a committed father.

With Jackie's support I decided to give away much of my practice to other anaesthetists. I weathered intense criticism from some of my colleagues for decreasing my workload, but I stood my ground. I knew the price of work addiction too well to ever go back there. I started to see success in a different light. Once I might have measured it by showy outward displays of expensive houses, clothes, cars. Now the only comparison I make with my colleagues' cars is whether theirs are still in the hospital car park while mine is taking me home to my family.

I began working only with surgeons who were flexible enough to allow me the time I needed to regain my children. Jackie had been living in a shared custody arrangement with her children Christopher and Jessica for several years, and I negotiated a similar arrangement with Amanda. Seeing much more of my children was wonderful. Being a hands-on father wasn't without its problems and, like all parents, there were times when I didn't know whether I was up to the challenge. But I love Ben, Daniel and Emma passionately, and being a part of their daily lives has nurtured me as I hope it has nurtured them. Having lost them for a while, once I had them back I vowed never to take them for granted.

From the earliest days of our relationship Jackie understood the deep sense of loss I felt about no longer being involved with Care-Flight. To me it had represented the greatest success that a doctor could achieve, and nothing else would compare with it. How could I be satisfied with the regular work of anaesthesia after the experience of helicopter rescue? I wanted to be back flying with CareFlight and yet I knew I could not live up to my responsibilities to my family if I became involved again. Still, I could no longer see that I made a difference and I seriously considered giving up medicine to do something more exciting, more rewarding, more worthwhile.

Jackie encouraged me to write down my experiences, and as the journey of this book neared its end I realised that the very act of telling my story was changing me in the most profound way. Finally the last word of the book was written. In that instant I just seemed to let go. Suddenly I no longer needed to look back to define myself. I wanted to look elsewhere. It was then that I went to have lunch with Paul Bowdler.

Having heard of Paul's miraculous recovery after the horrific injuries he sustained thirteen years ago, I wanted to meet him. I flew to Sydney and drove to the city's outskirts to have lunch with him and his mum Evelyn. The closeness of the whole family was evident. Paul was very humble, his mother even more so, but their hospitality and gratefulness for what I had done had me close to tears. Paul's little sister Hannah gave me a thank-you card and a medal she had made herself, and Evelyn presented me with a thoughtful gift.

In truth what they gave me was a most precious gift – they gave me back meaning to my career, something I seemed to have lost. In Paul I saw how I had touched another living person, how I had affected him and the people who love him. I started to realise how many others I had touched throughout my career.

I had anaesthetised over twenty thousand people. Each one of them I had touched, with my hands, my knowledge and, although at the time I wasn't conscious of it, with my heart. I thought of Care-Flight and the effect it had had on the lives of over eleven thousand people. I was proud of what I had contributed; today things like the stretcher bridge and rooftop helipads are taken for granted by retrieval services all over Australia, but it took a lot of effort to develop them. When CareFlight started we were challenged by the logistics of transferring an anaesthetised patient across the city. Now they do it regularly across the world.

Back at home, inspired by the philosophy of Rachel Remen, one of Jackie's heroes, I finally realised that, in learning to be cool and objective in the face of the horrendous experiences my patients endured, I had become immune to their triumphs. I threw away my old grey stethoscope and replaced it with a colourful new one. The first heart I listened to was my own. Now when I listen to a patient's chest I don't just hear heartbeats, I connect my aliveness with theirs.

Recently I anaesthetised a patient for a cataract operation. He had had the other eye done four weeks previously. I asked how it had changed his life.

'Doctor, now I can see leaves whereas before I could barely see the tree.'

I have anaesthetised perhaps three thousand people for similar operations, but this was the first time I really understood that I had contributed to a wonderful cause.

Now before I begin work anaesthetising my eye patients I squint till I can barely see the trees and for a moment I experience their dim world; then I open my eyes wide and look at the trees, the leaves, the lovely intricate detail. It fills me with a sense of enormous gratitude to be part of another team. One that gives people back their sight.

While I still strive for technical excellence, I have rediscovered the patients I treat. Decreasing my workload has given me time to connect with them as people; people who, like me, have their own unique story.

The joy of reconnecting with humanity has added so much to my life. Somehow I suspect that Jackie has been leading me to this point all along.

In the words of Douglas Adams, I may not have gone where I intended to go, but I had ended up where I intended to be.

For the briefest moment the cloud breaks. The Bell 47 swoops over Noosa National Park and my heart is lifted as the sun glints off azure water and white sand. From up here I glimpse the unexpected blessing in the work I have been doing for years. In a moment of blue-sky joy I realise I have never been happier. When we land I will turn my back on this powerful, seductive machine, its blades slowly winding down from flight, and know it is time to unfurl my own wings and catch a different breeze.

Acknowledgements

Special thanks to:

Dan Tyler, for not only his time devoted to assisting with research but also his friendship over many years. His support and encouragement with the writing of this book meant a lot to me.

Fran Smith, who shared the worst of days with me fighting to keep CareFlight alive, is a great friend and a great doctor.

Jo Bourke moulded my writing ability, as both my mentor in Toastmasters, and as a friend and chapter editor in the early days of writing. Thanks also for matchmaking me with my wife Jackie!

Ian Badham, for his review and editing of the final manuscript, and assistance with records and photos. Moreover, without his energy none of our dreams would have come true.

Peter Heath, Ken Vote and Frank Craven for their research surrounding the Barrington Tops mission.

Wysiwyg typing services at Nambour valiantly transferred my dictation to written words, which, considering the high jargon content, was a commendable effort.

Julia Stiles, who polished my manuscript and encouraged me to keep going when I felt overwhelmed.

Bernadette Foley who, as my publisher, saw a great story in the early work and whose advice and coaxing was the catalyst for my ideas becoming a finished product.

Brianne Tunnicliffe, my editor, who worked tirelessly to add the final polish.

Many others assisted, including Sean Beehan, Des Bokor, Jim

Campbell, Peter Cribbs, Mark Cruse, Bob Ford, Luis Gallur, Helen and Graham Gillies, Steve Grove, Marie Guthrie, Angela Hartman, John Hoad, Hayden Kenny, Terry Mortimer, Blair Munford, Andrea Nagle, Ian Paull, Jenny Ryan, Peter Underhill and Blair Weaver.

If I have missed anyone, sorry and thanks.

Finally I acknowledge:

The spouses and partners of these people, who kept our homes functional and put up with our addiction while we had fun.

The support crew of CareFlight. Many people work tirelessly on the ground to make it all happen while never getting to fly. Thank you for your dedication.

The community and individual sponsors of CareFlight, who give their hard-earned money so that New South Wales can have the best intensive care outreach service in the world. Government funds fall far short of what it takes to run an operation of this standard. Without your help CareFlight would never leave the ground.